THE PROBLEM

OF THE

PASTORAL EPISTLES

THE PROBLEM

OF THE

PASTORAL EPISTLES

BY

P. N. HARRISON, M.A., D.D.

WIPF & STOCK · Eugene, Oregon

Wipf and Stock Publishers
199 W 8th Ave, Suite 3
Eugene, OR 97401

The Problem of the Pastoral Epistles
By Harrison, P. N.
ISBN 13: 978-1-5326-0361-7
Publication date 7/29/2016
Previously published by Oxford University Press, 1921

PREFACE

THIS essay is an attempt to show how the language of the Pastoral Epistles can be used as a key to unlock the old secret of their origin.

It is not a complete Introduction to these epistles, but only a contribution towards that larger subject. On the other hand, it includes rather more than a series of linguistic studies pure and simple. In the matter before us, language is only one of several factors which are closely interconnected and refuse to be kept in separate water-tight compartments. The full significance of each is only seen in its relation to the rest.

This relation is indicated in Part I, where the problem is stated with the conclusion to which, in the mind of the present writer, every single item in the whole wide field of inquiry seems to lead. The principal items other than linguistic are named of necessity, for purposes of orientation; but as, in a number of cases, the evidence on which they rest is not submitted, no further stress is laid upon them in these pages.

Part II is devoted exclusively to linguistic evidence, and arguments based upon it, in support of the opinion that these epistles received their present shape at the hands, not of Paul, but of a Paulinist living in the early years of the second century.

Part III deals with the genuine Pauline elements embodied in these epistles. These are separated from the non-Pauline material, and classified under two main categories:

(1) Phrases borrowed from our ten Paulines, and (2) personal notes written by the real Paul to the real Timothy and Titus on various occasions which are specified. This is done without recourse to the hypothesis of a Release and Second Imprisonment; and it is argued that that hypothesis, being thus superfluous and otherwise without adequate support, falls to the ground, and with it, the entire modern case for the 'genuineness'—meaning the Pauline authorship—of these epistles as a whole.

In the effort to avoid tiresome repetition of clumsy periphrases and for the sake of brevity and convenience, the present writer has occasionally made use of terms like 'Conservative', 'Traditional', 'Orthodox', on the one hand, and 'Liberal' or 'Critical' on the other. In doing so, he wishes to disclaim the least shade of partisan suggestion, and to express the hope that these epithets will be taken, as they are certainly meant, without either prejudice or offence. While stating his own opinions quite frankly, it has been his constant desire to write at the same time very dispassionately, in all fairness, and with all due respect for the judgements, and regard for the feelings, of others.

The nucleus of the present work was read in November 1919 before the Oxford Society of Historical Theology. It was later expanded into a thesis, for which, in September 1920, the Senate of London University conferred on the writer the degree of Doctor of Divinity. It has since been revised throughout and to a large extent re-written, with material alterations and additions, especially in Part III and in the Appendices.

The Statistical data in Part II and in the Appendices are based upon Westcott and Hort's edition of the *New Testament in Greek*, Moulton and Geden's *Concordance to the Greek Testament*, and Goodspeed's *Index Patristicus* and *Index Apologeticus*. The text in Appendix IV follows that of A. Souter.

BEACONSFIELD,
 September, 1921.

CONTENTS

PART I. INTRODUCTORY

		PAGE
1.	The Problem of the Pastorals	1
2.	Principles of Investigation	2
3.	Thesis	5
4.	The name 'Pastoral Epistles': its origin, meaning, and application to the Epistles to Timothy and Titus	13
5.	Other titles by which they have been designated collectively	16
6.	Their Common Elements and Characteristics	16

PART II. UNPAULINE ELEMENTS

CHAPTER I. LINGUISTIC PECULIARITIES OF THE PASTORALS AS COMPARED WITH THE OTHER PAULINES

Introductory 18

1. Vocabulary:

    A. Words found in the Pastorals, but not in Paul (i.e., not in the ten Paulines):

        (1) *Hapax Legomena* 20
        (2) In other N. T. books 21

    B. Words found in the Pastorals and also in Paul:

        (1) Not elsewhere in the N. T. 24
        (2) In other N. T. books 26

    C. Words found in Paul, but not in the Pastorals:

        (1) Not elsewhere in the N. T. 31
        (2) In other N. T. books 31
            a. Nouns, verbs, adjectives, &c. . . . 31
            b. Particles, prepositions, pronouns, &c. . . 36

2. Grammar 38
3. Style 40

CHAPTER II. DIFFICULTY OF RECONCILING THESE PECULIARITIES WITH PAULINE AUTHORSHIP, EVEN BY REFERRING TO

	PAGE
1. The Writer	45
2. Circumstances	48
3. Subject-matter	50
4. Amanuensis	52
5. Recipients	54
6. Forgery	57
7. Literary Analogies	59
8. Derivatives	65
9. Septuagint	65
10. Classical Words	66

CHAPTER III. LANGUAGE OF THE PASTORALS AND OF PAUL COMPARED WITH THAT OF EARLY SECOND-CENTURY WRITERS

Introductory	67
1. *Hapax Legomena* in the Apostolic Fathers and Early Apologists	68
2. Other non-Pauline words in ,, ,,	70
3. Pauline words found in the Pastorals, but not in the A. F.	73
4. ,, found in the Pastorals and also in the A. F. and Apologists	74
5. Pauline words wanting in the Pastorals and A. F. and Apologists	74
6. General Analysis	77
7. Cognates and Derivatives	79
8. Patristic *Hapax Legomena*	79
9. The Residue: (*a*) Words occurring neither in Paul, nor in the A. F., nor in the Apologists, but found in non-Christian writers between A.D. 95 and 170	82
(*b*) Words found in no other writer of that period	83
10. Summary	84

CONTENTS ix

PART III. PAULINE ELEMENTS

PAGE

CHAPTER I. PHRASES TAKEN FROM THE TEN EPISTLES OF PAUL 87

CHAPTER II. PERSONALIA 93

Section 1. Reasons for refusing to regard the personal references in the Pastorals as fictitious 93

Section 2. The Second Imprisonment theory: its dependence on the mistaken assumption that they cannot be fitted into the known life of Paul 102

Section 3. The five genuine notes. Their several dates, birth-places, and occasions 115

EPILOGUE

Importance of present results, if accepted, for New Testament Criticism and Church History 136

APPENDICES

I. Analysed Vocabulary of the Pastoral Epistles and of Paul 137
II A. Stereotyped Phrases in the Pastorals 166
II B. Pauline Phrases in the Pastorals 167
II C. 1 Peter and the Pastorals 175
II D. 1 Clement and the Pastorals 177
III. Bibliography 179
IV. Text of the Pastorals, showing words which do not occur in the ten Paulines, *Hapax Legomena*, and Pauline Phrases
(*Erratum*. 1 Tim. v. 6 τέθνηκε should be printed red.)

LIST OF ABBREVIATIONS

A. A.	= Apostolic Age.
A C. L.	= (*Chronologie der*) *altchristlichen Litteratur.*
A. F.	= Apostolic Fathers.
Ap.	= *Apologia* I.
Apgts.	= Apologists.
App.	= *Apologia* II.
App.	= Appendix.
a. p. p.	= average per page.
Ar.	= Aristeides.
Ath.	= Athenagoras.
Barn.	= *Ep. of Barnabas.*
1 Clem.	= 1 Clement.
2 Clem.	= 2 Clement.
D. B.	= Dictionary of the Bible.
Dgn.	= *Epistula ad Diognetum.*
Did.	= *Didache, Teaching of the Twelve Apostles.*
E. B.	= Encyclopaedia Biblica.
Ep.	= Epistle or Epistula.
Epp.	= Epistles or Epistulae.
E. T. or E. Tr.	= English Translation.
Eus.	= Eusebius.
Exeg.	= *Exegetische* (*Abhandlung etc.*)
Gk.	= Greek.
G. T.	= Greek Testament.
Hap. Leg.	= *Hapax Legomena* or *Hapax Legomenon.*
H. E.	= *Historia Ecclesiastica.*
Herm.	= Hermas.
„	Man. = Mandate.
„	Sim. = Similitude.
„	Vis. = Vision.
H. N. T.	= Historical New Testament.
H. *PB.*	= Holtzmann, *Pastoralbriefe.*
Ign.	= Ignatius.
I. N. T.	= *Introduction to the New Testament.*
Jus.	= Justin.
Mar. or *M. P.*	= *Martyrdom of Polycarp.*
Mel.	= Melito.
N. T.	= New Testament.
N. T. I.	= *New Testament Introduction.*
O. N. T.	= Other books of the New Testament.
O. T.	= Old Testament.
Pap.	= Papias.
PB.	= *Pastoralbriefe.*
Pastls. or P. E.	= Pastoral Epistles.
Pline.	= Pauline.
Plp	= Polycarp *ad Philippenses.*
Ta.	= Tatian.
W. H.	= Westcott & Hort.
75/9	= 75 times in 9 Epistles.

CORRIGENDA AND ADDENDA

p. 36, l. 6, *for* erpetitions *read* repetitions

p. 38, l. 26, (i) The phrase ὁ μέν ... ὁ δέ &c. should be omitted in view of 2 Tim. ii. 20.

p. 92, l. 18, *for* 183 *read* 185

p. 137, l. 3, *before* Apostolic Fathers *insert* In

p. 180, l. 11, *after* 1911; *add* E. F. Brown, Lon. 1917;

p. 183, l. 1, *after* 1897; *add* J. Macpherson (*American Journal of Theology*, pp. 47 f.) 1900;

p. 183, l. 13; *after* 1911; *add* J. V. Bartlet, 'The Historic Setting of the Pastoral Epistles' (*Expositor*, 8th series, vol. v, pp. 47, 161, 256, 325), London, 1913 (superseding what is said on the subject in Dr. Bartlet's 'Apostolic Age').

PART I

INTRODUCTORY

(1) THE Problem of the Pastorals, as our New Testament Epistles to Timothy and Titus are now usually called,[1] is the problem of their origin.

In setting out to write an introduction to these Epistles, or a serious contribution towards that large subject, the nature of the task before us can be defined quite simply, though the task itself is anything but simple. It is to solve that problem. We must endeavour to promote a right understanding of their message and a just appreciation of their worth, by seeking first to ascertain and establish, as far as may be, the facts of their authorship, date, purpose, and composition.

Are they, or are they not, what on the surface and at first sight they give themselves out to be,—what official leaders of the Church, at any rate since the end of the second century, have declared them to be, and what so many millions of devout readers have believed them to be,—authentic first-hand products of the mind and heart of the Apostle Paul?

If so, at what moments in his life, under the stress of what special circumstances, and with what purposes in view, did he write them? Did he, as in the case of other epistles, use an amanuensis? If so, who or what manner of person filled this rôle; what degree of latitude did he receive, or take; and in what respects, if any, did he modify the original words and thoughts of his master? What further explanations can be given, and are they adequate to account for the many and marked differences, in form and in substance, between these and the other Pauline epistles?

[1] Chiefly on grounds of convenience, established custom, and for want of a better title. See further p. 13 ff. (4).

If not Paul, who then did write them? And as, in this case, it is hardly likely that the author's name can now be recovered, at any rate what sort of person was he? When did he live? In what circumstances, and with what aims, and in what spirit did he pen these epistles? Why did he conceal his own name and personality beneath that of the Apostle? To what extent must he be judged responsible for the mistake, if it be a mistake, into which so many generations of readers have been led? Was the deception deliberate and intentional, was it conscious, on his part? Did he actually in the first instance deceive anybody, or did the misunderstanding only arise after the matter had passed beyond his hands? How did he justify his procedure to himself and to his contemporaries? Did he or they feel that it needed any justification? From what sources of information did he derive his mental picture of the Apostle, of his life and death, his gospel and his methods of propagating it? What *was* his mental picture of the Apostle's life, more especially of his closing years? Did he believe that Paul was released at the end of the Roman imprisonment recorded in Acts, visited Spain, revisited Ephesus, Macedonia, Corinth, Troas, Miletus, Crete, wintered in Nicopolis, was imprisoned in Rome a second time, and only then suffered martyrdom? Or is the truth rather that he had never dreamed of any such extension of Paul's life, and that the imprisonment in which he makes Paul write 2 Timothy, was intended by him to be the same as we find recorded at the end of Acts, the same in which the epistles to Philemon, the Colossians, Ephesians, and Philippians had been written?

We speak of the 'author' in the singular. But whether these writings are all by the same author, whether they are each of them to be regarded as a unity or as composite, and as the work of one mind or of more than one, may not be taken for granted, but is precisely one of the questions we have to investigate.

More particularly, we have to consider and weigh carefully the evidence for and against the possibility that our author, if not Paul himself, may have had before him, and incorporated in his epistles, a certain quantum of genuine Pauline material. To what extent does he show acquaintance with our existing Paulines? Has he preserved any further authentic messages of the Apostle of which we should otherwise know nothing?

To all these questions an answer will be attempted, and the reasons for it given, in the ensuing pages.

(2) *Principles of Investigation.* In pursuing an inquiry of this kind, fraught with issues of such deep and far-reaching importance as this one obviously is, the writer of a modern Introduction is rightly expected, and in honour bound, to seek out and examine as far as humanly possible all the available evidence of every kind whatsoever, internal and external, with an absolutely open mind and a single eye to truth.

It would be highly improper for such a work calling itself historical, critical, scientific, or even simply honest, to begin by insisting on the necessity of any particular conclusion to any cause, however great or even sacred, in which the writer might be personally interested. The scholar who starts an investigation like this with the announcement that 'our whole position rests upon' the genuineness, meaning the direct Pauline authorship of these epistles, may or may not be able to establish what he sets out to prove. There is always the risk that his words may come back to him with the unfeeling retort that in that case he had better seek a safer position, or else make haste to set his present position on a more secure basis. Meanwhile he makes it difficult for those who perhaps do not altogether share that position to feel all the confidence they might desire in the complete impartiality of his investigation.

The one and only business before us is to discover by all means the truth, whatever it may be, whether or not it happens to coincide with our preconceived ideas, and whether or not it seems likely to prove convenient to the champions of any tradition, however august, or of any institution, however necessary in our eyes to human welfare. The practical, as well as the theoretical, results of whatever may ultimately prove to be the true solution to our problem, must be left to the end, if indeed they belong at all to the proper scope of a Biblical Introduction. Once the truth is established, it may be safely trusted to produce its own results; and these will probably be largely unforeseen, possibly embarrassing to some people, involving some readjustment, not to say reconstruction, but always in the long run for the sure, true, and lasting benefit of mankind.

In endeavouring to form an independent judgement on the

issues before him, the student of to-day must not ignore the labours of other men in the same field, but should faithfully observe the trend of previous investigations. In particular he must keep a very watchful eye for those points in the long controversy where two sets of equally learned and conscientious persons seem to have arrived at a deadlock,—pronouncing with equal conviction two quite contradictory verdicts. Inasmuch as both cannot be right, he must try to see whether either side has failed duly to note any pertinent facts adduced by the other. Where this cannot be demonstrated, he must try to see whether, by digging yet deeper, and pushing his investigations still further than either side has done hitherto, any issue that has so far remained a moot point may not be definitely settled one way or the other.

One great advantage following such a review of previous efforts is that it enables us to eliminate a number of hypotheses which may seem at first sight very promising and attractive, but to which unanswerable objections were at once pointed out; so that it would be sheer waste of time to pursue the subject any further in those directions.

Another good result that probably will, and certainly should, follow from this wider acquaintance with other men's labours, is a strong check to undue self-confidence and hasty dogmatism.

After seeing so many experienced and competent scholars arrive at what must be a false conclusion, apparently without being troubled by the shadow of a suspicion that they might after all be quite mistaken, it would be inexcusable, however natural, to let oneself fall into the very same error.

On the other hand, it would be no less grave an error to sink into a state of hopeless scepticism as to the possibility of ever finding out the truth. However presumptuous the claim to have finally solved a problem which has divided for more than a century the best scholarship of the world, it would be an even greater mistake to conclude that the problem is insoluble and the truth incapable of demonstration. Truth will out. After all the issue is in this case a clear one. Either Paul wrote these epistles substantially as they stand or he did not. It is true that the latter alternative holds within itself several widely different possibilities. But there is no need for these to obscure the main question. If not Paul himself, let the author have been who he may, it should be possible in the long run to find him out. Some hint of his own views and personality, some mark of the age to which he belonged, was bound to escape him, however skilful and, for a time, successful his attempt may have been to hide his own identity under that of the Apostle. The emergence of many such hints, or of many facts capable of such an interpretation, could not in any case be ignored. Nor would their significance seem to be lessened by their inobtrusiveness, nor by the fact that they are only now brought to light as a result of the most minute and searching investigation.

Whether or not the conclusion which must finally commend itself to all competent minds is now in sight, the future alone can decide. Those who have come nearest to the real difficulties will be the least inclined to indulge in over-positive assertions. Though it may not be given us to reach the goal, it is something to have pressed honestly towards it,—to have laboured with the one desire to know the truth. Those who so labour may not themselves arrive. At least they may know the satisfaction of having cut some of those steps in the rock, by which others in due time will gain the summit.

In its main outline the view put forward in these pages has no claim to originality. It is held by many scholars, including some of the very highest reputation. But certain new features are here embodied, and certain fresh considerations urged in its support. The effect of these is to encourage the belief that we have before us the true solution of this great problem, and the only one consistent with the whole of the evidence now forthcoming.

(3) *Thesis.* The precise character of these conclusions will appear gradually and in detail as the work proceeds; but it may be convenient to the reader, and may convey a sense of direction as he makes his way through the somewhat complicated mass of data which must come up for examination, if we set down here at the outset in barest outline the main thesis to which every single item in the whole variegated programme seems to point.

It is, first, that these epistles, in anything like their present form, cannot be the direct work of the Apostle. This negative result follows from a great number and variety of considerations including more than one group of facts which would by itself be sufficient to create the gravest doubts as to the Pauline authorship, but which, in their converging and cumulative effect, seem altogether overwhelming and decisive. These are partly chronological, partly linguistic, polemic, doctrinal, ecclesiastical, psychological, to name only the principal types of difficulty. But the fact is that from whatever point of view we approach these epistles, the further we carry our inquiry, the more impressive becomes the body of undeniable facts demanding explanation, and requiring the utmost ingenuity to reconcile them, if indeed they can be reconciled, with their apostolic origin. (Defenders of the traditional view are obliged to claim the benefit of the doubt, and insist on a shadowy 'off-chance', much too often.)

(i) It is now agreed by the overwhelming majority of conservative scholars that these epistles cannot by any means be fitted into the known life of Paul as recorded in Acts; and that if Paul wrote them, he must have done so during a period of release from that imprisonment in which the Lucan history leaves him, and at the close of a subsequent second Roman imprisonment. But this alleged release and second imprisonment, in spite of all great names and arguments in its favour, must be definitely dismissed as a legend without valid historical basis. So far from supporting this legend, the Personalia in the Pastorals provide, as we shall show, conclusive evidence against it. Even if the second imprisonment were generally accepted as 'an assured fact of history' (Harnack, *A. C.L.* i, p. 240) the remaining arguments against the Pauline authorship of these epistles would still be, as Harnack himself maintains, decisive (ib. p. 480).

(ii) The result of a close and comprehensive comparison of the language of the Pastorals with that of the ten Paulines on the one hand, and that of the Apostolic Fathers and early Apologists on the other, is itself fatal to the traditional opinion. Strong as the critical case here has long been admitted to be, the facts go far beyond any statement that has hitherto appeared even from the critical side, and still further beyond all that has ever yet been admitted or dealt with from the conservative point of view.

It is true that these epistles contain a considerable number of unmistakably Pauline phrases, such as could perfectly well have been taken direct from our ten 'Paulines' by a diligent student with these before him. And the 'Personalia' in 2 Tim. and Titus, when isolated from the main body of these epistles, and submitted to the same linguistic tests, are found to be thoroughly Pauline in vocabulary, idiom and style. But for the rest, the style of the Pastorals is radically different from Paul's, and their vocabulary is not that of the Apostle, but is that of early second-century Christendom as known to us from the writings of that period. See further the summary at end of Part II (p. 84 ff.).

(iii)[1] The whole ecclesiastical situation and atmosphere presupposed in these epistles represents a stage of development beyond that for which we have any evidence in the lifetime of Paul or in the Apostolic Age, but entirely in keeping with that of the period to which 'Liberal' criticism assigns them.

(*a*) The False Teaching which it is a main purpose of this author to counteract, in so far as a clear and coherent picture of it can be derived from the allusions in these epistles, is of a type which did not, so far as we know, exist in Paul's lifetime, but was certainly a real danger to the Church half a century or so later. And the very vagueness and generality of those allusions for the most part is not at all in the manner of the real Paul in dealing with the errorists of his own day.

(*b*) The positive doctrine of these epistles is professedly Pauline, but it is so in the sense rather of the Paulinism of the second and third generations than of the Apostle himself. Along with many undoubtedly Pauline features, terms and expressions, it includes certain elements which betray a later date, and omits others which are vital and central to the original Pauline gospel.

(*c*) The type of ecclesiastical organization presupposed, and the whole stress and emphasis laid on matters of Church polity, is foreign to all that we otherwise know of Paul's ideas on such matters. It may be accurately defined as more advanced than the state of things revealed in the Roman Clement, but less so than in the Ignatian Epistles.

(iv) It is psychologically inconceivable that the real Paul should have addressed the real Timothy and Titus in many of the terms, or in the general tone adopted by the Paul of these

---

[1] iii. *a–c*. These paragraphs are given for purposes of orientation, and as an expression of personal opinion. But as the evidence on which that opinion is based falls beyond the scope of this essay, and as these matters are disputed, no further stress is laid upon them here.

epistles. It is neither necessary nor just to disparage the personality and spirit of this author as it appears in his writing. But the fact remains that with all his excellent qualities and high gifts he was a very different type of person indeed, and for all his fervent admiration of the great Apostle, and loyal devotion to his name and memory, his was an altogether different kind of spirit from that which burns and throbs in every page of the genuine Paulines.

The *positive* conclusion, then, which forms the main thesis of the present work is that the real author of the Pastorals was a devout, sincere, and earnest Paulinist, who lived at Rome or Ephesus, and wrote during the later years of Trajan or (? and) the earlier years of Hadrian's reign. He knew and had studied deeply every one of our ten Paulines. In addition to these he had access to several brief personal notes written by the Apostle on various occasions (to be specified in due course) to his friends Timothy and Titus, preserved by them till their death, and then bequeathed as a priceless heirloom either to the Church or to some trusted friend.

There was also Paul's last letter and farewell to Timothy, written not long after Philippians, on the eve, or possibly on the very day, of his martyrdom. Our 2 Timothy, which was the first of the three to be written, consists of this last letter expanded and brought up to date by the *auctor ad Timotheum* to meet the requirements of his own day, with the three shorter notes, which had really been written earlier, two of them years earlier, added as a sort of appendix or postscript. In Titus also there is a genuine note to Titus dating from about the same time as 2 Corinthians, appended in iii. 12 ff. 1 Timothy, which is certainly the latest of the three, representing as it does a distinct advance on the others in the development of Church organization, opposition to heretics, &c., is destitute of such original fragments as enrich the others; the obvious and natural explanation of which fact is that, in responding to the demand for more letters of the same kind, our author had no more genuine notes in his possession, and was incapable of inventing such details. One or two half-hearted experiments in this direction (i. 3; iii. 14; v. 23) only illustrate the last remark, and are no exceptions to it.

Our author was acquainted with the Synoptic tradition

(Matt.–Luke) and perhaps with Acts, 1 Peter,[1] and 1 Clement.[2] He would naturally be acquainted also with current traditions touching the life and death of the Apostle. He believed honestly and wholeheartedly the Pauline gospel as he understood it. At the same time he shared the ideas of the Church of his own day on matters both of belief and of polity. These ideas represented, in fact, a perfectly natural development, due to the changed conditions of the times, in the direction of a more definite and formal statement of the Christian faith, and a more highly organized constitution of the Christian society and especially of its official leaders. Of this difference, however, from the original Pauline conceptions, the writer himself was no more aware than were his contemporaries. He and they regarded themselves as simply holding on to the genuine apostolic teaching.

For such a man and for such minds there was much in the circumstances of the Church to give grounds for grave concern. As at all other periods, the purity and spirituality of Christian belief and conduct alike were continually threatened by the pressure of forces from the outside world. These were partly Jewish and partly Pagan, and so included a variety of elements by no means all in harmony with one another. On the one hand there was a tendency towards some forms of asceticism, on the other to a recrudescence of pagan licentiousness. In the sphere of doctrine there was a proneness to wild speculation, leading to barren discussions, heated arguments and violent quarrels. An active propaganda was being carried on within the Church, taking the form partly of certain 'Jewish myths' and 'genealogies', partly of certain ceremonial restrictions having as their intellectual basis a dualistic philosophy. The propagandists showed a feverish activity, going from house to house, and finding no small measure of success, particularly among the women-folk. Some of them dabbled in the occult arts with the usual disastrous results. They asked and received money as the price of their teaching, and some had grown rich in this way.

All this was obviously incompatible with any real loyalty or respect for the memory and teaching of Paul. There was, in fact, a marked drift away from that type of Christian profession which still revered his name, and clung to what was believed to

[1] Appendix II C, p. 175.   [2] App. II D, p. 177.

be the pure original Pauline gospel. There was even in some cases an open depreciation of the personal influence and authority of the great Apostle of the Gentiles. And the new methods were equally inconsistent with any sort of respect for the authority of living representatives of the Pauline Church in general. Insubordination with all its attendant evils was spreading apace. Moral laxity was on the increase. And while the calm and happy fellowship of the Christian society was being marred by interminable wranglings, the Christian name and profession were being brought into disrepute with an outside world that watched with jealous eyes, only too ready to fasten on any occasion for scandal, or any excuse for active persecution.

In attempting to cope with this situation, experience seemed to force on earnest minds the necessity for a more precise and definite articulation of positive belief, greater care in the selection of those called to hold office in the Church, a quickening of zeal, a deepening of piety, and a revival of enthusiasm for the Pauline gospel. The best minds in the Church sighed for a return of the old apostolic fervour and sanctity. They had every reason to realize the need for a rekindling of the heroic courage with which Paul had faced tribulation, persecution, and finally martyrdom. And it seemed to some of them that nothing could be better calculated to promote such objects than a letter written in the spirit, bearing the name, and recalling the very familiar words of the great Apostle.

The time was ripe for such an effort. A circulation was guaranteed by the existence of a circle of readers, who were already familiar with at least the ten Paulines which have come down to us. It is even conceivable that the demand may have found definite expression in some such form as we find suggested by the story in the Muratorian Canon (ll. 9–15) describing the genesis of the Johannine Gospel, or by the statements of Dionysius of Corinth (c. A.D. 160, Eus. *H. E.* IV. xxiii), and Polycarp (Phil. iii. 1 f.), to the effect that they had written their epistles, not wholly on their own initiative, but at the explicit request of their brethren. It is, however, of course equally possible that the impulse to write may in the present instance have come purely from within or, why should we not say, from above, without the mediation of any human prompting?

There is at any rate no need for us to leave open the question as to the actual *occasion* which led to the writing of these epistles. The acquisition of those priceless relics, for the authenticity of which a responsible leader of the Church, say in A.D. 110, may perfectly well have had ample guarantees, was occasion enough for such a person as we have pictured him to be. Natural as it was, in view of their purely private character, that they had not been published earlier, it was equally natural in the circumstances just described for our Paulinist to feel of his own accord, even if it were not expressly laid upon him, that this was a sacred trust. He would neither desire nor dare to keep his treasure to himself, but would be only eager to discharge to the best of his ability the duty and privilege of passing it on to others in the form that, as it seemed to him, was likely to do the most good.

Had he lived in the twentieth century, no doubt he would have conceived and discharged his duty in this matter very differently. He would have handed in the original notes, exactly as they had come into his hands, to the curators of some great museum. And he would have issued to the public photographic facsimiles, with careful notes, detailing all relevant information. Where the text was defective he would have indicated the lacunae by asterisks. And if he ventured on an occasional conjectural emendation, he would have taken care that his readers knew exactly what he was doing.

But he lived in the early second century, and thought the greatest service he could render to his time and to the Church would be to issue Paul's farewell letter, and the other notes that came with it, not in their original bare brevity, with or without explanatory comments, but expanded somewhat into a message, an urgently needed message, to the Timothys and to the Church of his own day,—such as he believed the Apostle would have delivered, had he been still alive. His first page is a wonderful mosaic of phrases from the genuine Paulines, most carefully and skilfully fitted together. As he proceeds, and the necessity arises to make the Apostle speak still more clearly and directly to the heart and to the condition of this new time, he begins to compose more freely, and in doing so falls inevitably out of the Pauline style and phraseology into his own looser, less nervous, and less rugged style, and into the current vocabulary of his own day.

In all this he was not conscious of misrepresenting the Apostle in any way; he was not consciously deceiving anybody; it is not, indeed, necessary to suppose that he did deceive anybody. It seems far more probable that those to whom, in the first instance, he showed the result of his efforts, must have been perfectly well aware of what he had done. It is not to be supposed that he made any attempt to impose upon his friends, by inscribing his epistles on old and worn papyri or in old-fashioned writing! They went out for what they really were, and the warm appreciation with which the best minds in the Church received them, would not be tinged with any misunderstanding as to the way in which they had been written. Of course, they would then be copied and re-copied, and sent from church to church throughout the Christian world and,—in the absence of any footnotes, to explain the true facts of their origin; in the absence of books or papers, preserving a record of those facts; in the absence, further, of trained critical faculties, still more of any scientific apparatus, such as might have enabled the Christians of the last quarter of the second century to anticipate the conclusions of the twentieth century,—it was only natural that the true origin of these epistles should very soon be forgotten, and that they should come to be taken as being what, on the surface, they claim to be.

But if, on the other hand, we should feel obliged to say that the writer of these epistles wished and intended them to be read as authentic messages from the Apostle Paul himself, it still would not follow that we should be right in passing the same moral strictures upon his action as if he had been writing in the present day. A very different standard on these matters prevailed in those days. The theory of literary proprietorship was not held in anything remotely resembling its present form. It was a very common practice of ancient writers to appropriate, without any sort of acknowledgement, verses, sentences and whole paragraphs from any previous work they had before them. It was the custom of historians of the very front rank to put into the mouths of public men speeches of which they could not in the nature of things have had any verbatim report. It was not such a very great step from the speeches ascribed to St. Paul in the Acts, to the composition of letters in his name. In both cases the author believed himself to begiving a true representation, as far as it was in his power, of the sentiments and teaching of the Apostle. In neither case should we be justified in dismissing that representation as purely fictitious (see Moffatt, *H. N. T.*, p. 622 ff.).

(4)[1] The use of the word Pastoral in connexion with the Epistles to Timothy and Titus goes back at least as far as Thomas Aquinas († 1274), who says in his commentary (*Opera*, ed. Fretté, Paris, 1876, p. 454), 'est haec epistola quasi pastoralis regula, quam Apostolus tradit Timotheo, instruens de omnibus quae spectant ad regimen praelatorum'; and again in the Prologus in 2 Tim. (p. 502), 'in prima enim (epistola) instruit eum de ordinatione ecclesiastica, in hac autem secunda agit de sollicitudine tanta pastorali ut etiam martyrium sustineat pro cura gregis'.

In 1703 D. N. Berdot (*Exercitatio theol. exegetica in ep. S. Pauli ad Titum*, Halae, p. 3 f.) after quoting Augustine to the effect that those destined for the ministry ought to have Paul's epistles to Timothy and Titus constantly before his eyes, 'utpote quae de Pastoris Ministerii partibus agant', goes on to say of Titus 'in hac itaque Epistola, quae Pastoralis est, primo ostendit, qualis Minister sit eligendus . . . secundo quid et quomodo docere debeat'.

But the modern application of this term to these epistles collectively as a technical designation is rightly traced by Zahn (*Einl. N. T.* 1906, i. 447 n.) to a course of lectures delivered at the University of Halle in 1726-7 by Paul Anton, and edited in 1753-5 by J. A. Maier under the title *Exegetische Abhandlung der Pastoral-Briefe Pauli an Timotheum und Titum*.

As a matter of fact, Anton himself does not seem to have thought of limiting the word Pastoral in this special way. He describes his own lectures as 'Lectiones Pastorales on the Pauline epistles, and especially those to Timothy and Titus'. Starting from the large number of Pastoralia produced, since the Reformation, within 'our Evangelical Church', he shows how essential an element these are to a right preparation for the Christian ministry, and insists that the 'sap and strength to use them aright' must be drawn from the word of God itself. In this connexion he

[1] (4-5) An Excursus, not affecting the argument.

says that not only these three epistles, but also the seven epistolae apocalypticae or episcopales (Rev. ii, iii) are rightly to be described as Pastorals, in virtue of the divine guidance they contain for the leaders of Christian churches; and that, indeed, a great part of the Holy Scripture is in this sense a Pastoral. The title of the second volume runs *Exeg. Abhandlung der Paulinischen Pastoral-Briefe, samt einem Anhange der Sieben Pastoral-Briefe Christi an die Sieben Gemeinden in Asia*. Our epistles are thus regarded by Anton as *Pastoralia Scripta par excellence*, as the classical and supreme examples of writings serviceable to those who seek preparation for, and guidance in, the Christian ministry.

In accordance with this view of their character, the term Pastoral seems to have won its way into general acceptance in Protestant Germany as their recognized title and common designation, during the quarter of a century which intervened between the delivery of Anton's lectures and their publication by Maier, who refers to the usage and justifies it in his introductory pages ('die Pastoral-Briefe Pauli, wie sie insgemein, und zwar mit Recht, genennet werden'). Michaelis speaks of the 'so-called Pastorals' in his *Einleitung*, ³1777. Then in 1810 J. A. L. Wegscheider published his new translation and explanation of 1 Tim., as the first part of a larger work, *Die Pastoral-Briefe des Apostels Paulus*, in the preface of which he speaks of 'die sämmtlichen sogenannten Pastoral-Briefe des Ap. Paulus'. In Eichhorn's *Einleitung in das N. T.* (1812) they are called 'Die drey Pastoralschreiben, zwey an Tim. u. eines an Tit.'. From that time onwards the usage has been general among Continental scholars, and at any rate since Alford's *Greek Testament* (1849, ⁶1884) in this country also.

The facts about its origin were quickly forgotten, even in Germany. So that in 1826 the learned Heydenreich (*Die Pastoral-Briefe Pauli*) could write that they have been so called 'from the most ancient times' (*von uralten Zeiten her*, vol. i, p. 7), with reference to the fact that early Christian teachers were called Pastors, ποιμένας (Eph. iv. 11), after the prophets and teachers of the Jewish Church (Jer. ii. 8; Ezek. xxxiv. 2 f.), and like Jesus Himself (John x. 11 f.; 1 Pet. ii. 25; v. 4; Heb. xiii. 20).

With regard to the real fitness of this term as applied to our

INTRODUCTORY 15

epistles, opinions have been divided. 'They are', said the devout Maier, 'a living mirror reflecting the right organization of an entire Christian community, in every sort of state and circumstance, and in all public and special happenings,—showing not only what is necessary and proper, but also what is with the help of Divine grace perfectly "practicable" and possible.' 'Taken all together, our records of the Ministry (*Amtslauf*) of Christ in the gospels, and of the Apostles in Acts and of their successors in the teaching office in these Pastorals and other apostolic epistles, provide us with all that we need with regard to the teaching office and the planting of a Christian community, for the blessed instruction and imitation of the entire Church till the end of time.'

On the other hand, Heydenreich's acceptance of the term is much more qualified. 'It is true,' he says, 'that in earlier times these writings were wrongly regarded as a complete set of Pastoral instructions, and supposed to contain a sort of compendium of the entire body of Pastoral Theology. As a matter of fact, (1) they neither include all the occupations and duties which fall to a teacher of Christianity, nor (2) do they go deeply into special and single details, nor (3) do they bind themselves to the systematic arrangement which we might well expect in a real pastoral instruction, but not in brief letters; (4) there is much in them that refers to purely local circumstances, and to conditions peculiar to the period when they were written; ... (5) They are not exclusively concerned with matters connected with the teaching office. Quite other matters only very remotely connected with the pastoral instructions are woven into these confidential communications from the Apostle to his disciple and friend.' Nevertheless, he concludes that these epistles ought to be the handbook of every one who is, or expects to be, a teacher of religion. For here is to be found without fail a rich and open spring of teaching and exhortation (p. 8).

Zahn's verdict is that it suits 1 Tim. and Titus to a certain extent, 2 Tim. not at all. Holtzmann (*PB.*, p. 282 n.) remarks bluntly that 'of real pastoral teaching, i.e. of the theory of the individual cure of souls, our epistles contain little or nothing'. Moffatt (*H. N. T.*, 1901, p. 556 n.) goes still further. 'The inadequate and misleading title "pastorals", under which these writings have suffered for about ninety years, can only be retained (and used as seldom as possible) on the score of convenience.'

That they really do not contain all that might be desired from the modern point of view, in writings destined to be for all time the classical handbook on the cure of souls, for Christian ministers, is obvious enough. It is equally obvious that no such destiny was contemplated for them by their author (cf. 1 Tim. iii. 14 f.).

(5) That these three epistles call for some common designation, as forming a class by themselves, was felt as early as the beginning of the seventeenth century, when they were known as the Pontificial epistles, as being addressed to Timothy 'Ephesino Primati' and Titus 'Cretensi' by their apostolic superior. (*Operis Hierarchici, sive De Ecclesiastico Principatu, Libri iii, in quibus epist. tres B. Pauli Apostoli, quae Pontificiae vocari solent, commentariis illustrantur, autore P. Cosma Magaliona*, Lugduni, 1609.) At the beginning of the eighteenth we find them referred to by D. N. Berdot (p. 13) as 'epistolae ministeriales'.

(6) *Common Elements and Characteristics.* All three exhibit a close similarity, and to a remarkable degree identity, of contents and subject matter, of literary style, diction, vocabulary and grammatical peculiarities. All three name the Apostle Paul at the outset as their author, and are addressed to younger helpers of the Apostle, known to us otherwise from the pages of the N. T., and of the Pauline epistles in particular, as his close friends and intimate companions in travel and in service. These now appear as his legates and representatives, commissioned by him to superintend the life and organization of the churches, and to resist certain false teachers, whose pernicious doctrines bear the same characteristics whether at Ephesus or in Crete. For the true faith there is now substituted a morbid preoccupation with myths and speculations tending to wordy battles, strife and contention within the Church, and to mental degeneracy, loose living, and evil speaking, and finally to downright moral and spiritual ruin, in the individual. The representatives of this calamitous teaching are charged with the basest of motives,—the sordid greed of material profit which they hope to make, and are making, out of the gospel. They are to be opposed in each case

INTRODUCTORY

first by the resolute and courageous stand to be taken by the recipient of the letter, by his stern rebukes and relentless exposure of their presumptuous and hollow claims, and by his personal example of sober, pure and holy living; then by his loyal insistence on the wholesome doctrine committed to his charge; and thirdly by his careful zeal in carrying out the apostolic instructions for the guidance and organization of the Church, over which he is set in authority, more especially by seeing that the right sort of persons are associated with himself in the supremely vital task of handing on the sound apostolic doctrine. This sound doctrine is in each case conceived and presented as first and foremost Paul's own message, entrusted to him, heralded by him. It is the Word, the faithful Word, the Word of God,—the sound or wholesome teaching,—conveying to all who receive it knowledge of the Truth. It is the message of salvation in Christ Jesus our Lord,—given to us through faith, by grace,—taking effect in a life of true piety, faith, and love here, and holding the promise of eternal life,—or life and immortality,—hereafter, at His appearing.

In each of these short epistles the necessity for good works is insisted upon some half-dozen times; and in each the point of this is found to consist partly in the importance of making a favourable impression on an outside world only too ready to 'blaspheme'.

In addition to the number of *Hapax Legomena* and other non-Pauline words shared between two or more of the Pastorals (for which see Appendix I A, p. 137 f.), they are connected by a series of characteristic phrases which seem collectively to favour strongly the impression that, in their present form at any rate, they are the work of one mind, and that mind, another than Paul's (Appendix II A, p. 166 f.).

PART II

UNPAULINE ELEMENTS

THE LINGUISTIC EVIDENCE.

Introductory.

WHEN in the year 1807 Schleiermacher opened the Critical campaign against the authenticity of 1 Tim., he chose as the field for a first engagement with the forces ranged against him, the linguistic peculiarities of that epistle, and set in the forefront of his attack a great array of *Hapax Legomena*.

In his own less warlike metaphor, he found himself under the dire necessity of offering to his readers as the first course of their Critical banquet, no piquant hors-d'œuvre to whet their intellectual palate, but a dry list of words![1]

It is indeed far more as field-marshal[2] than as chef, that he shines in the present controversy. Few have relished the arduous lexical, grammatical, and statistical labour imposed on them by the form thus given to the inquiry from its outset. In every phase of the more than century-long conflict, to which the famous Sendschreiben, with the replies of Planck, Beckhaus, Wegscheider, &c., proved to be only a preliminary skirmish, there have been laments at so much counting,—not to say, discounting!—of *Hapax Legomena*; and the hope has been expressed fervently, but in vain, that we might now have heard the last of them.[3] The fact remains that these elements in the vocabulary of the Pastorals which are foreign not only to the Paulines, but to the entire N. T., form an essential part of the evidence on which the final decision must inevitably be based. It was neither the perversity of genius nor mere

---

[1] *Sendschreiben an Gass*, p. 28 f.
[2] 'Mit kritischem Feldherrnblick', Holtzmann, *PB.*, p. 7.
[3] Shaw, 1904, p. 439.

dialectical subtlety, which threw such emphasis upon them, but a true perception of their vital significance for the present issue. The process of collecting, sifting, and analysing these and other relevant linguistic data therefore still continues, and clearly must continue, until one side is compelled by sheer weight of evidence to quit the field, and a position of primary strategic importance in many and far-reaching issues, passes definitely into those hands to which it properly belongs.

Though not by any means the only, nor even the principal, ground on which subsequent critics, going beyond Schleiermacher, have rejected the Pauline authorship of all three Pastorals, the linguistic argument has all along been the one that has made the deepest impression on advocates of the contrary opinion; and it is at this point that these have expended the greatest pains and energy in its defence.

From a long line of workers in this department to whom we are indebted for positive information, or fruitful suggestion, we single out, on the Conservative side, Koelling 1882-7, Bertrand 1888, Workman 1896, Rüegg 1893, Findlay 1903, Wohlenberg 1906, Jacquier 1907, Robert Scott 1909, N. J. D. White 1910, Torm 1919, Parry 1920. Among the Liberals we name here only Mayerhof 1838, and H. J. Holtzmann 1880, from whose armoury many a critic has, in the interval, drawn some of his most effective weapons.

Though it is now forty years since the last-named scholar published his monograph on the Pastoral Epistles, that epoch-making work still holds the field as a classical statement of the case against the Pauline authorship of these epistles, and of the reasons for placing them in the second century. On the other hand it is now generally considered, even among those who find his main thesis unanswerable and decisive, that Holtzmann's own verdict requires revision in various details, and on at least one vital point. He failed to see in its true significance the fact that the language of certain passages in 2 Tim. and Titus, as well as their substance, unlike the rest of these epistles, is thoroughly Pauline in every respect. And so he made the mistake of dismissing these Personalia as mere fiction invented by the *auctor ad Timotheum et Titum* to lend colour and verisimilitude to his handiwork, on the basis of data found by him in Acts, the genuine Paulines, and a few scraps of second-century tradition. See Part III, Chapter II, pp. 93 ff.

The present essay represents one more attempt to marshal the relevant facts, and set them in such a light that the secret of their true explanation may be revealed. It is based first on some acquaintance with the work of previous investigators; but in the main on an entirely new and independent examination of the language (1) of the Pastorals, (2) of Paul and other N. T. writers, (3) of those second-century writers who belonged to the second and third generations after Paul's death, but were, on the 'critical' view, contemporaries of our author.

To a certain extent the effect of what follows is simply to exhibit from a fresh point of view facts that have long been known and frequently been pointed out. But much is here made public, so far as the present writer is aware, for the first time, and has to be added, for whatever it may be worth, to the already formidable mass of evidence which cannot easily, if it can possibly, be reconciled with the traditional opinion.

I. 1. THE VOCABULARY OF THE PASTORAL EPISTLES AND OF PAUL

The vocabulary of the Pastorals consists of some 902 words, of which 54 are proper names. Of the remaining 848, 306 or over 36 per cent. are not to be found in any one of the ten Paulines. See Appendix I, pp. 137 ff.

A 1. One hundred and seventy-five, the so-called 'Pastoral *Hapax Legomena*', appear in no other N. T. writing outside the Pastorals. Of these 1 Tim. has 96, that is 15·2 per page, 2 Tim. 60 or 12·9 per page, and Titus 43 or 16·1 per page.

Now Rom. has only four such words to the page, 1 Cor. 4·1, 2 Cor. 5·6, Gal. 3·9, Eph. 4·6, Phil. 6·2, Col. 5·5, 1 Thess. 3·6, 2 Thess. 3·3, and Philem. 4.

We are thus presented with a gradually ascending scale, approximating, though by no means exactly, to the chronological order, the maximum difference, between the two extremes, 2 Thess. and Phil., being 2·9 per page, and the intermediate stages, from 2 Thess. to 1 Thess. 0·3, Gal. 0·3, Philem. 0·1, Rom. 0, 1 Cor. 0·1, Eph. 0·5, Col. 0·9, 2 Cor. 0·1, Phil. 0·6,—in no single case so much as a word per page. Then comes 1 Tim.

with an *increase* over Paul's previous record, of 9 per page, 2 Tim. with an increase of 6·7, or else Titus with an increase of 9·9 per page. The gap between the lowest of the Pastorals and the highest of the Paulines would hold the entire series from Thess. to Phil. more than twice over. Even if we allow the

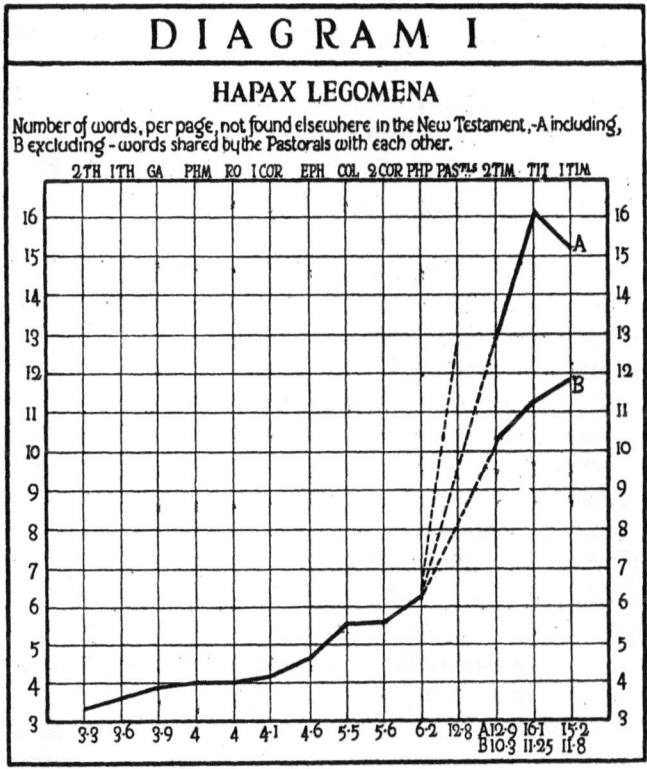

Pastorals to help one another, by eliminating all words shared by them with each other, they still refuse to be brought anywhere near the other ten epistles. But as they are all under a common suspicion, the number of such words rather strengthens than mitigates the case against them. See Diagram I.

A 2. One hundred and thirty-one words occur in the Pastorals and in other N. T. books, but not in any Pauline epistle. Of these 1 Tim. has 77, 2 Tim. 54, and Titus 38.[1] Sixty-one are shared with one N. T. author exclusively, viz. 3 with Matt., 2 with

[1] Appendix I A 2, p. 138 f.

Mark, 29 with one or both of the Lucan writings, 3 with John, 10 with Heb., 4 with 1 Pet., 7 (or ? 9) with 2 Pet., 2 with Jas., and one with Rev. See Appendix I D, p. 148 f.

Taking A 1 and 2 together, we find that 1 Tim. has 173 (out of 529) words that do not appear in any of the ten Paulines, that is one in three of its total vocabulary, or 27.3 per page, 2 Tim. 114 out of 413, or 24.4 per page, Titus 81 out of 293, or 30.4 per page.

In Rom. we find 261 words which do not recur in any other of the ten Paulines, or 10 to the page of Westcott and Hort, in 1 Cor. 11.1, in 2 Cor. 12, in Gal. 10.3, in Eph. 10.6, in Phil. 12.7, in Col. 9.7, in 1 Thess. 7.5, in 2 Thess. 8.7, and in Philem. 8 per page.

So here again we have a closely connected series, beginning with the earliest, 1 Thess., and moving by very easy stages of less than a word per page, till we come to the latest, Phil., which has, in proportion to its length, the largest number of such words. The maximum difference, between the first and the last member of this series, amounts to 5.2 per page, representing the actual development', or the extreme limits of variation, in Paul's working vocabulary in this respect, during the last eleven years or so of his recorded ministry, by the end of which he was an elderly man (Philem. 9). The intermediate stages are:—from 1 Thess. to Philem. 0.5, 2 Thess. 0.7, Col. 1, Rom. 0.3, Gal. 0.3, Eph. 0.3, 1 Cor. 0.5, 2 Cor. 0.9, Phil. 0.7.

We turn back now to the Pastorals, and find an *increase* over Phil. of 14.6 in 1 Tim., 11.7 in 2 Tim., 17.7 in Titus. This sudden and drastic interruption of a sequence hitherto so orderly is, if possible, even more arresting than the great gap of 22.9 words per page between 1 Thess. and Titus. (See Diagram II.)

The line A A follows, from 1 Thess. to Phil., a perfectly normal, easy, gradual curve, with an upward trend, and there is nothing whatever to suggest a doubt as to the common origin with the rest of any member in the series. But at this point it is not enough to say that the line bends suddenly at a sharp angle. It breaks off abruptly. And the Pastorals are represented by a different line altogether, on quite a new plane.

Thus the ten Paulines are seen to form a distinct group by themselves. And the Pastorals stand right outside that group

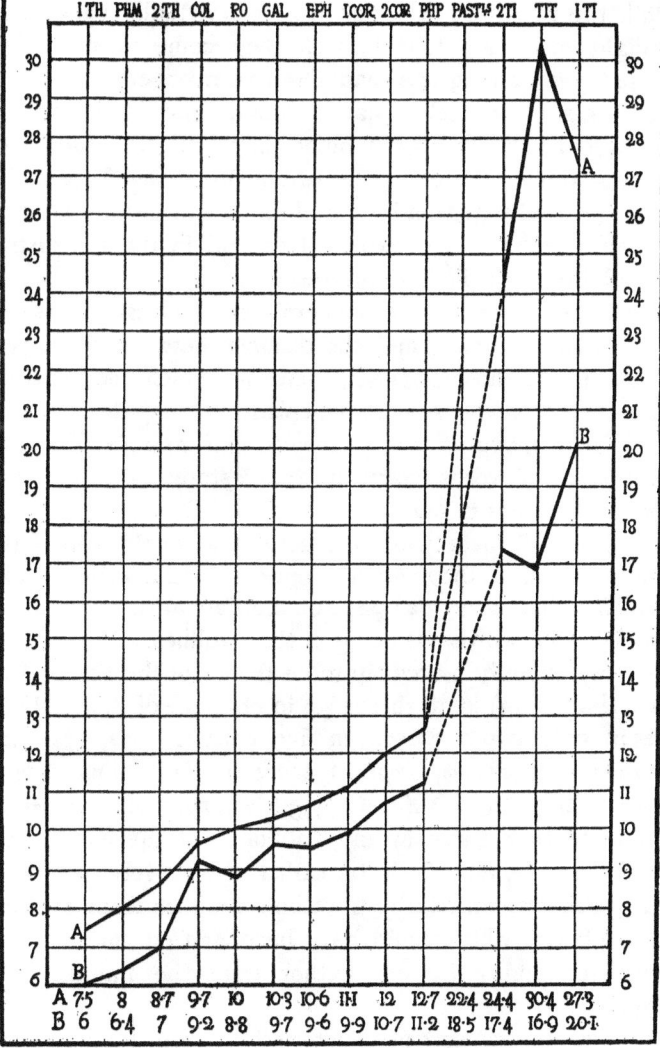

at such a distance as to create at once very serious doubts indeed, regarding the hypothesis of their common authorship with the rest.

In the same Diagram the second curve B B shows the result of eliminating in each case all words shared with one or more of the Pastorals, though with no Pauline epistle. From 1 Thess. to Phil. the two lines A A and B B run virtually parallel (with the slight exception that in Col. they come nearer than the average by something less than a word per page).

Now this is precisely what we might have anticipated in a writer who had them all ten before him, and had studied them with impartial reverence as the testament of his Apostle. But if they were really written by Paul himself some years after Phil., we should rather have expected to find in them a distinctly closer affinity with the later epistles.

When we come to the Pastorals themselves, the two lines spring violently apart; and the distance between them here is the measure of those linguistic elements which they share with one another, but with no Pauline epistle.

B. *Words found in the Pastorals and also in Paul.* The total number of words shared by the Pastorals with one or more of the ten Paulines is 542.

B 1. Fifty of these may be described as exclusively Pauline, in the sense that they do not appear in the other books of the N. T. That is 3·7 per page of the Pastorals, or 7·9 per cent. of the 632 such words occurring in the Paulines.

Of these 50, only 7 occur in more than 1 of the Pastorals, and only 1 (ἐπιφάνεια) in all three; 30 in only one of the Paulines, 10 more in only two; 3 occur in five epistles,—viz. ἔρις, μνεία, χρηστότης; 2 (ἀλοάω, σωρεύω) occur in Paul himself only in quotations from the LXX. Only 3 (ἀφθαρσία, οἰκέω, χρηστότης) occur more than twice in any Pauline. Of the handful which, rare as they are, may fairly be called distinctively or characteristically Pauline, practically the whole number form an integral part of phrases which could have been, and on our theory were, taken over bodily by our author from the Pauline epistles before him. See p. 90.

There is thus no sort of counterweight here to set against the great mass of facts which tell against the Pauline authorship of these epistles. (Further than this we do not need to go; and

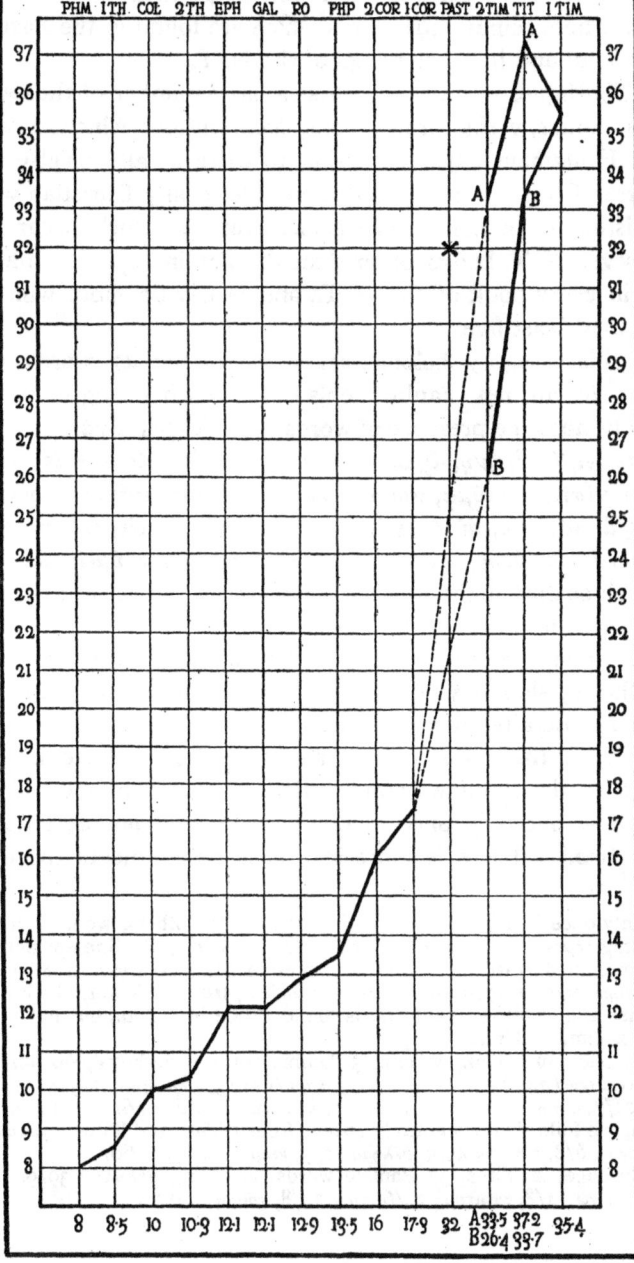

indeed must not, considering the small number of words in this class (113) shared by the ten Paulines themselves with one another,—from 1·8 per page in 1 Cor. to 4·8 in Col.)

B 2. There remain 492 words which are found in the Pastorals and in Paul and in other books of the N. T.

(*a*) This figure includes of course a large number of those commonest nouns, verbs, prepositions, &c., without which it would be, as Holtzmann says, impossible to write at all; or else those universal Christian terms indispensable to any Christian writer, and distinctive of none. We count over 230 which occur in at least seven N. T. books other than the Pauline epistles, many of them in every book of the N. T., and nearly 60 more which are found in at least five.

To this category belongs *every one* of the 47 words which appear in all ten Pauline epistles. Neither singly nor collectively does the presence of words like ἀδελφός, ἀγάπη, γίνομαι, εἰδέναι, εἰμί, εἰρήνη, ἔχω, εὐαγγέλιον, θεός, λέγω, πᾶς, κύριος, πατήρ, πίστις, πνεῦμα, ποιέω, χάρις, ἐκκλησία, πάντοτε, οὖν, ὑπέρ (gen.), ἀλλά, ἀπό, αὐτός, γάρ, δέ, διά, ἡμεῖς, εἰ, εἰς, ἐν, ἐπί, ἤ, ἵνα, καί, μετά, νῦν, ὁ, ὅς, ὅτι, οὐ, οὗτος, περί, πρός, τις, ὑμεῖς, ὡς, weigh so much as dust in the balance in favour of the Pauline authorship of any writing in which they occur.

The same may be said of all the 30 shared with 9 epistles, and the 25 shared with 8, as well as the 45 or so prepositions beyond those already mentioned.

(*b*) Then there are a great many of the most frequent and characteristic Pauline terms which occur, it is true, in the Pastorals, but only once in one of them, and not at all in the other two.[1] There is more in this fact than meets the eye at

---

[1] Only once in 1 Tim., and not in either of the others, we find 66 words, including νόμος (twice together; but 118 times in 5 Pauline epistles), σάρξ (89 times in 8 epistles), γνῶσις (22 times in 6), γράφω (62 in 8), δοκιμάζω 16/7, παράκλησις 19/7, προσεύχομαι 17/7, καθώς 75/9. Ἐκκλησία, which appears 59 times and in all ten Paulines, is found thrice in 1 Tim., but not at all in either 2 Tim. or Titus.

Only once, in 2 Tim., we find 53 Pauline words, including ἐγείρω 39/8, ζητέω 20/7, εὑρίσκω (bis) 14/5, θάνατος 44/5, καρπός 10/5, λογίζομαι 32/5, πληρόω 22/7, χαρά 21/7, οὕτως 72/9, πάντοτε 26/10, ὑπό with genitive 46/9. In addition to which, the following are entirely absent from 1 Tim. and Titus, ἀγαπάω 29/8, γιγνώσκω 46/8, δύναμις 45/9, θέλημα 22/7, νεκρός 42/8, μέν 60/8.

Only once, in Titus, 37 Pauline words, including ἀλλήλων 39/9, ἐξουσία 26/6, πέμπω 14/8, περιτομή 29/6, ποτέ 19/8, τοιοῦτος 31/8.

first. For, as we shall show later on (pp. 90, 97), a great many of these very words make their solitary appearance in the Pastorals precisely in those passages the Pauline authorship of which is not denied, but is on the contrary strongly affirmed as an essential feature of the 'critical' theory, as stated, e.g., in our introductory chapter, pp. 5-13. That is, they are contained either (1) in the phrases taken bodily, as we think, from the genuine epistles, or else (2) in the Personalia incorporated in 2 Tim. and Titus, mainly at the end of these epistles.

(c) Further this common vocabulary of Paul and the Pastorals is subject to a heavy discount in respect of the numerous words which carry a totally different meaning in the Pastorals from that which Paul gives them, or are used in a radically different way.

Thus ἀναλαμβάνω 1 Tim. iii. 16 of the Assumption, but in Paul = take up (spiritual weapons or armour, Eph. vi. 13, 16); ἀντέχομαι Titus i. 9 = hold fast (the faithful word), 1 Thess. v. 14 = support, aid, care for (needy members of the Church); γράμματα 2 Tim. iii. 15 = the sacred writings of the O. T., or, if we believe Holtzmann, theological study, exegesis of the O. T. text by discovery of the meaning hidden behind the letters—in any case, in a distinctly good sense; in Paul, γράμμα, always in a bad sense = the mere letter of the law, 'in a disparaging sense, as a hindrance to true religion' (Thayer, s. v.), Rom. ii. 27, 29, vii. 6, 2 Cor. iii. 6 f.; ἐπαγγέλλομαι 1 Tim. ii. 10, vi. 21 = profess, make a profession of, in Paul always of the Divine promises, Rom. iv. 21, Gal. iii. 19; ἐπέχω (sc. τ. νοῦν) 1 Tim. iv. 16 = take heed, Phil. ii. 16 = hold forth, hold towards as a light (Thayer); καθίστημι Titus i. 5 = appoint to office (act.), Rom. v. 19 = (pass.) be made, set down, constituted (*sisto*) i. q. declare, show to be (Thayer); κοινός Titus i. 4 = *communis* in good sense, of the general, universal faith of the Church, Rom. xiv. 14 = levitically unclean; μακάριος applied to God, 1 Tim. i. 11, vi. 15, never so in Paul, Rom. iv. 7 f., xiv. 22, 1 Cor. vii. 40; μόρφωσις 2 Tim. iii. 5 = mere form, semblance, in bad sense, Rom. ii. 20 = the form befitting the thing, or truly expressing the fact, the very form (Thayer), in good sense; οἶκος (θεοῦ) 1 Tim. iii. 15 = the Church, in Paul always of human dwellings, especially the private house in which a local church meets, never of 'God's House', Rom. xvi. 5,

Cor. xvi. 19, Col. iv. 15; παρατίθημι 2 Tim. ii. 2 = commit, entrust, to be religiously kept and taught to others (Thayer), in Paul only 1 Cor. x. 27 = set before, of food placed on a table; προσδέχομαι Titus ii. 13 = look for (the blessed hope), in Paul = welcome, of reception given to visiting saints, Rom. xvi. 2, Phil. ii. 29; πληροφορέω 2 Tim. iv. 5, 17 = fulfil one's ministry, or the Word, cause it to be shown to the full, in Paul always passive, = be convinced or persuaded, Rom. iv. 21, Col. iv. 12 (cf. 17); ὑποτίθημι 1 Tim. iv. 6 = put in mind of, Rom. xvi. 4 = lay down, risk (one's neck).

It is not of course to be expected of any author that he should invariably use every word in exactly the same sense. Paul himself, as well as the writer of these epistles, uses some words differently in different contexts. It is a question of degree as well as of kind. And it can hardly be denied that the instances given—and they might be considerably augmented—constitute no small difficulty in the way of assigning both groups of epistles to the same author.

(d) Conversely we are confronted with a series of passages in which Paul and the author of the Pastorals both say the same thing, but in different words. And once again we have to judge whether the instances, studied in detail and collectively, are favourable to, or even compatible with, unity of authorship. Thus in 1 Tim. iv. 12 Paul tells Timothy to let no one despise his youth, καταφρονεῖν, cf. Titus ii. 15 περιφρονεῖν. Now it happens that the real Paul had occasion to warn the Corinthians against exactly the same possibility, and with reference to this same Timothy. But although he knew the word καταφρονέω, and used it in other contexts, Rom. ii. 4, 1 Cor. xi. 22, he did not use it, but ἐξουθενέω, on this occasion—ἐὰν δὲ ἔλθῃ Τιμόθεος, βλέπετε ἵνα ἀφόβως γένηται πρὸς ὑμᾶς . . . μή τις οὖν αὐτὸν ἐξουθενήσῃ (1 Cor. xvi. 10). In 1 Tim. iv 12 we have the series ἐν λόγῳ . . . ἐν ἀγάπῃ . . . ἐν ἁγνείᾳ . . ., which corresponds with 2 Cor. vi 6 f., ἐν ἁγνότητι . . . ἐν ἀγάπῃ . . . ἐν λόγῳ . . ., except that for the Pauline ἁγνότης (cf. 2 Cor. xi. 3) is substituted ἁγνεία—a word foreign not only to Paul, but to the rest of the N. T., but very common in the Apostolic Fathers, whereas ἁγνότης occurs in these only twice, in Hermas.

In expressing his thankfulness to God, Paul consistently uses the word εὐχαριστέω (Rom. i. 8, 1 Cor. i. 4, 2 Cor. i. 11, Eph. i. 16, v. 20, Phil. i. 3, Col. i. 3, 1 Thess. i. 2, 2 Thess. i. 3, ii. 13, Philem. 4); this author never writes that word, but uses instead the Latinism χάριν ἔχω (= *gratiam habeo*) 1 Tim. i. 12, 2 Tim. i. 3. For the Pauline διό (27 times in 8 epistles) he substitutes δι' ἣν αἰτίαν (= *quam ob causam*) 2 Tim. i. 6, 12, Titus i. 13. Where Paul falls back on periphrases like εἰς ἕτερον εὐαγγέλιον μετατιθέναι, τὰ ὑψηλὰ φρονεῖν, τὰ ἑαυτῆς τέκνα θάλπειν, we now find the compounds ἑτεροδιδασκαλεῖν, ὑψηλοφρονεῖν, τεκνοτροφεῖν, of which the two first do not occur in extant literature till the second century. Instead of Paul's ἄμωμος or ἄμεμπτος, we find ἀνεπίληπτος, instead of ἀπὸ πατέρων, ἀπὸ προγόνων.

The expected coming of the Lord was bound to have a large place in the thoughts of any Pauline Christian; but the regular word for it in these epistles is ἐπιφάνεια (elsewhere in the N. T. only 2 Thess. ii. 8, τ. ἐπιφανείᾳ τῆς παρουσίας αὐτοῦ, but found in 2 Clement xii. 1, xvii. 4, Justin, *Apol.* xiv. 3, xl. 1, *Dial.* xxii. 3, 1 Tim. vi. 14, 2 Tim. i. 10, iv. 1, 8, Titus ii. 13), whereas Paul's word is παρουσία, 1 Cor. xv. 23, 1 Thess. ii. 19, iii. 13, iv. 15, 2 Thess. ii. 1, or ἀποκάλυψις, 1 Cor. i. 7, 2 Thess. i. 7, neither of which occurs in the Pastorals; while the act or state of expectation is expressed by the verb προσδέχομαι instead of the Pauline ἀπεκδέχομαι, Titus ii. 13 προσδεχόμενοι τὴν ... ἐπιφάνειαν τῆς δόξης τοῦ μεγάλου θεοῦ, cf. 1 Cor. i. 7 ἀπεκδεχομένους τὴν ἀποκάλυψιν τοῦ κυρίου ἡμῶν, Rom. viii. 19, Phil. iii. 20. Paul, as we have seen, uses προσδέχομαι to express quite another idea. Again the Paul of the Pastorals, as of the other epistles, makes mention of his friends in his prayers, but the former expresses this by μνείαν ἔχω, 2 Tim. i. 3, which the real Paul uses in the general sense of holding in remembrance, 1 Thess. iii. 6, while for the special sense of remembering in prayer he invariably says μνείαν ποιοῦμαι Rom. i. 10, Eph. i. 16, 1 Thess. i. 2, Phil. i. 3, Philem. 4. Both writers know of people whose very conscience has become defiled, but the writer of the Pastorals prefers μιαίνω (14 times in Hermas, e.g. *Man.* v. 1. 6, 7. 2, cf. Justin, *Dial.* xxi. 4, Aristeides, *Apol.* iv. 3, v. 1, xii. 1) to the Pauline μολύνω, Titus i. 15, μεμίανται αὐτῶν καὶ ὁ νοῦς καὶ ἡ συνείδησις, 1 Cor. viii. 7, ἡ συνείδησις αὐτῶν ... μολύνεται. The masters whom slaves are exhorted to obey are δεσπόται in these epistles (as e. g. in Hermas, *Sim.* v. 2. 8, 9), κύριοι in the Paulines, and the obedience enjoined is ὑποτάσσεσθαι in the former, but ὑπακούειν in the latter, Titus ii. 9, cf. Col. iii. 22, Eph. vi. 5 f. For further instances, see Holtzmann *P. B.*, pp. 105, 107.

C. It now remains to consider those elements in the Pauline vocabulary which are conspicuous by their absence from the Pastorals. The total number is 103 proper names and 1,635 other words, of which 582 are peculiar to Paul, and 1,053 occur also in other books of the N. T.

C 1. Of these 582 exclusively Pauline words, 469 occur in one epistle only, and have already been dealt with. The 113 found in more than one epistle include a majority used by Paul himself not more than twice or three times. Twenty-one occur in three epistles, ἁγιωσύνη, ἀνήκω, δοκιμή, ἔνδειξις, ἐξαγοράζω, ἐπιβαρέω, εὐσχημόνως, εὐωδία, κάμπτω, μετασχηματίζω, μόχθος, πάθος, πεποίθησις, προλέγω, συναιχμάλωτος, υἱοθεσία, φιλοτιμέομαι, (in 3 Homologoumena) θνητός, καταλλάσσω, κλίμα, φύραμα. Eight occur in 4 epistles, ἀγαθωσύνη, ἄπειμι, ἁπλότης, εἰκῇ, εἴπερ, ἐνέργεια, κενόω, ὑπερβολή. Though the aggregate number of these distinctively Pauline words is certainly considerable, it cannot be said that their absence from the Pastorals presents any serious difficulty for those who maintain the Pauline authorship, but only that there is still less difficulty here for the other side. See however below, p. 74 f.

C 2. There remain the 1,053 Pauline words, to be found in other N. T. books, but not in the Pastorals. Five hundred and thirty-two of these appear in more than one epistle. We select from these first (*a*) a number of the most frequent and characteristic terms in the Pauline vocabulary.

OF THE PASTORALS

C. Pauline Words wanting in the Pastorals.

C 1. Not elsewhere in the N. T., but in four Pauline Epistles:—
ἀγαθωσύνη, ἄπειμι, ἁπλότης, εἰκῇ, εἴπερ, ἐνέργεια, κενόω, ὑπερβολή.

C 2. In other N. T. books, and *in five Pauline Epistles*:

	Rom.	1 Cor.	2 Cor.	Gal.	Eph.	Phil.	Col.	1 Thess.	2 Thess.	Philem.	Total.
ἀδικέω	..	2	3	1	..	..	1	..	..	1	8
αἷμα	3	4	..	1	3	..	1	..	..	..	12
ἀκροβυστία	10	2	..	3	1	..	2	..	..	..	18
ἄλλος	..	23	4	2	..	1	..	1	..	..	31
ἀνάγκη	1	3	3	..	..	..	..	1	..	1	9
ἀξίως	1	..	..	..	1	1	1	1	..	..	5
ἀσθενής	1	9	1	1	..	..	..	1	..	.	13
δεξιός	1	..	1	1	1	..	1	..	..	..	5
διαθήκη	2	1	2	3	1	..	..	..	..	..	9
δοξάζω	5	2	2	1	..	..	..	..	1	..	11
ἐλεύθερος	2	6	..	6	1	..	1	..	..	..	16
ἐξέρχομαι	1	2	3	..	..	1	..	1	..	..	8
ἐξουθενέω	2	3	1	1	..	..	..	1	..	..	8
ἔπαινος	2	1	1	..	3	2	..	..	..	..	9
ἐρῶ	13	3	2	1	..	1	..	..	..	..	20
εὐλογία	2	1	3	1	1	..	..	..	..	..	8
ζῆλος	2	1	5	1	..	1	..	..	..	..	10
θυμός	1	..	1	1	1	..	1	..	..	..	5
καταλαμβάνω	1	1	..	..	1	3	..	1	..	..	7
καταρτίζω	1	1	1	1	..	..	..	1	..	..	5
κατεργάζομαι	11	1	6	..	1	1	..	..	..	..	20
καύχημα	1	3	3	1	..	2	..	..	..	..	10
κόπος	..	2	4	1	..	..	..	3	1	..	11
μέρος	3	7	4	..	2	..	1	..	..	..	17
νήπιος	1	6	..	2	1	..	..	1	..	..	11
νουθετέω	1	1	..	..	..	..	2	2	1	..	7
παλαιός	1	2	1	..	1	..	1	..	..	..	6
παράπτωμα	9	..	1	1	3	..	2	..	..	..	16
παρουσία	..	2	3	..	..	2	..	4	3	..	14
πλεονάζω	3	..	2	..	..	1	..	1	1	..	8
πλεονεξία	1	..	1	..	2	..	1	1	..	..	6
πλήρωμα	4	1	..	1	4	..	2	..	..	..	12
πνευματικός	3	13	..	1	3	..	2	..	..	..	22
σοφία	1	17	1	..	3	..	6	..	..	..	28
σταυρός	..	2	..	3	1	2	2	..	..	..	10
τέλειος	1	3	..	..	1	1	2	..	..	..	8
τρέχω	1	3	..	2	..	1	..	..	1	..	8
ὑπακούω	4	..	..	..	2	1	2	..	2	..	11
ὑπάρχω	1	5	2	2	..	2	..	..	..	..	12
ὑστέρημα	..	1	4	..	..	1	1	1	..	..	8
φοβέομαι	3	..	2	2	1	..	1	..	..	..	9
Carried forward ..	100	134	67	41	39	24	33	21	10	2	471

C. *Pauline Words wanting in the Pastorals* (continued).

	Rom.	1 Cor.	2 Cor.	Gal.	Eph.	Phil.	Col.	1 Thess.	2 Thess.	Philem.	Total.
Brought forward	100	134	67	41	39	24	33	21	10	2	471
In six Epistles:											
ἀκαθαρσία	2	1	..	1	2	..	1	2	..	..	9
ἀποκαλύπτω	3	3	..	2	1	1	..	..	3	..	13
ἀποκάλυψις	3	3	2	2	2	..	..	..	1	..	13
ἐπιστολή	1	2	8	..	..	..	1	1	4	..	17
εὐαγγελίζομαι	3	6	2	6	2	..	..	1	..	..	20
ἐχθρός	3	2	..	1	..	1	1	..	1	..	9
κατέχω	2	3	1	..	..	..	..	1	2	1	10
καυχάομαι	5	5	17	2	1	1	..	..	..	..	31
κοινωνία	1	3	4	1	..	3	..	..	..	1	13
μέσος	..	2	1	..	..	1	1	1	1	..	7
ὀφείλω	3	5	2	..	1	..	..	..	2	1	14
παραλαμβάνω	..	3	..	2	..	1	2	2	1	..	11
πορνεία	..	4	1	1	1	..	1	1	..	..	9
πρόσωπον	..	2	12	3	..	..	1	3	1	..	22
σκότος	2	1	2	..	3	..	1	2	..	..	11
στήκω	1	1	..	1	..	2	..	1	1	..	7
φρονέω	8	1	1	1	..	10	1	..	..	..	22
χαίρω	3	3	8	..	..	8	2	2	..	..	26
ὥρα	1	2	1	1	..	..	..	1	..	1	7
In seven Epistles:											
ἀποθνήσκω	22	7	5	2	..	1	2	2	..	..	41
βλέπω	6	7	7	1	1	3	3	..	..	..	28
γνωρίζω	3	2	1	1	6	2	3	..	..	..	18
ἐνδύω	2	4	1	1	3	..	2	1	..	..	14
εὐδοκέω	2	2	2	1	..	..	1	2	1	..	11
κενός	..	4	1	1	1	2	1	2	..	..	12
περισσεύω	3	3	10	..	1	5	1	3	..	..	26
πράσσω	10	2	2	1	1	1	..	1	..	..	18
συνεργός	3	1	2	..	..	2	1	1	..	2	12
ψυχή	4	1	2	..	1	2	1	2	..	..	13
In eight Epistles:											
δέχομαι	..	1	5	1	1	1	1	2	1	..	13
ἐργάζομαι	4	4	1	1	1	..	1	2	4	..	18
θλίψις	5	1	9	..	1	2	1	3	2	..	24
σῶμα	13	43	9	1	9	3	8	1	..	..	87
υἱός	12	2	4	13	4	..	2	3	1	..	41
χαρίζομαι	1	1	5	1	2	2	3	..	..	1	16
In nine Epistles:											
ἐνεργέω	1	2	2	4	4	1	1	1	1	..	17
εὐχαριστέω	6	6	1	..	2	1	3	3	2	1	25
οὐρανός	2	2	3	1	4	1	5	2	1	..	21
περιπατέω	4	2	5	1	8	2	4	4	2	..	32
Totals	244	283	206	96	102	83	89	74	42	10	1229

OF THE PASTORALS

Nor is it only single Pauline terms, however numerous, the absence of which makes itself felt in reading the Pastorals, but whole groups of such words derived from a common root: e. g. ἐνέργεια, ἐνεργέω, ἐνέργημα, ἐνεργής, one or other of which occurs 28 times and in all 10 epistles; also συνεργέω, συνεργός 14 times in 6 epistles, and ἐργάζομαι, κατεργάζομαι 38 in 9; εὐδοκέω, εὐδοκία, 17 in 9; περίσσευμα, περισσεύω, περισσός, περισσότερος, περισσοτέρως, 48/8; καυχάομαι, καύχημα, καύχησις, κατακαυχάομαι, 52/7; ὀφειλέτης, ὀφειλή, ὀφείλημα, ὀφείλω, ὄφελον, ὄφελος, 25/7; σταυρός, σταυρόω, συνσταυρόω, 20/7; ἐλευθερία, ἐλευθερόω, ἐλεύθερος, ἀπελεύθερος, 29/6; πρᾶγμα, πρᾶξις, πράσσω, 25/7; πλεονεκτέω, πλεονέκτης, πλεονεξία, 16/6; σκοτίζομαι, σκοτόομαι, σκότος, 14/6; σοφία, σοφός, 44/5; ταπεινός, ταπεινόω, ταπείνωσις, ταπεινοφροσύνη, 13/5; τέλειος, τελειότης, τελειόω, 10/5; ἐπαινέω, ἔπαινος, 13/5; εὐλογέω, εὐλογητός, εὐλογία, 19/5; κενός, κενόω, 18/8; μερίζω, μερίς, μέρος, 25/5; πνευματικός, πνευματικῶς, 23/5; ἀναγκάζω, ἀνάγκη, 13/6; ὑστερέω, ὑστέρημα, ὑστέρησις, 16/5; υἱός, υἱοθεσία, 46/8; ἀποκαλύπτω, ἀποκάλυψις, 26/7; ψυχή, ψυχικός, 17/7; λυπέω, λύπη, 22/5; φθαρτός, φθείρω, φθορά, 14/6; φρονέω, παραφρονέω, ὑπερφρονέω, φρόνημα, φρόνησις, φρόνιμος, 34/7 (on the other hand we find in the Pastorals, but not in Paul, περιφρονέω, φροντίζω, ὑψηλοφρονέω).

Now it goes without saying that the mere absence of any one, or any half-dozen, of these words from an epistle counts for very little indeed in this connexion. No writer can be required to use the whole body even of his own favourite expressions every time he puts pen to paper. It is always open to defenders of the Pauline authorship to say that the Apostle used the words that he wanted to express his meaning at the moment, and that the absence of any number of his usual expressions is due simply to the fact that he had no need for them in the present instance. But—apart from the fact already noted, that in these epistles there are plenty of passages, where a Pauline term would have come in admirably, but where we find instead some expression foreign to Paul's other writings—there must obviously be some limit here. And the whole contention at this stage is that, taken in the mass, as well as in detail, the omission of so very much that is most constant and characteristic in the Pauline terminology constitutes a very serious objection indeed to our acceptance of the Pauline authorship of these epistles. Not only does it go far and away beyond anything for which the variations in the ten Paulines had prepared us; it implies a change of perspective, a shifting of horizons, a profound modification of the whole mental and spiritual outlook for which two or three, or even five years would hardly be sufficient in any man, least of all an old man, and such a one as this Paul the aged, with such deep-rooted conceptions, and so definite a system of thought and expression as we know him to have reached, for all his receptivity and versatility. See Diagram IV.

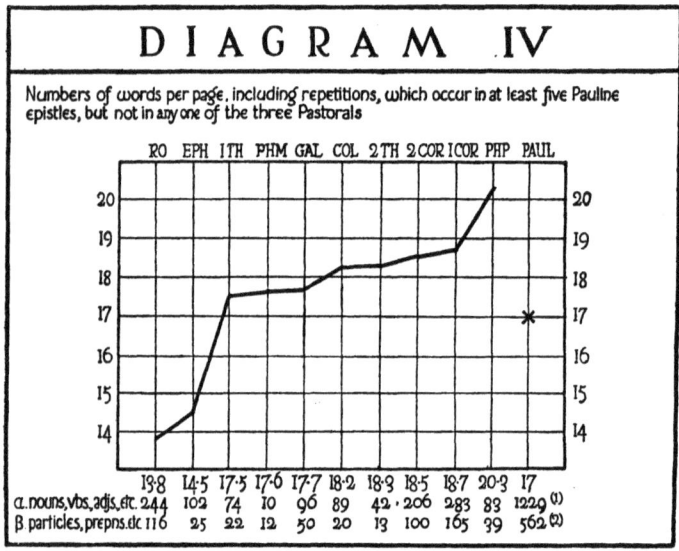

The Missing Particles.

(*b*) But we must now refer to another series of omissions, which is if possible still more striking and significant—the long string of Pauline particles, enclitics, prepositions, pronouns, &c., for which we look in vain in these epistles. Not only are the stones used by this builder of a different shape and substance from those of the Paulines, the very clamps and mortar that hold them together are different too. Holtzmann mentioned (*PB.*, p. 101) a couple of dozen or so of these, but the facts go far beyond anything that he or any one else has yet stated. In the table on pp. 36–7 there will be found a list of such words, showing the

[1] See p. 32.   [2] p. 37.

number of times that each occurs in the Pauline epistles singly and collectively. It is not suggested, of course, that the Apostle was under any obligation to use any one of these every time he wrote. But let any reader fully observe the facts here given in the mass, reflect on the evidence now produced touching Paul's habitual modes of thought and expression, and then consider the balance of probability against such a contingency as the traditional theory requires us to accept—viz. that within a very few years we should find the same writer producing three epistles without once happening to use a single word in all that list—

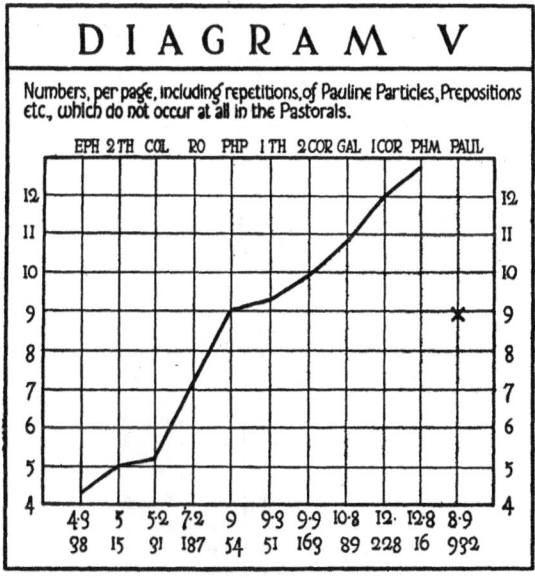

one or other of which has hitherto appeared on the average nine times to every page that Paul ever wrote.

It is certain that nothing to approach this list can be produced in the case of any Pauline epistle. Of the 112 Pauline particles, &c., on this page, Rom. has 58, 1 Cor. 69, 2 Cor. 53, Gal. 43, Eph. 22, Phil. 29, Col. 18, 1 Thess. 27, 2 Thess. 12, and even Philem. in its page and a quarter has 12. But we have to take into account not only the occurrence of such terms, but their frequent recurrence. One or other of these words appears in Eph. 38 times, or 4.3 per page, in 2 Thess. 15 or 5 per page,

Pauline Particles, Prepositions, Pronouns, &c., wanting in the Pastorals.

In one epistle:—C. 1. Not elsewhere in the N. T.: Rom. ἤτοι.—1 Cor. διόπερ 2 μήτιγε, νή, ὡσπερεί.—2 Cor. ἡνίκα 2, ὑπερλίαν 2. C. 2. In other N. T. books:

	Rom.	1 Cor.	2 Cor.	Gal.	Eph.	Phil.	Col.	1 Thess.	2 Thess.	Philem.	Times in Paul
In one Epistle	7	9	6	5	4	2	1	1	0	0	35
„ „ incl. erpetitions	7	12	11	5	8	2	1	1	0	0	47
In two Epistles:											
C. 1 ὑπερεκπερισσοῦ	..	..	..	..	1	..	..	2	..	..	3
τάχα	1	..	..	..	..	..	..	..	..	1	2
C. 2 δίς	..	..	..	..	..	1	..	1	..	..	2
ἕνεκεν	2	..	4	..	..	..	..	..	..	..	6
ἐπειδή	..	4	..	..	..	1	..	..	..	..	5
ἐφάπαξ	1	1	..	..	..	..	..	..	..	..	2
ἡλίκος	..	..	..	1	..	..	1	..	..	..	2
καθό	1	..	2	..	..	..	..	..	..	..	3
κἄν	..	5	1	..	..	..	..	..	..	..	6
κατέναντι	1	..	2	..	..	..	..	..	..	..	3
κατενώπιον	..	..	..	..	1	..	1	..	..	..	2
μενοῦνγε	2	..	..	..	..	1	..	..	..	..	3
ὁμοίως	1	3	..	..	..	..	..	..	..	..	4
ὅμως	..	1	..	1	..	..	..	..	..	..	2
οὗ	1	..	3	..	..	..	..	..	..	..	4
οὐθείς	..	1	1	..	..	..	..	..	..	..	2
οὔπω	..	2	..	..	..	1	..	..	..	..	3
πάντως	1	4	..	..	..	..	..	..	..	..	5
ποῖος	1	1	..	..	..	..	..	..	..	..	2
σός	..	2	..	..	..	..	..	..	..	1	3
τοσοῦτος	..	1	..	1	..	..	..	..	..	..	2
τοὐνάντιον	..	..	1	1	..	..	..	..	..	..	2
ὧδε	..	1	..	..	..	..	1	..	..	..	2
In three Epistles:											
ἄνω	..	..	..	1	..	1	2	..	..	..	4
ἅπαξ	..	..	1	..	..	1	..	1	..	..	3
ἔνι (= ἔνεστι)	..	1	..	3	..	..	1	..	..	..	5
ἐπεί	3	5	2	..	..	..	..	..	..	..	10
ἔπειτα	..	7	..	3	..	..	..	1	..	..	11
ἕως (prep.)	2	5	3	..	..	..	..	..	..	..	10
ὁποῖος	..	1	..	1	..	..	..	1	..	..	3
ὅπου	1	1	..	..	..	..	1	..	..	..	3
ὄφελον	..	1	1	1	..	..	..	..	..	..	3
πλήν	..	1	..	..	1	3	..	..	..	..	5
πόσος	2	..	1	..	..	..	..	..	..	1	4
ποῦ;	1	8	..	1	..	..	..	..	..	..	10
In four Epistles:											
ἄρτι	..	7	..	3	..	..	..	1	1	..	12
διότι	5	1	..	..	..	1	..	3	..	..	10
ἔμπροσθεν	..	..	1	1	..	1	..	4	..	..	7
ἔξω	..	2	1	..	..	..	1	1	..	..	5
ἔσω	1	1	1	..	1	..	..	..	..	..	4
ἰδού	1	1	6	1	..	..	..	..	..	..	9
Total words	25	35	22	18	8	11	8	10	1	3	76
„ repetitions	35	80	42	24	12	13	9	16	1	3	235

Rom. ἀπέναντι, δεῦρο, μεταξύ, μήπω, πού, ὡσεί.—1 Cor. δή, ἐπάνω, ὅλως 3, οὐδέποτε, τοίνυν.—2 Cor. ἔσωθεν, μήτι 2, τηλικοῦτος, τρίς 3.—Gal. ἄνωθεν, ἄρα, εὐθέως, ἴδε, πηλίκος.—Eph. εὖ, μακράν 2, ὑπεράνω 2, ἀμφότεροι 3.—Phil. ἐξαυτῆς, καίπερ.—1 Thess. τοιγαροῦν.—Col. ὑπεναντίος.

	Rom.	1 Cor.	2 Cor.	Gal.	Eph.	Phil.	Col.	1 Thess.	2 Thess.	Philem.	Times in Paul.	Times in Luke and Acts.
In four Eps. (ctd.):												
C. 2 καθάπερ	6	2	4	..	..	..	..	4	..	..	16	0
οὐ μή	1	1	..	2	..	..	..	2	..	..	6	20
ναί	1	..	6	..	..	1	..	..	..	1	9	6
ὁ μέν.. ὁ δέ..	..	1	..	1	1	1	..	..	..	..	4	4
οὖ..	3	1	1	..	..	..	1	..	..	..	6	14
οὔτε	10	15	..	5	..	..	..	5	..	..	35	22
οὐχί	3	13	1	..	..	..	..	1	..	..	18	21
παρά (acc.)	7	3	2	2	..	..	..	..	..	..	14	22
ὑμέτερος	1	2	1	1	..	..	..	..	..	..	5	3
C. 1 εἰκῆ	1	1	..	2	..	..	1	..	..	..	5	0
εἴπερ	3	2	1	..	..	..	..	..	1	..	7	0
μήπως	..	2	5	2	..	..	..	1	..	..	10	0
In five Epistles:												
C. 2 ἀντί	1	1	..	..	1	..	..	1	1	..	5	5
αὐτὸς ὁ..	3	3	2	..	..	..	..	3	2	..	13	13
ἄχρι	4	3	3	2	..	2	..	..	..	..	14	21
οὐκέτι	7	..	2	4	1	..	..	..	..	1	15	7
πάλιν	5	3	8	9	..	3	..	..	..	..	28	8
τε..	18	3	2	..	1	1	..	..	..	..	25	154
ὥσπερ	6	5	1	1	..	..	..	1	..	..	14	5
In six Epistles:												
ἄν..	7	8	5	3	..	1	1	..	..	..	25	56
ὁ αὐτός..	6	17	9	..	1	8	..	1	..	..	42	14
ἐμαυτοῦ	1	6	4	1	..	1	..	..	..	1	14	6
νυνὶ δέ..	7	4	2	..	1	..	2	..	..	2	18	2
ὅπως	3	1	2	1	..	..	..	..	1	1	9	22
ὑπέρ (accus.)	..	2	3	1	2	1	..	..	..	2	11	3
In seven Epistles:												
ἄρα	11	5	3	5	1	..	..	1	1	..	27	11
γε..	3	3	2	1	2	1	1	..	..	..	13	13
ἔτι	5	4	1	3	..	1	..	..	1	1	16	21
κἀγώ	2	10	9	2	1	2	..	1	..	..	27	12
τότε	1	6	1	3	..	..	1	1	1	..	14	36
ὥστε	5	14	7	5	..	3	..	3	2	..	39	13
In eight Epistles:												
διό	6	2	9	1	5	1	..	2	..	1	27	10
εἴτε	4	27	14	..	2	6	6	2	2	..	63	0
ἐμός	2	9	3	2	..	2	1	..	1	3	23	3
σύν	4	7	6	4	2	4	7	4	..	..	38	77
In nine Epistles:												
ἕκαστος	5	22	2	2	5	2	1	2	1	..	42	16
Total words	58	69	53	43	22	29	18	27	12	12	112	
,, repetitns.	187	288	163	89	38	54	31	51	15	16	932	Diag. V.
In at least five Epp. including rep.	116	165	100	50	25	39	20	22	13	12	562	Diag. IV.

in Col. 31 or 5.2 per page, in Rom. 187 or 7.2 per page, Phil. 54 or 9 per page, in 1 Thess. 51 or 9.3 per page, in 2 Cor. 163 or 9.9 per page, in Gal. 89 = 10.8 per page, in 1 Cor. 288 = 12 per page, and in Philem. 16 = 12.8 per page. The total number of occurrences for the whole ten epistles is 932, or on the average 8.9 per page. See Diagram V, p. 35.

Nor is it possible to redress the balance by referring to the 77 Pauline particles, &c., which do appear in the Pastorals. For of these—

(1) Every one occurs also in the Apostolic Fathers, and in the Apologists, and the great majority in practically every book of the N.T.

(2) Thirty-six occur in all three Pastorals, of which *all* occur in Rom., all but one in 1 and 2 Cor., Eph., Phil., Gal., 33 in Col., 30 in 1 Thess., 31 in 2 Thess., and 30 even in Philem.!

(3) Of the remaining 41, 7 occur in only one Pauline, 17 in only one of the Pastorals, and 10 only once in the Pastorals.

2. Grammatical Peculiarities.

But the familiar Pauline particles are not by any means the only grammatical forms which by their absence create in our minds a sense of strangeness and unfamiliarity as often as we come to the Pastorals fresh from a careful study of the genuine Paulines.

1. In his use of the definite article our author betrays a noticeably different method of literary craftsmanship.

(i) The phrase ὁ μέν ... ὁ δέ, which Paul finds so handy (cf. 1 Cor. vii. 7, Gal. iv. 23, Eph. iv. 11, Phil. i. 16), is not in these epistles.

(ii) Nor is the ὁ with nominative in place of a vocative which appears 9 times in Rom., 4 in Gal., 6 in Eph., 6 in Col., e.g. Rom. ii. 1 ὦ ἄνθρωπε πᾶς ὁ κρίνων, Gal. iv. 6 'Αββὰ ὁ πατήρ, Eph. v. 14 ἔγειρε ὁ καθεύδων.

(iii) Nor the ὁ with a numeral—cf. Rom. v. 17 τῷ τοῦ ἑνὸς παραπτώματι, 1 Cor. iv. 6, vi. 16, xiii. 13 τὰ τρία ταῦτα, xiv. 30 ὁ πρῶτος, xv. 5 τοῖς δώδεκα, 2 Cor. xiii. 2, Eph. ii. 15, v. 31, Phil. i. 23, 1 Thess. v. 11.

(iv) Nor the ὁ with an infinitive—34 times in Rom., 14 in 1 Cor., 18 in 2 Cor., 5 in Gal., 3 in Eph., 15 in Phil., 10 in

1 Thess., 7 in 2 Thess., e.g. Rom. i. 11 εἰς τὸ στηριχθῆναι ὑμᾶς, Phil. i. 21 Ἐμοὶ γὰρ τὸ ζῆν Χριστὸς καὶ τὸ ἀποθανεῖν κέρδος.[1]

(v) Nor the τοῦ with infinitive—9 times in Rom., 3 in 1 Cor., 4 in 2 Cor., 3 in Gal., 2 in Phil., e.g. 1 Cor. ix. 10 ἐπ' ἐλπίδι τοῦ μετέχειν, Gal. ii. 12 πρὸ τοῦ γὰρ ἐλθεῖν.

(vi) Nor the ὁ with an adverb—Rom. i. 13 ἄχρι τοῦ δεῦρο, viii. 22, xiii. 9 f., xv. 2, vii. 29, 2 Cor. iv. 16, v. 16, x. 16, xi. 28, xiii. 2, Gal. v. 14, vi. 17 τοῦ λοιποῦ, Eph. ii. 17, iv. 25, vi. 10, Phil. i. 5 ἄχρι τοῦ νῦν, iii. 14 τῆς ἄνω κλήσεως, iv. 8, Col. iii. 1 f., iv. 5, 9, 1 Thess. iv. 12, 2 Thess. iii. 1, cf. ix *infra*. (But cf. 1 Tim. iii. 7.)

(vii) Nor with an interjection—cf. 1 Cor. xiv. 16 τὸ ἀμήν, 2 Cor. i. 17, 20 τὸ ναὶ καὶ τὸ οὔ.

(viii) Nor with a whole sentence—cf. Rom. viii. 26 τὸ γὰρ τί προσευξώμεθα καθὸ δεῖ οὐκ οἴδαμεν, xiii. 9 *bis*, 1 Cor. iv. 6, Gal. v. 14 πεπλήρωται ἐν τῷ Ἀγαπήσεις τὸν πλησίον σου ὡς σεαυτόν, Eph. iv. 9 τὸ δὲ ἀνέβη τί ἐστιν εἰ μὴ ὅτι καὶ κατέβη, 1 Thess. iv. 1 καθὼς παρελάβετε παρ' ἡμῶν τὸ πῶς δεῖ ὑμᾶς περιπατεῖν, cf. 1 Tim. iii. 15 ἵνα εἰδῇς πῶς δεῖ ... ἀναστρέφεσθαι.

(ix) On the other hand we find ὄντως, which Paul uses adverbially 1 Cor. xiv. 25, Gal. iii. 21, converted by our author into an adjective by the preceding article, 1 Tim. v. 3, 5, 16 ἡ ὄντως χήρα, vi. 19 τῆς ὄντως ζωῆς. Cf. *Ep. ad Diog.* x. 7 τὸν ὄντως θάνατον, Aristeides, *Apol.* iv. 1 τοῦ ὄντως θεοῦ=Jus. *Ap.* xiii. 13, Athenag. *Suppl.* vii. 2 τὸ ὄντως θεῖον, xii. 2 τὸν ὄντως θεόν, xv. 3, xxiii. 4 τὸ ὄντως ὄν.

2. ὡς occurs fairly often in the Pastorals, generally followed by a substantive—e.g. παρακάλει ὡς πατέρα, 1 Tim. v. 1. But there is no trace in them of the Pauline uses of ὡς—

(i) with the participle, Rom. iv. 17 καλοῦντος τὰ μὴ ὄντα ὡς ὄντα, Col. ii. 20 ὡς ζῶντες ἐν κόσμῳ, 1 Thess. ii. 4 οὐχ ὡς ἀνθρώποις ἀρέσκοντες, Rom. xv. 15 ὡς ἐπαναμιμνήσκων ὑμᾶς, 1 Cor. iv. 7, 18, v. 3, vii. 25 (cf. 1 Tim. i. 13, 16) ὡς ἠλεημένος, vii. 30 f. οἱ κλαίοντες ὡς μὴ κλαίοντες, οἱ χαίροντες ὡς μὴ χαίροντες κτλ., 2 Cor. x. 2, vi. 9 ὡς ἀγνοούμενοι κτλ.

(ii) with the adverb—cf. Rom. i. 9 ὡς ἀδιαλείπτως μνείαν ὑμῶν ποιοῦμαι (contrast 2 Tim. i. 3 ὡς ἀδιάλειπτον ἔχω τὴν

---

[1] That is, 106 times in Paul. On this 'articular infinitive' see J. H. Moulton, *Grammar of N. T. Greek*, vol. i, p. 216, and Moulton and Geden, *Concordance to the G. T.*, p. 679.

περὶ σοῦ μνείαν, where as Holtzmann points out, *PB.*, p. 111, the change leaves no proper motive for the ὡς), 1 Cor. ix. 26 οὕτω τρέχω ὡς οὐκ ἀδήλως, οὕτω πυκτεύω ὡς οὐκ ἀέρα δέρων, Phil. i. 20 ὡς πάντοτε καὶ νῦν.

(iii) with ἄν—Rom. xv. 24 ὡς ἂν πορεύωμαι εἰς τ. Σπανίαν, 1 Cor. xi. 34 τὰ λοιπὰ ὡς ἂν ἔλθω διατάξομαι, Phil. ii. 23.

3. Another favourite construction of Paul's which is conspicuous by its absence from the Pastorals, is the series of prepositions in a single sentence with reference to some one subject, which is thus 'defined on every side' (Winer), e. g. Rom. i. 17 ἐκ πίστεως εἰς πίστιν, iii. 22 εἰς πάντας καὶ ἐπὶ πάντας, xi. 36 ἐξ αὐτοῦ καὶ δι' αὐτοῦ καὶ εἰς αὐτόν, Gal. i. 1 οὐκ ἀπ' ἀνθρώπων οὐδὲ δι' ἀνθρώπου, 2 Cor. xiii. 8 οὐ γὰρ δυνάμεθά τι κατὰ τῆς ἀληθείας ἀλλὰ ὑπὲρ τῆς ἀληθείας, Col. i. 16 ἐν αὐτῷ ἐκτίσθη τὰ πάντα . . . τὰ πάντα δι' αὐτοῦ κ. εἰς αὐτὸν ἔκτισται, Eph. iv. 6 εἷς θεὸς κ. πατὴρ πάντων ὁ ἐπὶ πάντων κ. διὰ πάντων καὶ ἐν πᾶσιν ὑμῖν (cf. 1 Tim. ii. 5 f.), 1 Cor. xii. 8 f. ᾧ μὲν γὰρ διὰ τοῦ πνεύματος . . . ἄλλῳ δὲ . . . κατὰ τὸ αὐτὸ πνεῦμα, ἑτέρῳ . . . ἐν τῷ αὐτῷ πνεύματι κτλ., 2 Cor. iii. 18 ἀπὸ δόξης εἰς δόξαν (Holtzmann, *PB.*, p. 101; Winer, *Grammar of N. T. Greek*, E. Tr., p. 521 f.).

3. STYLE.

But we have not yet finished with the missing particles, prepositions, and connecting words generally.

When we have asserted with complete confidence that their absence on the scale now demonstrated cannot by any possibility be dismissed as merely accidental, nor evaded by suggesting airily that the writer had no occasion to use them, nor explained away by any reference to changed circumstances, subject-matter, or readers, we are left face to face with the necessity of considering what is really involved in the facts before us.

This is nothing less than a radical peculiarity of style. It can hardly have been that the words in question were unknown to the writer! But his avoidance of them, whether conscious, deliberate or otherwise, is a strongly marked and highly significant feature in his mode of self-expression. Nor is it confined to any mere surface quality. It is intimately connected with his whole way of thinking and of reasoning, with his very temperament and, in a word, his personality. 'Le style, c'est l'homme.'

Now the style with which the ten Paulines have made us familiar, shows all the irregularities and abruptnesses—the tendency to fly off at a tangent, the sudden turns and swift asides, the parentheses and anacolutha, the frequent incursions of the unexpected—which mark the products of a mind carried along, and sometimes carried away, by the intensity of its own thoughts. Such minds are apt to be preoccupied with the substance of what they are trying to say, and somewhat careless as to its mere form. They tend to be oblivious, rather than scornful, of grammatical rules and precedents as such.

At the same time there runs through all these roughnesses the strong thread of a logical and reasoned argument. If the author does go off sometimes at a tangent, he comes back again to his main point, and takes up his thread, showing that he had never really lost sight of it. As Holtzmann says (*PB.*, p. 101 f.), 'the real Paul shows himself always equally possessed by his subject, or master of it, and carries his treatment of it through to a definite goal; so that even the smallest aside has ever its due relation to, and place in, the whole; hence it is a pleasure to observe how surely and purposefully this literary tactic proceeds (2 Cor. x. 5)'.

It is precisely here that our particles, prepositions, &c., come in. They are the links which bind the sundry and often variegated elements into a strongly compact and articulate unity; they are the tendons and ligaments 'by which the whole body is fitly framed and knit together through that which every joint supplieth'. That they do not aggressively thrust themselves forward, nor distract attention to themselves, but do their work quietly and unobtrusively, is just as it should be. Were they withdrawn, we should soon feel that there was something wrong, though we might not at once perceive what was the matter, unless we happened to be trained anatomists.

As a literary composition the Pastorals are admittedly less of a living organism, and more of an edifice—a somewhat rambling edifice.[1] In this structure the stones are less rugged than the Paul of Rom. or Phil. would have chosen, brick cast in

---

[1] 'Le style des pastorales n'a pas la vigueur et la force, la vivacité et l'impétuosité, la vie et la variété, l'âpre rudesse de celui des épîtres aux Romains ou aux Galates. Il est lent, monotone, pesant, diffus, décousu' (Jacquier, *Histoire des livres du N. T.*, i. p. 366).

a mould, instead of granite rough-hewn from the quarry, and they are laid more loosely one on the other than would have suited either the mind of Paul or the nature of his material. Like that spirit whose living garment it is, the style of the Paulines is nothing if not vivid, intense, dynamic, yes, often even volcanic and explosive, always impatient of any curb or restraint from man-made rules. The only bondage to which it will bow the neck is that of the life-giving Spirit 'bringing into captivity every thought to the obedience of Christ' (2 Cor. x. 5).

But the style of the Pastorals is by comparison sober, didactic, static, conscientious, domesticated. It lacks the Pauline impetus, the drive and surge of mighty thoughts never spoken before, struggling now for expression, and chafing against the limitations of human speech. It lacks too the Pauline grip and intellectual mastery, strong, clear, logical, sweeping and comprehensive—seeing the end of an argument from the beginning, and binding the whole tumultuous mass into a throbbing vital unity.

It is much rather the speech of a man greatly concerned to preserve intact the correct pattern of sound words, which must be diligently memorized, and faithfully recited, and so passed on from lip to lip as the one duly authorized expression of saving truth. Such with him is the sacred deposit to be handed on from one generation of accredited teachers to another.

But with Paul it was a blazing torch, passing from soul to soul, kindled in each from the same Divine fire which burns for ever on the great altar of the Cross. The Cross! Not once does our author write that word, nor any of its cognates. 'Still,' it may be said, 'he presupposes it in speaking of Him who gave Himself for all.' True, but it was many years since the real Paul made his great resolve to know nothing among his friends save Jesus Christ and Him crucified (1 Cor. ii. 2), many years since he wrote a letter (except the little note to Philemon) without some more explicit reference to that burning focus of the Gospel as he conceived it. (σταῦρος, σταυρόω, συνσταυρόω, 20 times in 7 epistles, in all 4 Homologoumena, and in all 3 epistles of the Roman imprisonment.)

The style of the Pastorals has also its irregularities, but these do not on examination tend to qualify in any way, but rather to confirm our impression, that it is a different order of mind which meets us here from that revealed in the grammatical *tours de force* of the Paulines.

We have (1) the passages in which he does, it is true, make use of Pauline prepositions, &c., but with a certain looseness and vagueness which only throws into relief the absence of any strong logical coherence. What logical connexion with the preceding passage necessitates the οὖν, 1 Tim. ii. 1? (Contrast Rom. ii. 21.) Wherein lies the similarity which we are led to expect by the ὡσαύτως, 1 Tim. ii. 9? (Contrast 1 Cor. xi. 25.) What is the point of the γάρ, 1 Tim. ii. 5? What has happened to the apodosis without which the καθώς, 1 Tim. i. 3 (our solitary instance of this favourite Pauline particle—84 times in 9 epistles), is left hanging in the air? It has (to quote Winer) 'escaped his attention' (E. Tr., p. 713).

But this last passage has been claimed as a clinching example of (2) the anacolutha which are so frequent and so marked a feature of the genuine Pauline style. Ramsay (*Expositor*, 1909, p. 481) finds here a proof that this is a genuine letter, inasmuch as the writer confidently assumed the ability of his correspondent to fill the gap correctly by sympathetic comprehension of the suppressed thought. The ingenuity of this theory may appeal to some. Others will find Winer's simpler explanation more convincing. But in neither case does this passage, even with the help of Titus i. 2 f. (ἣν ἐπηγγείλατο ... ἐφανέρωσεν δὲ ... τὸν λόγον αὐτοῦ) at all adequately balance the effect produced by a careful study of the long series of Pauline anacolutha to be found in any good Grammar of N.T. Greek, e.g. Winer (E. Tr., pp. 709–21).[1] It is no doubt difficult to avoid a certain degree of subjectivity in a comparison of this kind; but the composition of a passage like 1 Tim. i. 3 sqq., seems to differ from that of say Rom. v. 12, as the slow windings of a stream through flat country differ from the headlong rush of a mountain torrent. Nor do the very occasional brief and simple parentheses 1 Tim. ii. 7, 2 Tim. i. 18, iv. 7, 14, 16, by any means fill the place of such outbursts as Gal. ii. 4 f., 6 f. (apart from the fact that the first is taken bodily, as we shall see,[2] from Rom. ix. 1, while the remaining four occur in precisely those verses which most critics agree in regarding as fragments of genuine Pauline notes).

[1] Blass, E. Tr., pp. 282–6. [2] p. 90 f.

LINGUISTIC PECULIARITIES

(3) To the same order of construction, and arising from similar tendencies in the mind of Paul, belong the frequent instances of *Oratio Variata*, consisting of pairs of sentences running parallel and more or less synonymous with one another, and each complete in itself, cf. Rom. iv. 12, 1 Cor. vii. 13 γυνὴ ἥτις ἔχει ἄνδρα ἄπιστον, καὶ οὗτος συνευδοκεῖ οἰκεῖν μετ' αὐτῆς, μὴ ἀφιέτω τὸν ἄνδρα, 1 Cor. xiv. 1 ζηλοῦτε τὰ πνευματικά, μᾶλλον δὲ ἵνα προφητεύητε. Sometimes it takes the form of a transition from the singular to the plural, e. g. Rom. iii. 7 f., xii. 16 f., 20 ff., 1 Cor. iv. 6, 2 Cor. xi. 6 εἰ δὲ καὶ ἰδιώτης τῷ λόγῳ . . . ἀλλ' ἐν παντὶ φανερώσαντες κτλ. Of these heterogeneous periods too the Pastorals are innocent.

Yet another idiosyncrasy of our author is his curious fondness

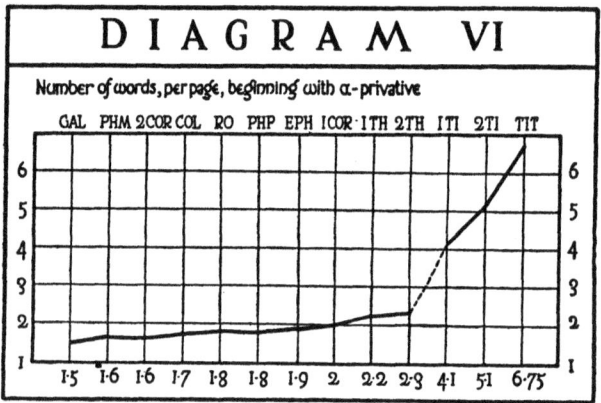

for certain types of compound, notably those bearing either the prefix φιλο- or α- privative. There is of course nothing unusual in the mere occurrence of either of these formations, both of which are found occasionally in Paul himself and in many other writers. What strikes our notice here is their quite extraordinary frequency. That this is no merely subjective impression may be seen from Diagram VI. Words beginning with α- privative appear not less than 1·5 and not more than 2·3 on the average to the page of any Pauline; but the average in 1 Tim. is 4·1, in 2 Tim. 5·1, in Titus 6·75.[1] It is not easy to find any satisfactory reason why the same writer who in ten epistles over eleven years kept within these narrow limits, should have gone beyond them to this extent in just these three instances.

[1] Appendix I G, p. 155 f.

II. DIFFICULTY OF RECONCILING THE LINGUISTIC PECU-
LIARITIES OF THE PASTORALS WITH THEIR PAULINE
AUTHORSHIP.

In vocabulary, grammar, and style, then, the Pastorals show a marked divergence from all other epistles bearing the name of Paul; and this divergence is now seen to be even wider and to go deeper than had been realized hitherto.

We have, therefore, to consider quite dispassionately—remembering the high demands of Truth and the grave issues involved—whether or not the facts before us are compatible with the hypothesis of Pauline authorship. Can they be adequately explained by taking into account the many-sided personality of Paul, the natural development of his thought and modes of self-expression, the changed circumstances and subject-matter, the persons addressed, the possible influence of an amanuensis, or any other of the considerations which have been, or can be, advanced in support of that hypothesis?

1. *The Writer.*

Complete uniformity of style, diction, and vocabulary must not, of course, be expected in any author, least of all in one with a mind so versatile, pliable, original, fresh, impressionable, and creative as the Apostle. A certain progressive modification was required by all analogy and by the laws of development, and is in fact visible in the existing Paulines, which fall into three clearly defined groups—(*a*) the earliest letters, 1 and 2 Thess., (*b*) the four 'Homologoumena', Rom., 1 and 2 Cor., Gal., and (*c*) the epistles of the Roman Imprisonment, Eph., Col., Philem., and Phil. With these last the Pastorals have quite a number of words in common. Given a further period of from two to five years, with the added experience they must have brought, then, it is argued, the evidence of yet further changes in the Apostle's diction ought not to surprise us half so much as would the absence of any such change.

Now we shall presently show reason to doubt whether room can be found in the life of the Apostle for this further development (Part III, pp. 102 ff.). But, waiving this point, the question still remains whether the actual *extent* of the departure from Paul's manner is not far too great to be accounted for along these lines.

(i) Paul's mind did not first begin to be versatile, original, or impressionable at the end of his career. It had all these characteristics, and showed them more clearly in many ways, in the earlier epistles. But, like all true genius, it moved within certain limits, and was subject to certain laws, some consciously self-imposed, others quite unconscious, imposed by the very nature of things.

The number of Greek words known to Paul, though considerable—far greater, doubtless, than the number actually used in his surviving ten epistles—was not by any means unlimited. His working vocabulary, as seen in those epistles over a period of eleven years, was drawn from within a circle, or series of concentric circles, which can be described with precision. It included 2,177 different words, of which 1,113 do not occur in more than one epistle, 396 occur in two epistles, 230 in three, 126 in four, 96 in five, 53 in six, 46 in seven, 35 in eight, 35 in nine, and 47 in ten. See Appendix I, p. 160.

The originality and freshness of Paul's mind is seen in the wonderful way in which it uses these limited materials to express such a series of new thoughts and boundless aspirations, and such a mighty conception of reality seen and unseen, as had never before been put into words at all.

To discard suddenly at the end of a lifetime such a host of favourite expressions, and introduce in their stead such a mass of new and unfamiliar terms, might indicate a certain kind of versatility, but not the kind which we have any reason for attributing to the Apostle.

We have certainly no wish to impose an arbitrary cast-iron standard on any human mind, least of all on Paul's mind. Deissmann is perfectly right in saying that one must not try 'to mechanize the wonderful variety of the linguistic elements in the Greek Bible'.[1] But Deissmann would be the last to commit us or himself to the principle that there are no limits at all to the probabilities of variation in an author's style and vocabulary. It may have been physically possible for Paul to have composed a trio of letters in which not only 21 per cent. but 90 per cent.

[1] *Bibelstudien*, 1895, p. 66.

of the words were *Hapax Legomena*. But it remains equally incredible that he should have done so, whether by accident or by design.

(ii) Each of the Paulines, and each of the three groups into which they fall chronologically, has naturally a certain number of expressions peculiar to itself, and lacks some that appear more or less frequently in the others. But that this is so to a degree comparable for a moment with that obtaining in the case of the Pastorals can hardly be asserted in the face of the evidence now forthcoming, and must be dismissed as a subjective impression in direct conflict with the objective facts. Under test after test the Pastorals are shown to be divided from the other epistles by a great gulf, to which the actual differences among these afford no sort of analogy.

(iii) But, 'we do not demand that Shakespeare's *Sonnets* or *Cymbeline* should exhibit a certain percentage of *Hamlet* words. ... Antecedently we should not expect that an author's favourite expressions would be distributed over the pages of his book like the spots on a wall-paper pattern.'[1]

Still, if the authorship of a play supposed to be Shakespeare's were open to very serious doubts on other grounds, those doubts would hardly be allayed by the discovery that it contained an extraordinarily low percentage of the commonest and most characteristic Shakespearean terms, and a correspondingly high percentage of words found in no Elizabethan playwright, but current among those of the late seventeenth century.[2] And having observed carefully the actual extent and the actual limits of variation among all the other known writings of an author, over a long period of years, we do certainly look for some sort of approximation to his normal line of development, in a work purporting to come from the same author after a brief interval.

(iv) A 'development' there is indeed from 1 Thess. to Phil., not quite mechanical in its regularity, but real and natural, with the fluctuations which so often mark a natural process. But applied to a transition like that from Phil. to the Pastorals, this word, implying as it does a certain degree of orderly continuity, would seem to be a misnomer.

[1] N. J. D. White, *Expositor's G. T.*, 1910, p. 68.   [2] See below, pp. 67 ff.

(v) It is quite true that the Pastorals have a certain number of words in common with the epistles of the Roman imprisonment and with these only. The actual figure is 28, as against 160 shared exclusively with the group Rom., Cor., Gal., and 13 with 1 and 2 Thess. Allowing for the differences in length, we get an average of 1·5 per page of the Thessalonian epistles shared by the Pastorals with these exclusively, 2·1 per page with the four Homologoumena, and only 1·2 with the four prison-letters. They have thus rather *less* exclusively in common with the latest than with the earlier groups, which is hardly what the idea of development would have led us to expect, supposing them to have been written by Paul a few years after Philippians.

(vi) On the same hypothesis 2 Tim. must, of course, be the last of the three; and we should in that case have expected to find in this epistle still further progress than in 1 Tim. and Titus *away from* Paul's earlier manner. Instead we find that 2 Tim. stands much the nearest of the three to the other Paulines—a fact which agrees perfectly with the theory that this epistle contains much the largest amount of genuine Pauline matter. See Diagram III, p. 25.

2. *Circumstances.*

But, it is urged, 'circumstances alter cases'. (*a*) The changed environment of the Apostle, further travels, fresh experiences, new acquaintances, would naturally lead to a further modification of vocabulary, &c., especially in one so 'sympathetic and open to influences from without'.[1] 'Weariness, ill-health, gloomy prospects, and growing years and cares, might all be important factors in the case.'[2] The Apostle's lengthy sojourn in Rome might perhaps account for the number of Latinisms which make their appearance in these epistles.[3]

This line of explanation, like the last, is of course closed to those who believe that Paul wrote the Pastorals during the period recorded in Acts, i. e. the same period as the other epistles.

But even if we assume a second imprisonment, and grant the abstract principle that new experiences beget new expressions, and that changed surroundings would tend to exercise a certain influence over the language of any impressionable writer, it still

---

[1] White, 1910, p. 59.   [2] Shaw, 1904, p. 440.   [3] James, 1906, p. 148.

remains more than doubtful whether the facts before us can be adequately explained in this way. For—

(i) the ten Paulines themselves were not all written under identical circumstances, nor was the life of the Apostle altogether monotonous during those eleven years. He had already passed through many vicissitudes, made many new friends, travelled far, knew bodily sickness and pain, mental distress and disappointment, suffered many losses and hardships, cares and sorrows, trials and dangers, had spent at least two years as a prisoner in Rome, and had come to feel the burden of advancing age, before he wrote Phil. Yet the ten epistles show no such far-reaching changes among themselves.

(ii) Assuming their Pauline authorship, the Pastorals must have been written under circumstances as different from one another as from those in which some of the others were composed,—and in fact more so. Almost the only circumstance common to the three, but foreign to the ten, would be found in Paul's added years—that is supposing, what is strongly denied, that he survived his first Roman imprisonment. But, even so, as Otto pointed out long ago, in reply to Guericke, it is not the usual result of old age to produce a new vocabulary.

For the rest it must be asked, which of the circumstances now under consideration was really new to the Apostle? He was no stranger to most of these influences when he wrote 2 Cor. xi. 12-30, but their effect upon his style and diction was then quite different.

(iii) Some of the Latinisms ($\mu\epsilon\mu\beta\rho\acute{a}\nu\alpha$, $\phi\alpha\iota\lambda\acute{o}\nu\eta s$) occur in passages the Pauline authorship of which is not disputed. The residue may be explained by supposing, with Holtzmann[1] and others, that Rome was the birthplace of these epistles. In any case Rome was not the only place in the world where an occasional Latin word would be quite natural and intelligible in a Greek composition.

(b) Conditions within the Church, too, were different in various ways from those prevailing when Paul wrote his earlier epistles. We have to consider the possible influence of this upon his choice of words and general mode of expression. In particular there is the appearance of the False Teachers, and the necessity for

---

[1] Holtzmann, *PB.*, pp. 109, 271.

choosing special terms to describe them and their novel theories, and to suit the new atmosphere of debate and acrimonious strife created by their presence.[1] Moreover, the Church had itself developed, by the time these epistles were written, in organization, polity, discipline, liturgy, and practical Christianity.

The specific circumstances here named are themselves among the principal grounds of objection against the Pauline authorship of these epistles. But the question whether their introduction within the lifetime of the Apostle is, or is not, in the nature of an anachronism, does not fall within the scope of the present linguistic argument. In any case, Paul was not now for the first time forced to breathe the heated atmosphere of doctrinal discussions, nor to deal with opposition on the part of false teachers coming in and leading weak minds astray. We do not find this particular type of linguistic phenomena in Galatians nor yet in Colossians.

3. *Subject-Matter.*

The same remarks apply in part to the suggestion that we should refer peculiarities of diction to the new subject-matter. Thus we have (i) a whole series of what have been described as technical terms belonging to (*a*) the heresies to be rejected (γενεαλογία, γνῶσις, ψευδώνυμος), (*b*) the true doctrines to be inculcated (διδασκαλία, παραθήκη, ὑγιής), (*c*) the ecclesiastical rules to be enforced (γυμνάζειν, διδακτικός, ἐπισκοπή, νεόφυτος), (*d*) the religious and moral situation presupposed (βέβηλος, εὐσέβεια, σεμνότης).[2]

The reasons for and against regarding precisely these matters as marks of a later age belong to another field of inquiry, about which the most fundamental differences of opinion remain. But there is no need to reserve our judgement on the present issue until those vexed questions of Church History have been settled. For, even supposing that the whole ecclesiastical situation might have developed in Paul's mind and experience along the lines, and to the extent, indicated in these epistles,—it still would not by any means follow that we should have here a satisfactory explanation of the varied, deep, and far-reaching contrast now

---

[1] Wohlenberg, *PB.*, 1906, pp. 55 ff.
[2] Jacquier, *Histoire des livres du N. T.*, 1903, p. 363.

demonstrated between the language of the Pastorals and that of the ten Paulines.

The very wide range of subjects covered by the ten Paulines themselves has not, in their case, resulted in similar discrepancies.

And it has been pointed out many times[1] that the vagueness and generality of many of these 'technical terms' is unlike Paul, who was accustomed to meet the errors of his day in a more thoroughgoing and concrete fashion, coming to closer grips with the fundamental ideas of his antagonists, and showing how and where they were wrong. It was not his way to content himself with disparaging epithets and labels to the extent that we find in these epistles. Many of these terms are wide enough and vague enough to have fitted equally well the disturbers of the churches of Galatia or of Colossae; but they do not appear in Paul's letters to those communities. The residue of more precise and definite expressions coincides significantly with the terminology of second-century writers in characterizing the heresies, church-institutions, &c., of their day.

(ii) Least of all would any change in subject-matter seem to account for that strange absence of more than a hundred Pauline particles, &c., or for those radical differences in grammar and style, to which reference has been made on pp. 34–44.

Can this very disuse of particles, conjunctions, &c., be explained by referring to the absence of dialectic discussions, and by suggesting that the Pastorals consist mainly of instructions, disciplinary rules, and regulations, rather than detailed arguments or expositions?

Hardly, for the Pauline prepositions, &c., missing from the Pastorals are not by any means confined to argumentative or keenly logical contexts. The absence, e.g., of ἄν, παρά with the accusative, τότε, τε, ἕκαστος, ἔτι, ἐμαυτόν, κἀγώ, οὔτε, σύν, &c., &c., does not so much as begin to be explained by any such considerations.

(iii) A certain number of the unique words in the Pastorals must certainly be written off on the ground that their uniqueness is obviously quite accidental. Their presence is necessitated by the introduction of sundry matters of which the Apostle had no occasion to speak in his earlier letters, though he might

---

[1] e.g., by McGiffert, *A. A.*, p. 402; Moffatt, *I. N. T.*, p. 409.

perfectly well have done so, had occasion required; e.g. ἀγωγή, ἀκαίρως, ἀνάλυσις, βέλτιον, μάμμη, μεμβράνα, στόμαχος, φαιλόνης, χαλκεύς.

But the number of these is strictly limited, and a certain number of unique words under this heading must similarly be written off from each of the other epistles also, if the comparison is to be drawn fairly. Most of them occur, as it happens, in the admittedly genuine paragraphs. The elimination of the remainder would not materially lessen the mass of non-Pauline expressions.

4. *Amanuensis.*

We know that Paul did not write all, if he wrote any, of his earlier letters with his own hand, but dictated them to an amanuensis (Rom. xvi. 22 ἐγὼ Τέρτιος ὁ γράψας τὴν ἐπιστολήν), only taking the pen to add a few words of personal greeting at the close (1 Cor. xvi. 21, 2 Thess. iii. 17 f., Gal. vi. 11 ff., Col. iv. 18).

A prima facie explanation of the linguistic peculiarities of the Pastorals, which does not at the same time prejudice their apostolic authority, has been found in the suggestion that, in this case, the amanuensis may have been allowed more freedom than usual as to the precise form and wording, while faithfully reproducing the substance of the apostolic message.

That the name of Luke should have been thought of in this connexion[1] was almost inevitable, in view of the fact that he alone was with Paul at the time when 2 Tim. iv. 11 was being written.

Those who adopt this explanation bear witness as a rule explicitly, as well as by the very fact that they find such a hypothesis necessary, to the reality and weight of the difficulties in the way of an unqualified belief in the direct Pauline authorship.[2] At the same time they point out quite clearly that it must have been Luke *if any one* who filled this rôle.[3]

---

[1] H. A. Schott, *Isagoge Historico-Critica in Libros Novi Foederis Sacros*, 1830, p. 325: 'vir quidam apostolicus, unus ex sodalibus Pauli (forsitan Lucas), ipsius Apostoli nomine et auctoritate has litteras exaravit'.

[2] J. D. James, *Genuineness and Authorship of the P. E.*, 1906, pp. 144, 154 f. Robert Scott, *Pauline Epistles*, 1909: 'It is not for a moment imaginable that Paul ... could have written these three moral charges ..., and have written them in a new terminology' (p. 350 f.).

[3] James, p. 154: '"Only Luke is with me"—stares us on the written page'. Cf. Scott, p. 333, Luke is 'the one companion of Paul whom we know to have possessed the two qualifications of literary ability and Gentile birth'.

But as a real solution of our problem this hypothesis can hardly be said to pass the necessary tests. The phenomena before us are not by any means of such a nature that they can be accounted for by imagining a superimposition of the Lucan style and vocabulary upon the Pauline. The *Hapax Legomena* are of course as foreign to Luke as to Paul. The total absence of such particularly frequent and characteristic Pauline words as ἀδικέω, -ος, ἀκάθαρτος, ἀποθνήσκω, ἀναγκάζω, ἀποκάλυψις, -πτω, βλέπω, γνωρίζω, διαθήκη, ἐνδύω, ἐργάζομαι, ἐξουθενέω, εὐδοκέω, εὐλογέω, ζῆλος, καταρτίζω, κενός, κοινωνία, οἰκοδομέω, οὐρανός, ὀφειλέτης, περισσεύω, πράσσω, σταυρός, σῶμα, υἱός, ὑπάρχω, φοβέομαι, χαρίζομαι, ὥρα, does not become any more intelligible when we presuppose as the amanuensis a writer who in his own works uses every one of these words, some of them with great frequency. Still less does the Lucan hypothesis help us to understand the strange omission of Pauline particles, &c., seeing that Luke himself uses ἄν 56 times, ἀντί 5, ἄρα 11, ἄχρι 21, γε 13, διό 10, διότι 8, ἐγγύς 6, ἕκαστος 16, ἐμαυτόν 6, ἔμπροσθεν 12, ἕνεκεν 8, ἔξω 20, ἐπεί 3, ἐπειδή 5, ἔτι 21, ἕως 30, ἰδού 79, κἀγώ 12, ναί 6, ὁμοίως 11, ὅπου 7, ὅπως 22, οὗ 14, οὐθείς 6, οὐχί 21, οὐκέτι 7, οὔτε 22, πάλιν 8, παρά with accus. 22, πάντως 4, πλήν 19, πόσος 7, ποῦ; 7, σός 7, σύν 77, τε 154, τότε 36, ὥσπερ 5, and ὥστε 13 times.

It is not easy to see how the co-operation of two such minds as Paul's and Luke's should have led to the introduction of so many terms utterly foreign to them both, and the omission of two such large and important series of words which they had both found indispensable. Nor can the stylistic divergencies of the Pastorals from the Pauline manner be fairly said to point towards the peculiar grace, literary charm, and finish so conspicuous in the Lucan writings.

It seems nearer the mark, therefore, to hold that, while the affinity between our author and the writer of the Third Gospel and of Acts is clear and indisputable, their identity would be quite incredible on linguistic grounds alone, and cannot be accepted as a possible explanation of the facts with which we are now concerned.

5. *Recipients.*

The Pastorals are addressed to individuals, not to churches. May not this be the true explanation of their peculiarities as compared with the other Paulines?

Promising as this way of escape from our difficulties may seem at first sight, it is beset, from the start, with pitfalls for the unwary, and leads at last to a veritable morass of shifting speculations, where we are obliged to leap from one precarious hypothesis to another in the vain hope of reaching firmer ground.

Stated in general terms, and without further qualification,[1] it is met at once by the obvious and fatal objection that the Epistle to Philemon, which really is a private letter in a far fuller and truer sense than either of these, shows no trace of the special features now under consideration; on the contrary, it keeps remarkably close to the normal Pauline type, and well inside its natural allowance of unique words.

We must therefore retrace our steps and begin again, exercising greater care this time to avoid the mistake of putting more weight on the private character and destination of our epistles than it will carry. They are—shall we say—private communications about matters concerning the Church as a whole, addressed to personal friends in their official capacity, thus differing on the one hand from Philemon, which is addressed to a private member on a purely private matter, and on the other hand from the other nine Paulines, which are addressed to churches? By this necessary distinction the maximum distance is left between the Pastorals and the letters to churches, consistent with immunity from the awkward analogy of Philemon. But when we have thus succeeded in framing a formula which excludes *all* other Paulines, while it includes the Pastorals, we have still to show just *how* and *why* this explains the many and great differences already noted.[2]

---

[1] e.g. Gloag, *Introduction to the Pauline Epistles*, 1874, p. 380.

[2] Koelling (*1 Tim. auf's Neue untersucht u. ausgelegt*, 1882–7, p. 24) regards this distinction as 'wholly central to the present field of investigation, and the key to their linguistic peculiarity'. Similarly Rüegg (*Zur Echtheitsfrage der P.B.*, 1898, p. 62 f.): 'We are dealing here with an entirely new class of epistle to which we possess no analogue among the undisputed

Can we say that the superior education of Timothy and Titus made it possible and natural for the Apostle to write to them in a literary style, and use a number of more or less technical terms, which would have been unsuitable in writing to churches, because unintelligible to the majority of simple and ignorant folk of which they were composed?[1]

This matter of the 'technical terms' has partly been dealt with already (p. 50 f.), and partly falls outside our present inquiry. Meanwhile, regarding the theory of a 'linguistic dualism' in Paul's epistles, analogous to that between Schleiermacher's beautiful letters to his wife and his sister, and his correspondence with scientific friends like Gass and de Wette on technical subjects, we have to inquire, does it meet the case?

Can it be maintained that the style and diction of the Pastorals bear evidence of being addressed and adapted to a more highly educated type of mind than, say, the Epistle to the Romans? True, he tells the Corinthian brethren that he has been obliged to speak to them as to babes, and to feed them with milk suited to their *spiritual* (he does not say *mental*) capacity (1 Cor. iii. 1 f.). But neither the ancient Church (2 Pet. iii. 15 f.) nor the modern has ever yet derived from these epistles to churches the impression that their author was writing down to the mental level of ignorant and illiterate readers.

On the other hand we must avoid putting too much stress on the superior educational qualifications of Timothy and Titus, and the personal, intimate, and confidential character of the letters addressed to them, or we shall soon find ourselves involved in

Paulines.... A writing made up of Pastoral instructions was bound to show an essentially different linguistic character'.

[1] 'In Paul's letters to communities he had to take account of the fact that οὐ πολλοὶ σοφοί, οὐ πολλοὶ δυνατοί, κτλ., 1 Cor. i. 26.' The rank and file were 'largely uneducated, slaves, &c.'. ' In writing to them he needed to exercise the greatest care in the structure of sentences, and the utmost sobriety and detail (*Ausführlichkeit*) in the development of his thoughts, and to avoid in his expressions, especially in his choice of words, everything which in any way went beyond the popular means of knowledge, circle of ideas, and range of diction' (Koelling, p. 27). 'But in writing to Timothy, he was addressing a man who like himself had no mean scientific qualifications' (p. 41 f.). 'Men with a literary education write in a different fashion to one another than they do to simple folk' (p. 44). The great bulk of the *Hapax Legomena* in 2 Tim. are 'scientific termini', and 'as such, it is thoroughly natural for them to appear in a letter whose author and recipient alike undoubtedly possessed the scientific qualification' (p. 150).

very serious difficulties with regard to the tone of these epistles, which now seems all the more strangely pedagogic.[1]

The problem is to find a way out of these difficulties without wholly sacrificing the private letter hypothesis as a satisfactory explanation of the linguistic peculiarities. A solution which has commended itself to some minds is that we should regard the Pastorals as *semi*-private communications of which certain portions were intended for Timothy and Titus alone, while others were to be produced by them as their authority when issuing instructions to the Church at large.[2]

Presumably Titus i. 12 (Κρῆτες ἀεὶ ψεῦσται, κακὰ θηρία κτλ.) would be one of the parts reserved by Titus for his own private information. However that may be, it is clear that the present hypothesis can only be maintained at the expense of the last. Communications which were intended to be used as a sort of credentials cannot at the same time have been meant for the eyes of Timothy and Titus alone. They are now shown to be private only in form, and the whole argument based on the superior education and scientific equipment of Timothy and Titus falls to the ground. We cannot possibly have it both ways.

But now what of our new position? In avoiding Scylla, we are drawn back inexorably into Charybdis. For we are left without any adequate explanation of those glaring linguistic discrepancies which the private letter theory recognizes and was designed to meet.

It is inadequate, for instance, to suggest that, as 1 and 2 Thess. have an average of 5 *Hapax Legomena* to the *chapter*, Rom.

---

[1] Shaw, p. 442: 'Timothy is addressed as an immature youth who needs very elementary lessons in life and duty. ... It also sounds strange that to him above all Paul should think it needful to make strong assertions regarding his apostleship and his truthfulness. In short he tells Timothy a great deal that he must often have told him before, and he tells it in rather a stern manner on the whole. ... It must be confessed that there is much in such objections that is very hard to explain, and sufficiently justifiable of doubt.'

[2] Findlay, *Appendix to the English Transl. of Sabatier's St. Paul*, p. 369: 'Why, it is asked, should he write to his old assistants and familiars, his "true children" in the Faith, with so much stiffness and formality, and such an air of authority? ... The answer lies partly in the fact that these epistles, especially 1 Tim. and Titus, are "open" or quasi-public letters, written with the Churches of Ephesus and Crete in view, and such as it would be suitable to read, in part at least, at their assemblies.' Cf. Dummelow's *One Volume Bible Commentary*, 1909, pp. 992, 1006: 'private correspondence, not strictly confidential.... The author is writing with his eye on the community.'

nearly 7, Eph.-Col. 8, Phil. 10, and the Pastorals 13, 'the regular progression of the above figures marks them as belonging to one and the same series'.[1] For the chapter is an artificial and an *elastic* standard of measurement, and its use for the present purpose would tend to obscure the state of things revealed in our Diagram I (p. 21).

Nor can we recall any really convincing account of the Missing Particles from this point of view,[2] nor one that does justice to the facts set forth in our table (p. 36 f.).

Still less is the final verdict of scholarship likely to be influenced by any argument based on the use of our Saviour's name in the Pastorals,[3] which omits to mention the very important fact that whereas Paul uses Ἰησοῦς alone at least 38 times, and in every epistle except Philem., Χριστός alone and without the article 126 times, and in every epistle except 2 Thess., and ὁ Χριστός 79 times, and in every epistle except Philem., the author of the Pastorals, according to Westcott and Hort's text, *never once* uses either Ἰησοῦς alone or Χριστός alone, and ὁ Χριστός alone only once, 1 Tim. v. 11. If the reading Ἰησοῦς in 2 Tim. iv. 22 be correct (so W. H.^{m} and v. Soden's text), this is the exception which proves the rule. For this verse is admittedly Pauline.

6. *Forgery.*

But may it not be that these very difficulties, which offer such a stubborn resistance to all frontal attacks, may yet succumb to a flanking movement, or better still, an assault from the rear, and so prove to be 'not insuperable' after all?

Why should it not be argued that such obvious and striking discrepancies, when set in the right light, tell rather in favour of the Pauline authorship than against it? What forger would have dared to run such a risk of detection? Who else but the Apostle himself could afford to indulge in such a patent departure from the normal and familiar style and diction of the Apostle? What could have been easier for a clever *falsarius* than to avoid every non-Pauline expression, and confine himself strictly to words and

---

[1] Findlay, p. 354.
[2] id., p. 359. He mentions *four*! (Similarly J. D. James, p. 134.)
[3] id., p. 361.

idioms for which a parallel could be produced from within the genuine epistles?[1]

Now the whole question of pseudonymity in ancient writings generally, and in the second century in particular, requires a chapter to itself, where the procedure, motives, ethic, and psychology of this very interesting and important literary method could be dealt with in more detail than is possible here.[2] Meanwhile it is certain that those who deny the Pauline authorship of the Pastorals do not as a rule use the terms 'forger' and *falsarius* in this connexion. Nor would they admit for one moment that these terms, with their distinct implication of moral depravity and of the deliberate will to deceive, represent the only alternative to the Pauline authorship of these epistles.

But how should it ever have entered the head of any second-century Christian writer—even of a 'forger' of the deepest dye —to sift out from his original every little particle and preposition, and to pepper his own composition with them, for the more thorough deception of his readers? Would such a procedure really have been quite so easy in those days as has been suggested? Without a concordance it would not be just the simplest task in the world even now. And what would have been the use of it? What second-century reader would ever have noticed such a point, or allowed it to influence him in the least? We know that the absence of Pauline particles did not in fact prevent the acceptance of these epistles as Paul's by the Church towards the close of that century. It was not by such canons that the early Church determined the apostolic authority of any work, but by its practical value for edification, and its faithfulness to the apostolic teaching as then held and under-

---

[1] 'If the logical particles of the argumentative epistles are missing, this is in favour of authenticity rather than otherwise. Nothing would have been easier for a man steeped in Paulinism like our author, than to sprinkle his pages with catchwords of this kind' (Findlay, p. 359).

'A clever *falsarius* would not have omitted such obvious marks of his master's style. A writer who could have reproduced the parenthetical sentences of St. Paul would not have failed in such a minor detail' (James, p. 154).

'For a forger would have been at pains to keep as closely as possible to the admitted style of the writer whose name he was fraudulently assuming' (Bowen, *Dates of the Pastoral Epistles*, 1900, p. 6 f.).

'In fact, the only man who can afford to differ largely from previous compositions is the author himself' (Shaw, p. 439).

[2] See Moffatt, *H. N. T.* (1901), pp. 619 ff.; *I. N. T.*, pp. 40 ff., 415 ff.

stood. So far from its being 'obvious', many centuries had to pass before this mark of the master's style could be recognized as such; and even now it would certainly escape the notice of the vast majority of readers, unless it were pointed out to them.

But the certain fact that a point of this kind lay right outside the mental scope and interests of early Christendom, makes it none the less valuable as a test for our present purpose. Indeed the very unconsciousness of the symptoms renders them all the more significant. This applies still more forcibly to the facts brought to light in our diagrams.

7. *Literary Analogies.*

If the sharp contrast between the language of the Pastorals and that of the ten Paulines cannot be denied, and if all attempts to explain it consistently with their Pauline authorship prove unavailing, can the position still be turned by referring to analogous variations among the works of any other writer ancient or modern?

The difficulty with so many of the ancients is that the true origin of their reputed works is wrapped in an obscurity as deep as, or deeper still than, that which we are now seeking to penetrate. So that it is a case of explaining 'ignotum per ignotius'.

On the other hand, any modern writer is divided from Paul by so vast an abyss of time, so many incalculable changes resulting from the invention of printing (to name only one all-important factor), that, even supposing that any real resemblance were apparent, it would be largely nullified by the obvious differences between the two cases.

A great majority of the analogies which have actually been suggested in this connexion are much too indefinite to affect in any way the issue before us, which is one of degree and of concrete detail. General observations about the liability of an author's style and diction to vary with his subject-matter, &c., coupled with vague allusions to Luther, Klopstock, Dante or any other versatile writer whose name happens to occur,[1] are powerless against the great body of facts now specified.

[1] 'Why should not a certain change and development in mode of expression and of writing have taken place in Paul, just as in others?' Wohlenberg,

For, as J. S. Mill showed long ago, the force and value of an argument from analogy may amount to anything or nothing (*Logic*, III. xx). Everything depends upon the precise extent and character of the *resemblance* upon which the inference is based, as compared 'first with the amount of ascertained difference, and next with the extent of the unexplored regions of unascertained properties'.

Considering the possibilities of such an inquiry, it may seem somewhat surprising that there should have been so few attempts to produce concrete examples of linguistic variations analogous to those which distinguish the Pastorals from all other Pauline epistles. But the labour involved is considerable, and in itself not very exhilarating. A reliable word-index is indispensable, and is only forthcoming for a very limited number of authors. It may have been partly the existence of such an index which led W. P. Workman to select Shakespeare as the subject of an experiment in this direction, which some have found reassuring (*Expository Times*, vol. vii, 1896, p. 418 f.).

In this article Workman sets out 'to exhibit, with an approach to scientific accuracy, the real value or valuelessness of the numbers in question'. He proceeds to state the numbers of *Hapax Legomena* per page in the Pastorals and in the Paulines, and continues, 'It is no longer possible for any candid man to say that there is no case for investigation. These epistles are now seen to present twice as many unusual words as any other of Paul's, and three times as many as most.'

Having indicated the 'unsatisfactory' nature of previous explanations, he now provides the 'true answer', which is twofold. '(1) The epistles stand roughly in the order of age, the latest coming first. The general tendency of a writer, as he advances in knowledge of a language, and mastery of its possibilities, is to use more unusual words and more involved constructions.... .(2) The number of unusual words in the writings of an author is a very variable quantity, and as a matter of fact, there is nothing to excite comment in the fact that one writing contains three times as many as another.' Then follows in tabular form a list of Shakespeare's plays, showing in each case the number of words

Die Pastoralbriefe, 1906, p. 53, and instances Luther, Klopstock, Schiller, and Goethe.

per page not found in any other play nor in the poems—all based on the lists in the Irving edition. From these it appears that 'the frequency in Shakespeare varies from 3.4 (*Julius Caesar*) to 10.4 (*Hamlet*), a range almost exactly the same as in Paul where it varies from 3.6 to 13'.

'This striking fact seems (to Workman) to be almost fatal to the argument against authenticity as drawn from *Hapax Legomena*.' And with this view quite a number of subsequent writers concur, e.g. James (1906), R. D. Shaw (1904).[1]

(i) The writers are indeed, as Shaw admits, 'very dissimilar'. Apart from the fact that both were men of high genius, it would be difficult to name two authors more unlike, or two series of writings presenting a sharper contrast in form, length, purpose, subject-matter, and spirit, or produced under circumstances more remote.

'But', Shaw continues, 'he is not comparing Paul with Shakespeare. He is comparing Paul with Paul, and Shakespeare with Shakespeare. He shows that each is an illustration of his general principle.'

Still, he is comparing a certain variation in 'Paul' with what he regards as a similar variation in Shakespeare. And his method of drawing the comparison is open, as we shall show, to more than one fatal objection.

(ii) But he has appealed to Shakespeare, unto Shakespeare let him go! And first of all, that we may visualize the evidence on the strength of which he claims to have exhibited 'sufficiently the utter weakness of the argument' (from *Hapax Legomena*), let us turn to the diagrams, VII and VIII, on pp. 62 and 63, in which the Pauline and the Shakespearean variations, as indicated by his own figures, may be taken in at a glance.

We observe, to begin with, that chronological development has little or nothing to do with the actual variations in the numbers of Shakespearean *Hapax Legomena*. The latest play stands lower than the earliest, and the play with the largest number stands next in order of time to that with the smallest number—not a very good illustration of the 'general tendency' alleged by Workman as 'surely beyond dispute'!

But the two main points to be considered are (*a*) the maximum

[1] *The Pauline Epistles*, p. 438: 'legitimate and forcible'.

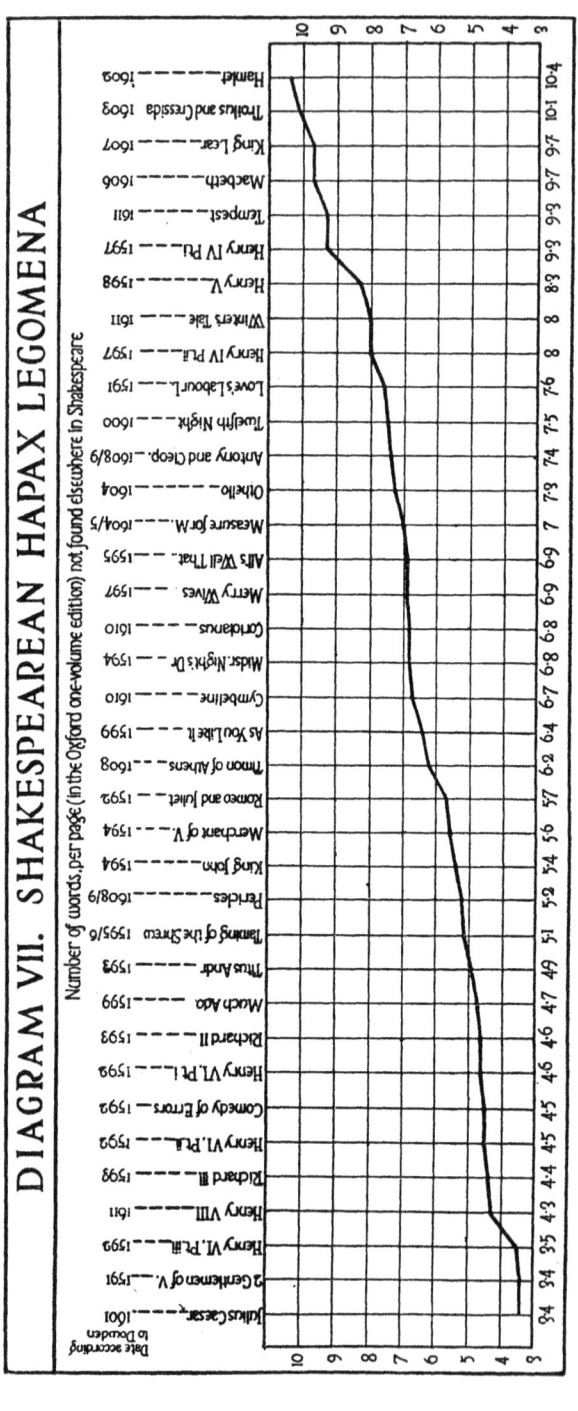

limits of variation in each series, and (*b*) the nature of the intermediate stages.

As regards the first (*a*), Shakespeare's 'range', in Workman's sense of the word, and according to his own figures, is seen to fall short of Paul's in the ratio of 7 : 9·4 (assuming the Pauline authorship of the Pastorals).

But we have been told that he 'is comparing Paul with Paul and Shakespeare with Shakespeare'. That is precisely what he

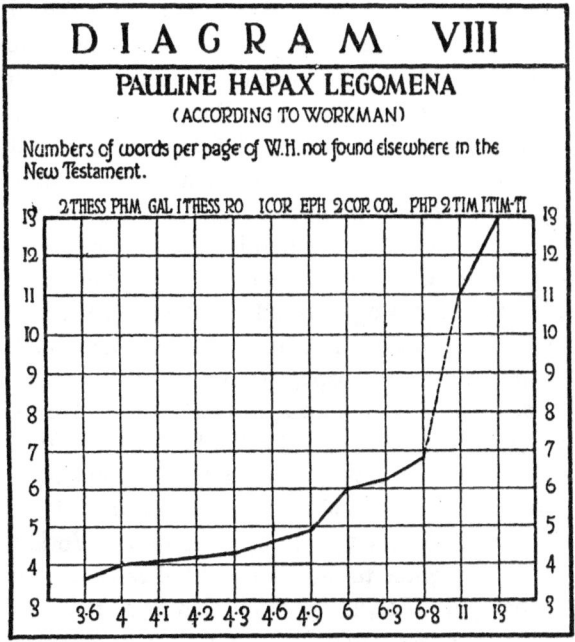

has not done. He has compared Shakespeare with Shakespeare and Paul with the whole body of N. T. writers! To make his comparison what it is claimed to be, he ought to have given us the number of words per page in each Pauline which are not to be found in either of the others—including by all means for the sake of argument the Pastorals. These will be found in our Diag. II, line B B, p. 23.

We now see (1) that assuming the Pauline authorship of the Pastorals, the Pauline 'range' amounts to no less than fourteen words per page, or exactly *twice* that of Shakespeare; (2) that it does so simply and solely by virtue of one tremendous leap at the end accomplished in worn old age; whereas (3) if we confine our attention to the other ten epistles (line A A), the Pauline 'range' is 5.2, or less by 1.8 than the Shakespearean, and the general trend of the two curves is remarkably similar. Finally, (4) by granting, as we have done, for the sake of the experiment, the very point at issue—the Pauline authorship of the three Pastorals—we have ruled out the very considerable number of non-Pauline words shared by each of them with one or both of its fellows. If these are taken into account, then the number per page of non-Pauline words in the Pastorals treated as a unit is 22.4. Or if, refusing to let them help one another, we take each separately on its merits, then Titus alone is found to have no less than 30.4 such words per page, and the Pauline 'range' rises to 23, *or more than three times the Shakespearean!*

(*b*) As regards the second, which is really the crucial point (the nature of the intermediate stages), between the two extremes mentioned, the remaining thirty-five plays form an absolutely orderly and unbroken sequence. In no single instance is there a gap of more than one word per page, the average distance between one play and another being about 0.2, and our 'curve' barely diverges from a straight line. Whereas the Pauline curve, after following for ten epistles a course very similar to the Shakespearean, on reaching the Pastorals, makes a sudden and violent leap upwards from 6.8 to 11 and 13 (taking once more Workman's own figures), a phenomenon to which the Shakespearean line offers no sort of analogy. For, in the transition from the 3.4 of *Julius Caesar* to the 10.4 of *Hamlet*, for $\frac{6}{7}$ths of the way Shakespeare was only returning to the level (9.3) which he had already attained in *King Henry IV*, Pt. I. The increase on his own previous record was thus only 1.1. Whereas Paul's transition from the 6.8 of Phil. to the 11 of 2 Tim. or the 13 of 1 Tim.—Titus starts from the highest, instead of the lowest, point he had ever touched, thus exceeding his previous record by a greater distance than he had covered during the whole period of his previous literary career. The contrast is, of course, here too, still further accentuated, if we take into account the necessary correction of Workman's figures indicated above (*a*).

For these reasons the present writer is unable to regard the analogy from Shakespeare as being in any way detrimental, let alone 'fatal', to the argument against the Pauline authorship of the Pastorals, as drawn from *Hapax Legomena*. At the same time he desires to make full acknowledgement of his own indebtedness to Mr. Workman for having actually pointed the way, by his very interesting and suggestive experiment, to those further statistical investigations which play so large a part in this Essay.

8. *Derivatives.*

Jacquier (1903, p. 362 f.) urges that many of the *Hapax Legomena* in the Pastorals are derivatives of Pauline words, and that most of the new compounds have their analogies in the other epistles.

But this is an argument that cuts both ways, and cuts deeper against the conservative view. For if derivatives are to be taken into account—and it is quite right that they should be (due caution being observed)—then they must obviously be taken into account all round. In that case it will be found that the number of unique words in the other epistles also will be similarly, and in fact still more largely, reduced; and the net result will be to leave the comparison more unfavourable than ever for the Pastorals. But furthermore the same consideration must be applied to the relation between the Pastorals and the Christian writers of the early second century. And the result will then be to reduce almost to the vanishing point those elements in the vocabulary of the Pastorals which cannot be shown to belong to the current phraseology of the period to which our criticism assigns them. See below pp. 79, 83 f.

9. *Words found in the LXX.*

Jacquier (l. c.) thinks it important that many of the *Hapax Legomena* are found in the LXX and must therefore have been known to Paul. (So too Rüegg, 1898, p. 65.) But the 'critical' view does not rest on any contention that Paul was necessarily ignorant of all the words in question. Some words have a long life but a short vogue. As certain words current in the religious speech of one period tend to drop out, and are replaced by others, this does not imply that those words pass completely out of knowledge, nor that these others have all been newly coined. And the fact that a given word, or group of words, is known and its meaning understood, does not at once prove that it is likely to be used, by a given author, or at a certain time. Nor can it be conceded as self-evident that Paul must have been familiar with every Greek word in the LXX and Apocrypha.

10. *Classical Words.*

The long list of expressions occurring in these epistles, but not elsewhere in the N. T., includes a considerable number of classical words. Can this be explained by the suggestion that Paul may have devoted some leisure hours during his second Roman imprisonment to a study of the Classics?

Against this conjecture, and in favour of a different explanation, we have to weigh certain concrete facts. (1) Whatever Paul may have done during the sixties, some eminent Greek writers and teachers in the earlier years of the second century are known to have steeped themselves in the Classics. (2) The literature of that period shows a marked revival of classical diction. (3) The particular classical words now in question were demonstrably one and all in actual use during that period—which cannot be said, by a long way, of Paul's lifetime. See Chapter III and Appendix I, esp. 'Residue', pp. 83 f., 161 ff.

On the other hand, more than a few of the unique words in the Pastorals, so far from being in any sense 'classical', belong definitely to the vocabulary of a later Hellenism. Several of them are actually mentioned by the Atticist Moeris in a list of Hellenist substitutes for the correct Attic of his classical models. They are used, as he puts it, not Ἀττικῶς, but Ἑλληνικῶς, e.g. ἀνδροφόνος (*Attic Lexicon*, ed. Koch, 1830, p. 364), αὐθέντης (p. 54), βαθμός (90), κνήθειν (215), μάμμη (237), ξενοδοχέω (248), παραθήκη (286), περίεργος (also Acts xvi. 19, p. 205), ὑδροποτεῖν (346).

III. THE LANGUAGE OF THE PASTORALS AND OF PAUL COMPARED WITH THAT OF THE APOSTOLIC FATHERS AND APOLOGISTS.

It is, then, admitted on all hands that the language of the Pastorals, compared with that of the other Pauline epistles, has a very considerable number of strongly marked peculiarities, and that these are such, both in kind and in degree, as to require a good deal of explanation, if they are to be reconciled with the traditional view. And while various explanations have been forthcoming which satisfy not only their authors but also a very large and influential body of scholars, members of the 'critical' school still remain entirely unconvinced, and persist in maintaining that the facts are incompatible with the Pauline authorship of these epistles. The result is for the moment a deadlock, each side holding its ground in more or less strongly entrenched positions, but failing to dislodge the other.

And yet both opinions cannot be right. One must be in the main true, and the other false. Either Paul wrote these epistles in substantially their present form, or else he did not. If they were really written during the first half of the second century by some ardent Paulinist, using and quoting largely from our ten Paulines, let his motives and abilities have been what they may, we should expect his work to have retained some mark of its true origin, and to yield up its secret sooner or later to persistent research and accurate observation. Some fresh body of evidence, emerging as the result of inquiries pushed further than before in some particular direction, may reasonably be expected at any moment to settle the matter once for all, one way or the other, in the minds of all who know the facts and desire only the truth whatever it may be. We should expect, for instance, to find our second-century Paulinist falling back unconsciously from time to time into the speech, as well as the ideas, of his own time. He could say much, but not all, that he had to say, in the *ipsissima verba* of his master.

Does our author in his choice of words, when diverging from the known phraseology of Paul, show such a marked affinity or identity of expression with those Christian writers who would on the 'critical' theory be his contemporaries, as would seem natural on that theory, but highly improbable on the traditional hypothesis? Or does he not? That is a question of fact which has never yet been dealt with in any thoroughgoing fashion. Yet it is vital to the whole issue before us. And it can be answered on a scale, and with a degree of scientific accuracy hitherto out of the question, with the help of E. J. Goodspeed's excellent *Index Patristicus* (Leipzic, 1907) and *Index Apologeticus* (1912). We proceed therefore to supplement our comparison of the two vocabularies, Pauline and Pastoral, by a comparison of both with this *tertium quid*—the vocabulary of the Apostolic Fathers and Apologists. We take primarily the former, as covering approximately the period of fifty years A.D. 95-145; in the second place the latter group as showing the trend of Christian diction during the next thirty years, say A.D. 140-170.

It will be useful to bear in mind from the outset the relative bulk of the documents in question. The text of the Apostolic Fathers occupies some 200 pages in Lightfoot's smaller edition. The text of the N.T. fills 516, the ten Paulines 105, the Pastorals $13\frac{2}{3}$, and the other books of the N.T. say 395 pages of approximately the same length in Westcott and Hort. So the length of the Apostolic Fathers is rather less than twice that of the Paulines, and just two-fifths that of the entire N.T. The vocabulary of the Apostolic Fathers comprises some 4,020 words other than proper names, as compared with 2,177 in Paul and 848 in the Pastorals. The length of the Apologists is rather more than three-fifths of the N.T., and their vocabulary still larger than that of the Apostolic Fathers.

1. Of the 175 *Hapax Legomena* in the Pastorals no less than 61 occur in the Apostolic Fathers, and 61 in the Apologists, including 32 which are not in the Apostolic Fathers, making a total of 93. See Appendix I, A I, p. 137 f. In the great majority of cases these appear not in any sense as possible quotations from the Pastorals, but in a distinct context of their own, proving that they did in fact belong to the current speech of the Church and to the working vocabulary of Christian writers and thinkers in this period.

The Pastorals share with the Apostolic Fathers from 4.4 words per page (1 Tim.) to 7.1 (Titus) which are foreign to the rest of the N. T.; the Paulines, from 1 (Rom.) to 2·4 (Philem.), the majority having less than 1·5 per page. See Diagram IX, B.

With the Apostolic Fathers or Apologists, or both, the Pastorals share from 7·5 (2 Tim.) to 8·6 per page (Titus); the Paulines, from 1·6 (Eph.) to 3·2 (Phil.), with the rest under 2·5 per page. See Diagram IX, A.

These words are distributed over the whole body of writings

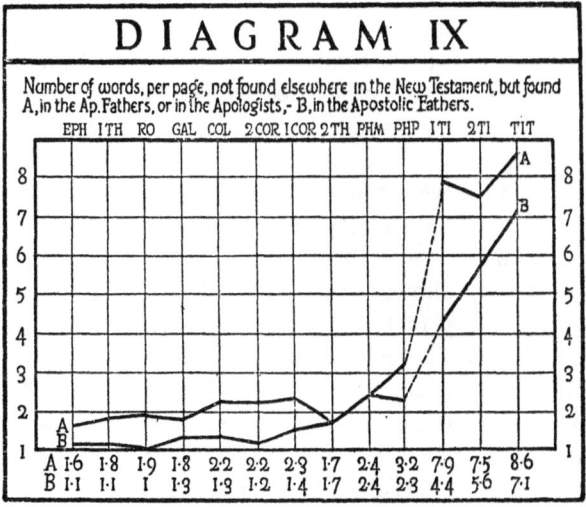

before us, without exception; even the brief fragments of Papias, Melito, and Dionysius of Corinth adding their small quota to the general mass of evidence. Clement of Rome has 21, 2 Clem. 7, Ignatius 13, Polycarp 6, the Martyrdom of Polycarp 4, the Didache 3, Barnabas 4, Hermas 21, the *Ep. ad Diognetum* 7, Papias 1, Aristeides 1, Tatian 19, Justin 40, Athenagoras 22, Melito 2, and Dionysius of Corinth 2. The lists are given in our Appendix I, E, pp. 150 ff. Twenty-nine occur in both groups.

If, in a number of instances, the word in question appears seldom, or only once, the same is true to a still greater extent of the Pauline *Hapax Legomena*. On the other hand we find more than a few of the Pastoral *Hapax Legomena* recurring again and again in one writer after another. Thus e. g. ἁγνεία appears in 1 Clem., Ign., Plp., and Herm.—a dozen times; ἔντευξις 18 times, in 1 Clem., 2 Clem., Herm., and Jus.; ἄλλως 15 times, in Herm.,

Ta., Jus., Ath.; ἐνδύνω 41, in 1 Clem., Barn., Ign., Herm., Jus.; θεοσέβεια 13, in 2 Clem., Dgn., Ta., Jus., Ath.; πραγματεία 13, in Herm., Ta., Ath.; φιλαργυρία 7, in 2 Clem., Plp., Ta.; σωτήριος 18, in 1 Clem., Dgn., Jus.; φροντίζω 11, in Ign., Jus.; χρήσιμος 9, in Ign., Herm., Jus., Ta.; μηδέποτε 7, in Mar., Barn., Herm., Jus.; ἀνόσιος 7, in 1 Clem., Jus., Ath.; διάγω 7, in Ign., Jus., Ath.; πρόγονος 7, in Mel., Jus., Ath.; σεμνότης 10, in 1 Clem., Herm., Ta.; σώφρων 12, in 1 Clem., Ta., Jus., Ath.; ὠφέλιμος 5, in 1 Clem., Herm., Ta., Jus.

The author of the Pastorals does speak the language of the Apostolic Fathers and Apologists, while diverging from that of other N. T. writers, to a degree wholly without parallel in the genuine Paulines.

2. But we have seen that, in addition to these *Hapax Legomena*, he uses a large number of words which, while they occur in other books of the N. T. (i. e. in Christian writings of the forty years or so following the death of Paul), are foreign to the working vocabulary of the Apostle, in so far as this is known to us from the ten surviving epistles.

Out of 131 such words, 100 occur in the Apostolic Fathers, 95 in the Apologists, 118 in one or the other, and 77 in both. See Appendix I, A 2, p. 138 f.

1 Clem. has 42 of these, 2 Clem. 21, Ignatius 26, Polycarp 14, the Martyrdom of Polycarp 18, the Didache 18, Barnabas 24, Hermas 54, the *Ep. ad Diognetum* 20, the fragments from Papias 3.

Aristeides has 6, Tatian 42, Justin 76, Athenagoras 37, and Melito (fragments in Eusebius) 3. See Appendix I, E, pp. 150 ff.

Combining these results with those in the last paragraph, we see that the Pastorals share with the Apostolic Fathers 161 words which do not appear in the Pauline epistles, with the Apologists 156, with both groups 106, and with one or the other no fewer than 211.

Each of the Pauline epistles has also naturally a certain number of words which do not appear elsewhere in the ten epistles, but do appear in one or both of the second-century groups. But whereas the Pastorals share with the Apostolic Fathers from 13.6 to 18.7 such words per page, the Paulines share from 4 to 7. See Diagram X, B, p. 71. So once again we find the ten Paulines forming a close, gradual, and orderly sequence among themselves. Once again the Pastorals show a violent break away from that sequence. Only now, to the negative observation that the words in question were missing from the other Paulines, we have added the positive fact that they are present, some of them very frequently, in the pages of those Christian teachers who were, on our theory, the contemporaries

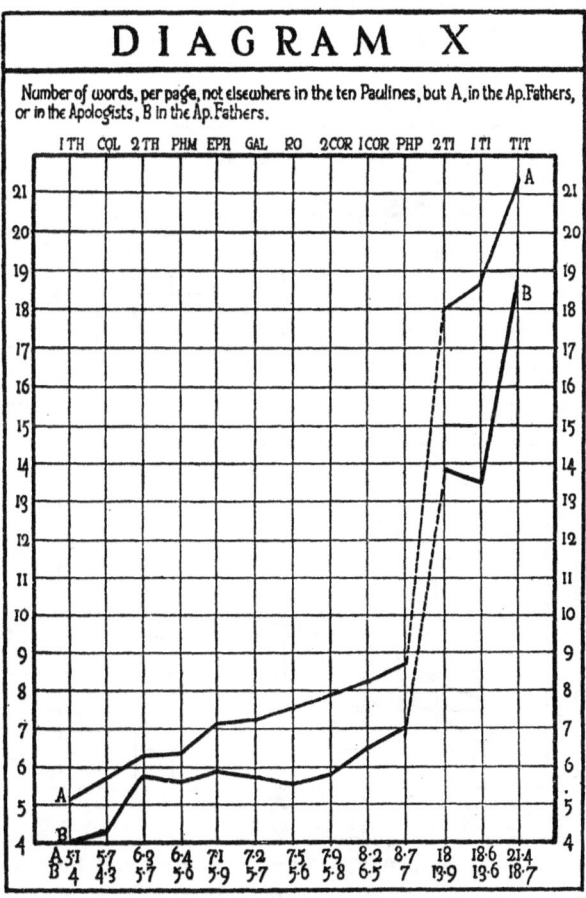

of this author, but on the traditional view, were writing from 30 to 80 years after his death.

If the validity and significance of this result needs any further confirmation, it seems to find it in the entirely similar result of our parallel experiment with the Apologists. The Pastorals share with this second group of writers from 13.3 to 16.5 non-

Pauline words per page; while the corresponding figures for the ten Paulines range from 4·2 to 6·6 per page. See Diagram XI, C. In the same Diagram, line D, we show that the Pastorals have in common with *both* these second-century groups from 9·2 to 13·9 per page, the Paulines from 2·8 to 4·9. Finally with *one or the other* of these groups the Pastorals share from 18 to 21·4 per page, the Paulines from 5·1 to 8·7. Diagram X, A, p. 71.

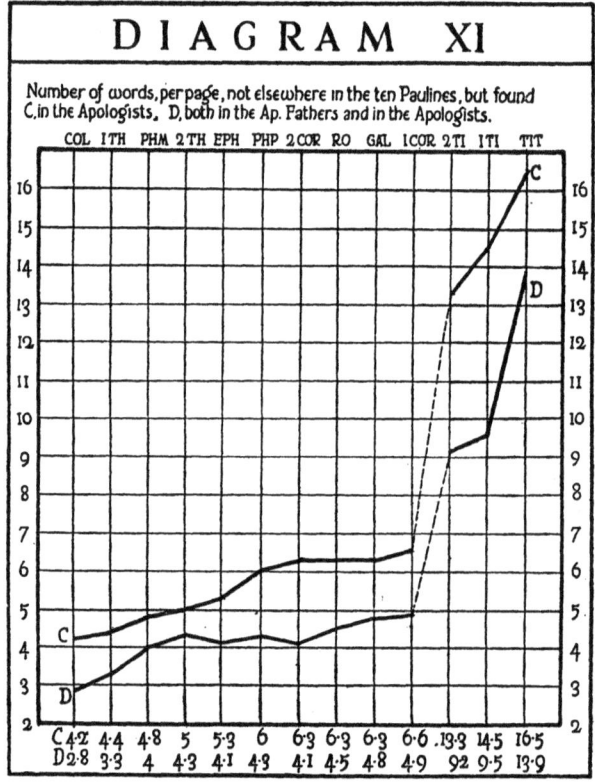

This contrast between Pastorals and individual Paulines is still further accentuated, if we take into account the frequency with which the words in question recur in these later books.

We have shown (Appendix I, E, pp. 150 ff.) that Clement of Rome uses in common with the Pastorals 63 words never so far as we know employed by Paul, 2 Clem. 28, Ignatius 39, Polycarp 20, the Martyrdom of Polycarp 22, the Didache 21, Barnabas 28, Hermas 75, the *Ep. ad Diognetum* 27, and the fragments from Papias 4;

while Aristeides has 7, Tatian 61, Justin 116, Athenagoras 59, and the fragments from Melito 5.

The corresponding lists and numbers for the books of the N. T. are given in Appendix I, D, p. 148 f., as follows:—Matt. has in common with the Pastorals 34 non-Pauline words, Mark 32, Luke 56, John 25, Acts 60 (including 32 which are also in Luke), Heb. 39, 1 Pet. 17, 2 Pet. 18 (that is more than any other N. T. book, in proportion to its length), Jas. 15, the Johannine epistles 8, Jude 8, and Rev. 16.

Thus 1 Clement, Hermas, and Justin have each a larger number of such words than any N. T. book; Tatian and Athenagoras have as many as Acts and Luke, which have much the largest number in the N. T., and the total in the Apostolic Fathers exceeds that in the whole body of non-Pauline N. T. books by 30 (or 22·9 per cent.); while the total in the Apostolic Fathers and Apologists combined exceeds that in the N. T. books by 80 (or 61·1 per cent.). Yet the entire bulk of the Apostolic Fathers (200 pages in Lightfoot) is rather more than half that of these non-Pauline books of the N. T. (say, 395 pages). In proportion to their length, the Apostolic Fathers have more than twice as many non-Pauline words in common with the Pastorals as have the other books of the N. T. (The ratio is as 127 to 52.)

But the outstanding fact here is that one word in every four throughout the Pastorals, 211 out of 848, while foreign so far as we know to the vocabulary of Paul, is now proved to form part of the working vocabulary of Christian writers between the years A.D. 95 and 170—including many words which recur with some frequency in these writers (e.g. ἀρνέομαι, δεσπότης, εὐσέβεια, μῦθος, παραιτέομαι, ὠφέλιμος—all of which are found in all three Pastorals).

It does not seem possible to regard any one of the series of facts adduced in this section as merely accidental—still less the whole number.

3. But now what of the converse relation? In what numbers and in what proportions do the Pastorals share with the other Paulines words foreign to the vocabulary of these second-century writers? The total number is 18, of which 7 are to be found elsewhere in the N. T., viz. (ἅλυσις, εὐαγγελίστης, παραχειμάζω), ἀνυπόκριτος, μεσίτης, *ὀνειδισμός, *φιμόω. There remain 11

shared exclusively with Paul, viz. 6 in 1 Tim. *ἀλοάω, ναυαγέω, ὀδύνη, προκοπή, στρατεία, ὑβριστής, 4 in 2 Tim. ἄστοργος, μόρφωσις, (σπένδομαι), *σωρεύω, 1 in Titus ἀποτόμως.

Not one of these occurs in Paul himself more than twice, and only 3 more than once, 4 (marked by *) occur in his epistles only as part of quotations from the LXX, and 4 (in brackets) occur in the Pastorals in verses which are admittedly genuine.

4. Of the 50 words found in Paul and in the Pastorals, but not elsewhere in the N. T., 33 occur also in the Apostolic Fathers, 26 in the Apologists, 20 in both second-century groups, and 39 in one or the other.

Of the 492 common to Paul, the Pastorals and other N. T. books, 470 are in the Apostolic Fathers, 459 in the Apologists, 444 in both, and 485 in one or the other.

Of the 106 words found in all three Pastorals, 97 are also in Paul, 102 in both Fathers and Apologists, and 105 in one or other of these second-century groups. And the remaining word, ὑγιαίνω, occurs in non-Christian writers of this period, e. g. Lucian, in a similar figurative sense to that which it bears in the Pastorals. See Appendix I, 'Residue,' p. 165 (7).

Of 542 words common to Paul and the Pastorals, 503 or 92.8 per cent. are in the Apostolic Fathers also, 485 or 89.5 per cent. in the Apologists, and 524 or 96.7 per cent. in one or the other.

Of Paul's 2,177 words, 1,543 or 70.9 per cent. are in the Apostolic Fathers. Of the Pastorals' 848 words, 664 or 78.3 per cent. are in the Apostolic Fathers.

5. We have seen that 634 words used by Paul in his ten epistles have disappeared entirely from the current speech of second-century Christendom, as represented by the writings of the Apostolic Fathers. If we ask how many of these same words are conspicuous by their absence from the Pastorals, the answer is, no less than 595 or 92.3 per cent. One hundred and thirty-two occur in more than one Pauline epistle, and of these 123 are wanting in the Pastorals also. See Appendix I, F, pp. 153 ff.

Among these are included seventy-three words all found in more than one Pauline epistle, but never once in the Apostolic Fathers, nor in the Apologists. Seventy-two of these are wanting in the Pastorals also. Sixteen occur in three epistles—δοκιμή, ἔνδειξις, ἐπιβαρέω, εὐσχημόνως, καταλλάσσω, μετασχηματίζω, συναιχμάλωτός, υἱοθεσία, φιλοτιμέομαι (none of which occur elsewhere in the N. T.), and ἀνάθεμα, ἀσπασμός, ἐκδίκησις, πανουργία, περιποίησις, προερῶ, ἔνι, 3 in 4 epistles—ἀπεκδέχομαι, εὐδοκία, περισσοτέρως, 1 in 6 epistles—στήκω, and 1 in 7 epistles—συνεργός.

In view of the linguistic affinity already noted between the Pastorals and the writings of the Apostolic Fathers, the question is worth asking, whether or not the latter show a corresponding tendency to dispense with that same series of Pauline particles, &c., on the absence of which from the Pastorals so much stress has been laid in these pages.

The answer is that while none of them exhibits this tendency on quite the same scale as our author, it is nevertheless in varying degrees quite unmistakably present among them all.

Of the 'missing particles, &c.' mentioned on p. 36 f., the following are entirely absent from the Apostolic Fathers also; διόπερ, ἤτοι, ἴδε, μήτιγε, νή, πηλίκος, ὑπεναντίος, ὑπεράνω, ὑπερλίαν, ὡσπερεί. ἐφάπαξ, καθό, μενοῦνγε, οὗ, ὅμως, τάχα, τοὐναντίον, ὑπερεκπερισσοῦ. ἔνι, ὄφελον, πλήν. μήπως. Only once altogether in the Apostolic Fathers, we find δεῦρο, ἐξαυτῆς, ἡνίκα, μήπω. δίς, ἡλίκος, κατενώπιον. εἰκῇ, εἴπερ, ἄχρι. Most of these, it is true, occur but seldom in Paul himself. But this cannot be said of e. g. ἕκαστος, which occurs 42 times and in 9 epistles, but not at all in the Didache, once each in Polycarp (in a quotation), and in the Martyrdom of Polycarp, twice in Ignatius and in 2 Clem.; nor of σύν (38 times in 8 Paulines), which our author seems to go out of his way to avoid as a preposition, though he uses it frequently as a prefix.[1] It occurs once each in 1 Clem., Polycarp, and the *Ep. ad Diognetum*, and not at all in 2 Clem., the Didache, Barnabas, nor even in Hermas. With these writers too it might almost be said to have dropped out of use in favour of μετά, as a preposition, though still (as in the Pastorals) very common as a prefix. εἴτε occurs 63 times in Paul, and in 8 epistles, but not at all in 1 Clem., 2 Clem., Barn., Mart., Did., and only once each, in its double form, in Ignatius, Polycarp, and Hermas. ἐμός (23 times in 8 epistles)

---

[1] συναπεθάνομεν 2 Tim. ii. 11 for ἀπεθάνομεν σύν Rom. vi. 8; ἀσπάζονταί σε οἱ μετ' ἐμοῦ πάντες Titus iii. 15 for ἀσπάζονται ὑμᾶς οἱ σὺν ἐμοὶ πάντες Phil. iv. 21; μετὰ τῶν ἐπικαλουμένων τὸν κύριον 2 Tim. ii. 20 for σὺν τοῖς ἐπικαλουμένοις τὸ ὄνομα τοῦ κυρίου 1 Cor. i. 2.

is wanting in 2 Clem., Barn., Plp., Mar., Did.; and in 1 Clem. it appears in one passage only, repeated there half a dozen times, but all in quotation. διό (27 times in 8 epistles) is found neither in 2 Clem., nor in Mar., nor in Did., nor yet in Hermas, and only once in Dgn. and Ignatius. ὥστε (39 in 7) is not in Polycarp, nor in Dgn., nor in the Didache, and only once in Ignatius. κἀγώ (27/7) is missing in Plp., Did., Dgn., and occurs once each in 2 Clem., Mar., Barn.; twice in 1 Clem., but in quotations. ἔτι (16/7) is missing in Plp., Mar., Did. γε (13/7) is not in 2 Clem., Ign., Plp., Mar., Did. ἄρα (27/7) is not in Plp., Mar., Did., Dgn.—and once in 1 Clem. νυνί (18/6) is not in Barn., Ign., Plp., Mar., Herm., Did., Dgn. ὅπως (9/6) is not in Barn., Plp., Mar., Herm., Dgn. ἐμαυτοῦ (14/6) is not in 1 Clem., 2 Clem., Mar., Did., Dgn. ὥσπερ (14/5) is not in 2 Clem., Plp., Mar. οὐκέτι (15/5) is not in 1 Clem., Did., Plp., Mar., Dgn. ἄχρι (14/5) is not in 1 Clem., 2 Clem., Barn., Ign., Plp., Mar., Did., Dgn. οὐχί (18/4) is not in 2 Clem., Plp., Mar., Dgn. καθάπερ (16/4) is not in 1 Clem., 2 Clem., Barn., Did., Ign., Plp., Mar., Herm.

The conclusion which we can hardly help drawing from these facts, is that a marked tendency to drop a considerable number of the Pauline particles, prepositions, &c., is shared by our author with the Christian writers of the early second-century, and forms one more link between him and them; while it is carried by him so much further than by any of them as to constitute a distinct idiosyncrasy of his style and diction.

Comparatively scanty as is our author's equipment in words of this class, it still includes several which lie outside the Pauline vocabulary, but inside that of the early second-century writers. We find μηδέποτε 2 Tim. iii. 7, nowhere else in the N. T., but in the Martyrdom of Polycarp, Hermas (several times), and Justin; ἄλλως 1 Tim. v 25, another *Hapax Legomenon*, very common in Hermas, and several times also in Justin, Tatian, and Athenagoras; μέντοι 2 Tim. ii. 19, and in the Catholic Epistles, Papias, Hermas, Justin, and Athenagoras; μήποτε 2 Tim. ii. 25, Gospels, Acts, Heb., 1 Clem., Barn., Ign., Did., Herm., and Justin; δι' ἣν αἰτίαν 2 Tim. i. 6, 12, Titus i. 13, Luke, Acts, Heb., cf. διὰ ταύτην τὴν αἰτίαν Heb., 1 and 2 Clem., Herm. (αἰτία not in Paul).

But, it may be urged, the Pastorals have a considerable number of such words—particles, &c.—in common with Paul. That is true. The actual number is 77. They are in fact the irreducible minimum without which it would be difficult to compose a telegram, and impossible to write a book or letter. The great majority of them occur not only in Paul, but also in every book of the N. T., and with barely an exception these 77 words are found both in the Apostolic Fathers and in the Apologists.

6. The entire vocabulary of the Pastorals has 542 words in common with Paul, 623 with the other books of the N. T., 664 with the Apostolic Fathers, 641 with the Apologists, 673 with the entire N. T. including Paul, and 735 with the Apostolic Fathers and Apologists combined. We may summarize the totals shared by these epistles with the other groups of early Christian writings.

	Pastorals.	Paul.	O. N. T.[1]	Apos. Fath.	Apologists.	Both A. F. and Apgts.	Either A. F. or Apgts.	N. T.[2]
A 1	175	0	0	61	61	29	93	0
A 2	131	0	131	100	95	77	118	131
B 1	50	50	0	33	26	20	39	50
B 2	492	492	492	470	459	444	485	492
Total	848	542	623	664	641	570	735	673
Pages		105	395	200	318		518	503

The Pastorals share with the—

Ap. Fathers, but not with Paul	161,	with Paul but not with Ap. Fathers	39
Apologists	,,	,,	156,	,,	,,	Apologists	57
Both[3]	,,	,,	106,	,,	,,	Both[3]	78
Either[4]	,,	,,	211,	,,	,,	Either	18
Either	,,	N. T.	93, with N. T.	,,	Either	31

If now, for the purpose of our comparison, we choose to leave out of account the fragments of Aristeides, Quadratus, and Melito, and confine our attention, in the case of the Apologists, to the *Dialogue* and *Apologies* of Justin, the *Or. ad Graecos* of Tatian, and the *Supplicatio* of Athenagoras, we have in these and the Apostolic Fathers together a volume of about the same length as the N. T.—and the above figures will not be materially

---

[1] O. N. T., i. e. other books of the N. T., not counting Paul.
[2] N. T., i. e. whole N. T. including Paul.
[3] i. e. both with the Apostolic Fathers and also with the Apologists.
[4] i. e. either with the Apostolic Fathers or with the Apologists.

altered. A reduction of one word only[1] representing what is shared by the Pastorals with the fragments in question exclusively. Here then are two volumes of about the same size, one comprising the Christian writings of the first two generations, say, the second half of the first century, including the ten epistles of Paul himself—the other, the Christian writings of the third and fourth generations, from A.D. 95 to 170. And the significant fact is, that the vocabulary of the Pastorals has actually sixty-one words more in common with the later than with the earlier group—a truly amazing circumstance, if Paul wrote them.

Again, taking the three groups of post-Pauline Christian writings, (*a*) the non-Pauline books of the N. T., (*b*) the Apostolic Fathers, (*c*) the Apologists, we find that (*a*) is nearly four times, (*b*) nearly twice, and (*c*) three times the length of the ten Paulines. Now (*a*), which is thus much the largest of the three groups, and stands nearest in time to Paul, has the smallest number of words in common with the Pastorals: whereas (*b*) which is decidedly the smallest of the three, but coincides with the period to which our criticism assigns the Pastorals, has in common with them easily the largest number of words—another circumstance difficult to explain on the traditional hypothesis.

Further, of the individual books contained in (*a*) it is with those which, on the 'critical' view at least, are dated last, towards the end of the first century, and after, that our epistles show much the closest affinity—especially the Lucan writings and 2 Pet. See Appendix I, D, p. 148 f.

If therefore the Pauline authorship of our epistles is still to be maintained, some explanation has to be produced for the curious fact that the other works not only of the same period, but of the same author, have considerably less in common with the epistles to Timothy and Titus than have those of the next three generations, and that too, in a degree which increases steadily as time goes on, till a climax is reached in the writings of the next generation but one after the death of their supposed author.

While we ransack the literature of the first century in vain for many of the characteristic expressions used by this author, we find most of them in the Greek literature of the first half of the second century. To find the rest, all that is necessary (as we

[1] ἐπιπλήσσω, Melito.

EARLY SECOND-CENTURY WRITERS 79

shall show in full detail presently), is to extend our researches to a point still farther away, by twenty years, from Paul's lifetime— i. e. to the year A.D. 170.

7. Of the remaining 113 words in the Pastorals which are not to be found in Goodspeed's *Indices Patristicus et Apologeticus*, we have at least the cognates of fully the half, e. g:

If not ἀδηλότης, we have ἄδηλος in 1 Clem. and Ath.
„ ἀπόβλητος, we have ἀποβάλλω in 1 Clem., Herm., and ἀποβολή Ta.
„ ἀποθησαυρίζω, we have θησαυρίζω Jus., and ἀποθήκη Herm., Jus.
 γραώδης, we have γραίδιος Ath., cf. γραολογία Ta.
„ γυμνασία, we have γυμνάζομαι 2 Clem., γυμνητεύω Ta., -όομαι Dgn.
„ κοινωνικός, we have κοινωνός Herm., &c., -ωνέω Barn., Mar.
„ πυκνός, we have πυκνότερον 2 Clem., Ign., -ῶς Ign., Herm., Did.
„ σκέπασμα, we have σκεπάζω 1 Clem., Herm., Jus.
„ στόμαχος, we have ἀστομάχητος Herm.
„ ἀπαίδευτος, we have ἀπαιδεύτως Ta.
„ ἐπανόρθωσις, we have ἐπανορθόομαι Mel.
„ σωφρονισμός, we have σωφρονίζομαι Jus., -έω 1 Clem., &c.
„ αἱρετικός, we have αἱρετίζω 2 Clem., αἵρεσις Ign., Mar., Herm., αἱρεσιώτης Jus.
„ ἱεροπρεπής, we have ἁγιοπρεπής 1 Clem., Plp., ἱερατεύω 1 Clem., &c.
„ κενοφωνίαι, we have κενοδοξία 1 Clem., Ign., Herm., ὁμοφωνίαι 1 Clem.
„ νομίμως, we have νόμιμα 1 Clem., Herm., &c.
„ γενεαλογία, we have γενεαλογέομαι Ar.
„ νηφάλιος, we have νήφω Ign., Plp., &c.

For further instances see pp. 83 ff., and Appendix I, 'Residue,' pp. 161 ff.

8. We have now applied to the vocabularies of Paul and of the Pastorals respectively a number of tests, the result of which has been in every case to show that the ten Paulines form a closely connected series, from which no single epistle stands out in such a way as to suggest a doubt of its common origin with the rest. It is not even the case that any particular epistle

stands invariably at the top or the bottom of this series. From one point of view 1 Thess., from another 2 Thess., from another Col. takes the lowest place. Now Phil. and now 1 Cor. heads the list. The Pastorals on the other hand one and all consistently refuse to be brought anywhere near this series. They stand invariably at a greater distance from the nearest Pauline, than divides that epistle from the farthest of its fellows.

This being so, one final experiment remains. We have now to inquire whether, under similar tests, the Pastorals fall inside or outside the group of Christian writings to which, on our theory, they belong chronologically and in other important respects—

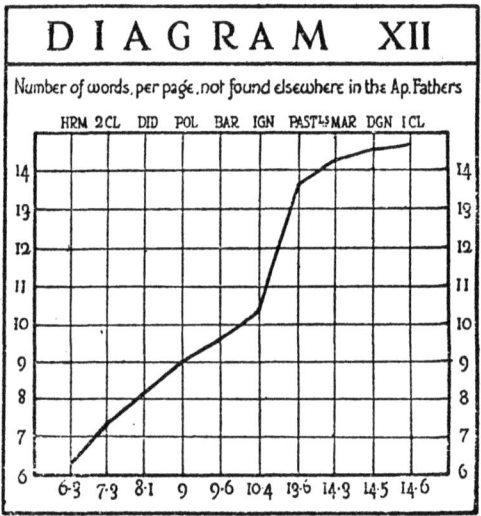

not including their intrinsic worth, canonical authority, or inspiration. These belong of course to an entirely different field of inquiry, and must not be dragged in here to confuse the real issue.

Each of the writings grouped under the title Apostolic Fathers, has naturally a certain number of words not to be found in any of the others. They too form from this point of view a fairly connected series, and the Pastorals prove on examination to fall well inside it. They have a larger number of unique words to the page than Hermas, 2 Clement, Ignatius, or the Didache, but a smaller number than 1 Clement, the Martyrdom of Polycarp, or the Epistle to Diognetus. See Diagram XII.

There is thus no counterweight on this side to set against the mass of positive evidence produced in the foregoing pages, not to mention those which follow. We do not of course regard the result of this last experiment as having any particular *positive* importance, taken by itself. For this is obviously one of those facts which, when first isolated and then unduly emphasized, could be most misleading, and only yield their true significance, when studied in connexion with the great body of related facts to which they belong. Thus, it is also a fact, that every one of the ten Paulines, when examined from the same point of view, has a still smaller number of unique words per page, not only than the Pastorals, but also than any of the Apostolic Fathers themselves. From this a too hasty logic might draw the paradoxical inference that, if the Pastorals are to be assigned to this period, much more must the Paulines one and all belong to it too! As an *argumentum ad hominem*, that would break down over the fact that we have refrained from basing our opinion on so insecure a foundation. As serious reasoning, it would be to ignore, not only the whole of the evidence produced in these pages, but various other known and relevant facts, e.g. that Clement of Rome writing before the end of the First Century, names and quotes the First Epistle to the Corinthians explicitly as the work of the Apostle Paul (xlvii. 1), and shows certain acquaintance with Rom. (xxxv. 5 f., xxxiii. 1, &c.). The combined vocabulary of these early Christian writers is very extensive, and includes the majority of Paul's written words, not only as the greater includes the less, but as we might expect remembering that they possessed, studied, and revered his epistles. We do not propose to meet one paradox with another, and suggest that the relative frequency in the Pastorals, as compared with the Paulines, of words which do not appear in the Apostolic Fathers is a further argument against the theory that they were as well known, and as assiduously read, as the Paulines, by these writers, or were included by them in a *Corpus Paulinum*. We prefer to take our stand on the more moderate statement that we have found nothing in the vocabulary of the Pastorals to conflict with the opinion that their author lived and wrote between the years A.D. 95 and 145, whereas many facts hitherto unknown, if not unsuspected, have emerged in the course of our comparative studies, which strongly support, if they do not finally confirm, that opinion.

It has already been pointed out (p. 68) that in the vast majority of cases, the context, in which these Pastoral *Hapax Legomena* occur in the Apostolic Fathers and Apologists, is such as to exclude any thought of a quotation or direct reference to these epistles. If, in face of this fact, it should still be argued that the words in question may have come into the current speech of second-century Christendom *via* the study of these, along with other Pauline epistles, at any rate it will not be suggested that Epictetus, Appian, Galen, Polyaenus, M. Aurelius, &c., all enriched their Greek vocabulary in this way!

9. THE RESIDUE.

There remain eighty-two words (marked • in Appendix I, A 1) in the Pastorals, which are not to be found elsewhere in the N. T., nor in the Apostolic Fathers, nor in the Apologists, i. e. in no Christian writing prior to A. D. 170.

The question which naturally suggests itself at this point is: Are these words, or any large proportion of them, to be found in non-Christian writings of the same period, and more especially during the first half of the second century? This again suggests the larger question: Does the vocabulary of the Pastorals as a whole, but more particularly in its non-Pauline elements, coincide to any large extent with that of Epictetus, Dio Chrysostom, Dioscorides (*c*. A. D. 100), Plutarch (who died A. D. 120), Arrian (pupil and friend of Epictetus), Appian, Aelian, Philo Byblius, Ptolemaeus, Lucian, Polyaenus, Galen, the Emperor Marcus Aurelius Antoninus, and their contemporaries?

The answer to both these questions is in the affirmative. See Appendix I, 'Residue,' pp. 161 ff., where it is proved that at least fifty-seven of these 'Residue' words do occur, some of them with great frequency, in books usually dated between the years A. D. 95 and 170.

In the same literature our 'A' words generally—(A 1) *Hapax Legomena* and (A 2) non-Pauline words found in later books of the N. T.—appear, we might almost say, on every page. It is certainly no uncommon thing to find several of them in a single sentence.[1]

---

[1] It has not seemed possible to print the large volume of evidence

EARLY SECOND-CENTURY WRITERS

We are left with 25 (out of the 306 non-Pauline words in the Pastorals), the occurrence of which in Greek writings of the period to which we have assigned these epistles, we have to admit our inability at present to demonstrate with chapter and verse. For several of these we have cognates so close that we feel justified in regarding them, in each case, as simply another form of the same word. Thus, (i) in 1 Tim., if we do not actually find αὐθεντέω between the stated limits (except in Papyri), αὐθέντης appears in Hermas and in Moeris, αὐθεντικός in 2 Clem. The unique διαπαρατριβή is represented by διατριβή (Dio Chrys., Justin, Lucian, &c.), and παρατριβή (Athenagoras), cf. ἀποδιατρίβω (Schol. in Lucian). Instead of ἑδραίωμα we have ἑδραῖος in Ignatius, ἑδράζω in 1 Clem., Ign., Jus., Ath., ἑδραιότης in Dio Chr., (cf. Reizenstein's *Poimandres*, p. 343[4], ὁ βαθμὸς οὗτος, ὦ τέκνον, δικαιοσύνης ἐστὶν ἕδρασμα), ἑδραιόω in Lucian.

For τεκνογονία (*Anth. P.*ix.22) we have in the *Ep. ad Diognetum* τεκνογονέω. For ἐκζήτησις we have ἐκζητέω very often in the Apostolic Fathers and in Justin, and ζήτησις in John, Acts, Justin, and Melito and Lucian. For (Anon. *ap.* Suid.) πρόκριμα (=*praeiudicium*) there is προκρίνω in Justin and Melito. The use of ὑψηλοφροσύνη and ὑψηλόφρων by Hermas, while 1 Clem. and Hermas have both ταπεινοφροσύνη and ταπεινοφρονέω, shows that the absence of ὑψηλοφρονέω is purely accidental.

(ii) in 2 Tim.: ἀντιδιατίθεμαι is represented by Justin's ἀντιτίθεμαι in the same sense, and his διατίθεμαι, cf. ἀντιδιατάξομαι (Epictetus). We have not found the word itself before Longinus (c. A.D. 250). For ἀφιλάγαθος there is φιλάγαθος in Plutarch, and a host of words like ἀφιλόκαλος (Plut.), ἀπειράγαθος (Diod.), ἀφιλοξενία (1 Clem.), ἀφιλόσοφος (Jus.), while ἀφιλοκἀγαθία is found in a second-century papyrus. συνκακοπαθέω is represented by συμπαθέω (Jus.) and κακοπαθέω (2 Clem. and Lucian).

(iii) in Titus. If not ἀφθορία, Justin (as well as Diodorus and Artemidorus v. 95) uses the adjective ἄφθορος, or in case the reading ἀδιαφθορία were preferred, we have ἀδιάφθορος in Plutarch and Galen. καλοδιδάσκαλος seems to be unique, but κακοδιδασκαλέω occurs in 2 Clem., κακοδιδασκαλία in Ignatius.

summarized in these four lines. But it is before us as we write, and is to our mind overwhelming.

Similarly ματαιολόγος may be confined to Titus, but ματαιολογία is used by Polycarp and by Plutarch.

For several more of these 'Residue' words we have formations only a little less closely related, or at least so entirely analogous as to leave no shadow of difficulty in the way of our belief that they all belong to one family, and formed a part of the same working vocabulary. Thus λογομαχέω and λογομαχία have their counterpart in the λογοποιέω and λογοποιία of Athenagoras. ὀρθοτομέω has its complements in the καινοτομέω of Tatian and Lucian, and the ὀρθογνώμονες of Justin. The word itself occurs in the LXX, Prov. xi. 5. ἔλεγμος also occurs fairly often in the LXX, while the form ἔλεγχος, as well as the verb ἐλέγχω, is common in this as in other periods. διδακτικός occurs so far as we know only in Philo, but its cognates in our period especially are legion. Another unicum, ἐπιδιορθόω Boeckh, *Inscr.* ii. 409, is represented by the διορθόω of 1 Clem. and others, as well as the ἐπανορθόω, -ωσις of Epict., Galen, &c. ἀκατάγνωστος, which occurs in 2 Maccabees, has its close analogies in Justin's ἀκατασκεύαστος, and the ἀκατάληπτος of 1 Clem. and Athenagoras. With αὐτοκατάκριτος (Philo) compare 1 Clement's αὐτεπαίνετος, and the κατάκριτος of Ignatius.

Finally, καταστρηνιάω occurs in the 'Ignatian' *Ep. ad Antioch.*, c. 11; φρεναπάτης is a derivative of the Pauline φρεναπατάω (Gal. vi. 3), but akin also to the φρενήρης of M. Antoninus and Lucian; καυστηριάζομαι is found in Strabo, in a second-century papyrus, and in the Schol. in Lucian; νεόφυτος ('neophyte') does not appear elsewhere, so far as we know, in this sense, till much later; and μεμβράνα is a Latin word and occurs in the 'genuine' verse 2 Tim. iv. 13. We do not think that any one will venture to deny, on the strength of any or all of these, the thesis which we now lay down as rigorously proved scientific fact—the language of the Pastorals is the Greek of the first half of the second century.

10. *Summary of Linguistic Argument.*

1. The language of the Pastorals shows on the face of it certain strongly marked peculiarities as compared with the other Paulines. A close and methodical examination very greatly

accentuates this contrast, and reveals further discrepancies none the less significant for being largely beneath the surface.

2. It is true that every Pauline epistle, and every sub-group of Paulines, is distinguished from the rest by its use of certain characteristic expressions, and its disuse of others. But when every allowance has been made for this wholly natural and obvious consideration, the fact remains that, under similar tests, the ten Paulines are still found to maintain among themselves a close and unmistakable family likeness. They form a clearly defined series; and the actual variations among them keep within certain limits, and are obedient to certain laws. The freedom and originality of the genuine Pauline spirit is in no way hampered by its obviously unconscious observance of these laws, and shows itself quite otherwise than by any transgression of these limits. The Pastorals refuse utterly to be brought within or near this series, and at every point exceed these limits and break these laws.

3. For such a discrepancy within the authentic works of a single author there is at present no known analogy in literature. Certain instances which have been alleged prove on examination to be no exception, but rather, most striking examples of those same laws which we have found governing the relations between the ten Paulines, but not between these and the Pastorals.

4. It is universally admitted that the linguistic peculiarities of the Pastorals are such as to call loudly for some explanation. But while numerous explanations have been forthcoming from the side of those who still adhere to the traditional view of their origin, neither singly nor collectively are these sufficient, in the judgement of 'critics', to neutralize the overwhelming cumulative effect of the great body of evidence pointing in an entirely different direction. The true explanation, they maintain, and the only one consistent with all the known facts, is that the Pastorals were not written by Paul, but by a devout and earnest Paulinist with our ten Paulines and, as many think, other genuine notes before him, during the half century A.D. 95-145.

5. In support of the critical view, it has now been demonstrated that these peculiarities of diction do in fact coincide with actual developments in the current speech of the Christian

Church, and in the working vocabulary of Christian leaders and thinkers during this very period. A large percentage of the words and expressions in the Pastorals which are foreign to the vocabulary of Paul, in so far as this is known to us by his genuine epistles, is found to belong to the vocabulary of the Apostolic Fathers. Of the Pauline words which appear to have dropped out of use among these writers nearly 94 per cent. are wanting in the Pastorals also. When the individual Paulines are submitted to similar tests, the result is once again to prove that among themselves they show a natural variation, but within certain fairly narrow limits. Once again they form a series. And the Pastorals stand outside that series but inside the series presented by the Apostolic Fathers. They have linguistically as much in common with these as these have with one another. And they have actually many more words in common with these and the Apologists together, than with the entire N. T. including the ten Pauline epistles.

6. Finally, it is proved that of those comparatively few remaining words in the vocabulary of the Pastorals, which do not occur in Christian writers between A. D. 95 and 170, practically the whole number did, nevertheless, belong to the current Greek speech, and are actually used by non-Christian writers of that period.

PART III

GENUINE PAULINE ELEMENTS IN THE PASTORALS

MORE than once in the preceding pages we have drawn attention to the fact that, along with so many expressions foreign to the diction of Paul, the Pastorals do unquestionably contain a notable quantity of definitely Pauline matter bearing the unmistakable stamp of the Apostle. The only question is—Who put it there? For, stated in these general terms, this fact is of course perfectly consistent with the theory formulated in our opening chapter (pp. 5 ff.), and is indeed essential to it, no whit less than it is to the view that Paul wrote the whole of these epistles, as they stand. We have now, therefore, to examine the relevant data more closely and in fuller detail, with a view to determining which explanation they seem to favour.

These elements in the language of the Pastorals, on the Pauline origin and character of which practically all parties are now agreed, fall under two distinct categories, one of which, the so-called 'Personalia', will come up for consideration presently.

I. PAULINE PHRASES.

The other, to which we must now turn our attention, is the extraordinary number of *phrases*, consisting sometimes of half a dozen or more words together, which coincid more or less closely, many of them exactly, with Paul's own most characteristic expressions in the ten epistles.

The vital issue here is, whether these correspondences are simply what we ought to expect between different writings by the same author, or whether they point rather to the intermediate activities of another mind, weaving the words of his great exemplar, along with his own, into one web and one design.

The actual phrases now in question may be seen by turning first to our text of the Pastorals (Appendix IV), where they are underlined, and references given in the margin, next, to (*a*) the Pauline Parallels (Appendix II, B), where they are collected and classified under the different Pauline epistles with which they show connexion. This is supplemented by (*b*) a list of words shared by the Pastorals with each single Pauline exclusively. See Appendix I, B 1 (and B 2).

Some of the correspondences produced are of course more striking than others. Some are only convincing when taken in conjunction with the whole body of evidence in which they play a very minor part. But taken as a whole, the facts here arranged seem to leave no room for doubt that our author must in any case have been deeply versed in those Pauline writings which have come down to us, and actually incorporated a number of words and phrases from each of them into his own three epistles.

While we have echoes from every period of Paul's epistolary career, and from every specimen of his literary craftsmanship, the most numerous and striking of these are taken, not from the latest group—as would have been natural, if he had written the Pastorals during and shortly before a second Roman imprisonment—but from Romans and 1 and 2 Corinthians, precisely those epistles which were fitted both by their length and their character to make the strongest impression, and with which, as a matter of fact, the Roman Clement and other Christian writers of the early second century show the closest and most certain acquaintance.[1] Even 2 Thess. and Philem., short as they are, furnish several examples of what we should have to regard as very curious coincidences, if nothing more. With a helping hand from the other epistles, to which they are bound by so many ties, even these make a strong bid for recognition as giving evidence of definite literary filiation. But for the rest the proofs of such a connexion as we have suggested seem to us quite conclusive.

Now is there anything whatever, in the parallels and agree-

---

[1] Cf. The Oxford Society of Historical Theology, *The N. T. in the Apostolic Fathers*, 1905, p. 137, &c.

ments here adduced, inconsistent with the theory that the Pastorals were written early in the second century by a devout Paulinist, with the genuine epistles of Paul either directly before his eyes, or, as the result of close and reverent study, well in his mind?

If this question is answered, as we think it must be, in the negative, we may proceed a step further, and inquire whether the facts before us are not better explained in this way than on the supposition that Paul wrote the whole of these epistles in substantially their present form. It is, to say the least, somewhat surprising to find the Apostle quoting himself to such an extent as must, on the latter hypothesis, be admitted to be the case. It can hardly be called an illustration of that remarkable freshness and originality of expression, as well as of thought, which is so conspicuous in the other Pauline epistles, and is sometimes said to explain the very numerous and striking divergences from the phraseology of those epistles, which we have found in the Pastorals. It is true that Paul himself has, like most other writers, his own favourite turns of speech which keep cropping up in one epistle after another. But we have not found between any one genuine epistle and the others anything like the great series of such composite links connecting the Pastorals with them all. Indeed so numerous and striking are these verbal agreements that it becomes a very serious question whether Paul himself would have been able, or likely, to reproduce, purely from memory, such a variety of extracts from letters which he had dictated seven or eight years previously. Supposing that the Pauline authorship of the Pastorals were fully established, we should almost feel driven to conclude that the Apostle must have obtained, or retained, copies of his own earlier epistles, and refreshed his memory of their contents before setting to work on the Pastorals. Even granting that very remote possibility, and setting aside the whole of the evidence produced in our previous section (Part II), it seems particularly surprising that the Apostle should have thought it necessary to instruct Timothy to such an extent in identically the same terms as had been used, so many years before, in those letters (to the Thessalonians, Romans,[1] Corinthians,[2] Philippians,

[1] xvi. 21.   [2] 1 Cor. iv. 17, xvi. 10, 2 Cor. i. 1, 19.

Colossians, and Philemon) in which this very Timothy had been expressly associated with himself.

It is in these very phrases that we find not a few of those undoubtedly Pauline words which appear, as was pointed out pp. 24, 26 f., once and only this once in the Pastorals, e.g. in 1 Tim.: B 1. ἐξαπατάω, ἀλοάω, βοῦς, φιμόω, ἀφορμή, ὄλεθρος. B 2. ἁγιασμός, ἀόρατος, ἄφθαρτος, γράφω, δύο, τρεῖς, ἐκτός, διαλογισμός, μεσίτης, παράκλησις, παρρησία, παραδίδωμι, οἰκονομία, σάρξ, τέλος, ἐπιτρέπω, ψεύδομαι.

In 2 Tim.: B 1. ἀτιμία, ἀλαζών, ἄστοργος, ἀδιάλειπτος μνεία, μόρφωσις, ὀστράκινος, συνβασιλεύω, συνζάω. B 2. ἀπιστέω, δέσμιος, δεσμός, δέω, ἐγείρω, ἐπιποθέω, ἐπικαλοῦμαι, καταργέω, θάνατος, κλῆσις, λατρεύω, πληρόω, χαρά, σκεῦος, σπέρμα, συναποθνήσκω, (νεκρός).

In Titus: B 1. χρηστότης. B 2. ἀρχαί, ἐξουσίαι, ἐντρέπω, οἰκονόμος, κληρονόμος, περιτομή.

But supposing that the presence of these Pauline expressions really did come about in the way here suggested, might we not reasonably expect to find at one point or another some indication of that fact? Would not our second-century Paulinist be almost bound to reveal himself sooner or later, if not by any downright blunder, at any rate by the occasional introduction of some Pauline phrase in a context to which it might be made to apply, but not with quite the same fitness as in its original setting, and not without some modification of its original meaning improbable in Paul, but natural in a secondary writer? Are there in these epistles any indications of this kind? We think there are.

Take, for instance, the familiar Pauline parenthesis, 1 Tim. ii. 7 ἀλήθειαν λέγω, οὐ ψεύδομαι = Rom. ix. 1—a remark which was wholly natural and convincing in its original setting. In telling the Christians at Rome of the intense spiritual agony and travail with which he longed incessantly for the conversion of his fellow-countrymen, and his readiness to lose his own soul for their sake (if that would have helped!), he felt quite reasonably that to people who did not yet know him personally such a statement might seem extravagant. Yet it was neither more nor less than the truth. So too when he was giving the Galatians an outline of his life and movements subsequent to his conversion, in order to convince them that his apostolic authority had indeed come to him directly from God, and through no human mediation, it was entirely to the point for him to add the solemn asseveration Gal. i. 20 ἰδού ἐνώπιον τοῦ θεοῦ ὅτι οὐ ψεύδομαι. And no less appropriate was it, when declaring, paradoxically, as it might well sound to the Corinthians, that he gloried in his very weaknesses, for him to insist, 2 Cor. xi. 31 ὁ θεὸς ... οἶδεν ... ὅτι οὐ ψεύδομαι.[1] But now the Apostle is writing neither to strangers who have never set eyes on him, nor to foolish and unstable minds bewitched and misled by influences foreign to the gospel (Gal. i. 6 ff., iii. 1, 2 Cor. xi. 4), but to his true and trusted friend, the loyal comrade of so many years. What was the point, and where the necessity of assuring Timothy, of all people in the world, that he really was speaking the truth, and not telling lies, when he asserted that he, Paul, had been appointed an Apostle and teacher of the Gentiles? By what conceivable possibility could it have occurred to Timothy to have denied or doubted that? But as addressed to the Timothys of our author's time this solemn reminder, in the familiar phrase of the Apostle, has edge and point. It was needed, and there was some hope that it would not prove altogether ineffective.

Again, the ὡς in 2 Tim. i. 3 is certainly awkward and difficult to account for grammatically. There is much to be said for Holtzmann's explanation (*PB.*, p. 111) that it arises from the combination here of two Pauline phrases, one from Rom. i. 8 f. εὐχαριστέω τῷ θεῷ ᾧ λατρεύω ... ὡς ἀδιαλείπτως μνείαν ὑμῶν ποιοῦμαι κτλ., and one from 1 Thess. iii. 6 ἔχετε μνείαν ἡμῶν ἀγαθήν, ... ἐπιποθοῦντες ... νυκτὸς καὶ ἡμέρας, κτλ. 2 Tim. i. 9 οὐ κατὰ τὰ ἔργα ἡμῶν looks like a slip for the Pauline οὐκ ἐξ ἔργων Rom. ix. 11, xi. 6, Gal. ii. 16, iii. 2, 5, 10, Eph. ii. 9. Paul says more than once, quoting Ps. lxii. 13 = Prov. xxiv. 12, that God will reward every man κατὰ τὰ ἔργα αὐτοῦ Rom. ii. 6, 2 Cor. xi. 15, 2 Tim. iv. 14 (a genuine verse!).

Again, 2 Tim. ii. 11 f. εἰ γὰρ συναπεθάνομεν, καὶ συνζήσομεν, agrees almost verbatim with Rom. vi. 8 εἰ δὲ ἀπεθάνομεν σὺν Χριστῷ, πιστεύομεν ὅτι καὶ συνζήσομεν αὐτῷ. But whereas in Romans the aorist is perfectly natural, for he is speaking of the death to sin which took place at conversion, here the reference is

---

[1] If these words are taken as referring rather to the statement of fact which follows them, our argument remains the same.

clearly to literal physical death in martyrdom, which for the real Paul was not yet accomplished, though so near at hand when he wrote, if indeed he did write this verse to Timothy. This, and the significant transference of σύν from preposition to prefix (see p. 75), seems once more to suggest the secondary writer quoting a familiar saying of the Apostle in a way in which we cannot quite think that the Apostle would have quoted himself. This impression would be still further confirmed if we were sure that the usual translation of πιστὸς ὁ λόγος is correct. It seems a little strange to find even an apostle quoting his own 'sayings' with so much solemnity as 'faithful'. But elsewhere in the Pastorals ὁ λόγος consistently means the Word of God, the Gospel message of salvation; and we incline to believe with Holtzmann that it does so here.[1] In that case the γάρ introduces not a 'faithful saying', but a sort of proof-text, showing that the Divine Promise is, like the God who gave it, worthy of all trust.

A glance at our text (Appendix IV, pp. 183 ff.) will show that these borrowed Pauline phrases are distributed throughout the whole body of the Pastorals. Not quite evenly, however. There are passages like 2 Tim. i. 1-15 which consist almost exclusively of such phrases, so that practically the whole of the materials are, in this sense, not only Pauline, but are Paul himself, his *ipsissima verba*, and only the arrangement, and an occasional touch of foreign colour, betrays the later mind. On the other hand, there are pages, like 1 Tim. v. 1-19, vi. 7-21, 2 Tim. ii. 15-iii. 6, Titus i. 13-ii. 15, in which the Pauline echoes almost die away, where our author is evidently composing more and more freely, and in doing so falls unconsciously but inevitably into the vocabulary of his time, and into a general type of composition, syntax, grammar, style, and diction which we come to recognize as peculiarly his own. Here the number of words foreign to the genuine Paulines rises to its maximum—40 to 46 per page; two lines together, at most, free from such words; and sometimes four or five lines together with hardly a Pauline word in them, e.g. 1 Tim. vi. 18-21a, 2 Tim. iii. 2-5, Titus i. 7b-8, ii. 1-5a, iii. 9-11.

---

[1] And in the four other verses where this phrase occurs.

And yet again there are places where phrases from the genuine Paulines, and non-Pauline terms in use among second-century writers, alike recede, and we find ourselves suddenly back in the familiar atmosphere, listening to the familiar accents, no echo this time, but the real Paul, or else the most marvellous imitation in all literature! It is precisely this last observation which leads us to lay down our second thesis,—

II. PERSONALIA.

This author must have had before his eyes, and has incorporated bodily into his epistles and so has preserved for all time, a certain amount of genuine Pauline material, which cannot be identified with any of the surviving epistles, and would otherwise, in all human probability, have been lost beyond recall.

In proof of this proposition it will be best to take as our starting-point those verses about which there is the greatest unanimity among critics and least room in fact for differences of opinion as to their authenticity—2 Tim. iv. 6-22 and Titus iii. 12 f. There is absolutely no trace here of the doctrinal controversies, nor of the ecclesiastical situation, with which the bulk of these epistles is occupied. Instead we find a series of personal details, greetings, messages, items of news, small commissions, names—some referring to people and places already familiar to students of Paul's life, others to companions and fields of service of which we otherwise know nothing. These Personalia are so vivid, so concrete, so entirely in the vein of the references to be found in every letter that Paul ever wrote, that, we may safely assert, no one would ever have dreamed of doubting their authenticity, had it not been for the context in which they occur.

1.

With regard to these Baur wrote, 'One must admit that in this respect the epistle (2 Tim.) does not lack colour and life. But this is only the happy thought of invention; and we must not let ourselves be led away by it into mistaking what is mere appearance and copy for truth and reality' (*PB.*, 1835, p. 68).

Similarly Holtzmann, 'Whoever once undertook to write in Paul's name, was bound in the nature of things to do what he could to render the fiction as convincing as possible. The analogy of the genuine epistles was bound to suggest to him a certain quantum of personal notices' (*PB.* 125).

But what if he had the real thing ready to his hand in the form of actual notes written by the Apostle himself to one or another of his companions? In that case it would have been superfluous, and a waste of energy, to say the least, if he had set these aside in favour of laborious imitations of his own.

Holtzmann had considered this hypothesis (which had been put forward as early as 1843 by Credner and Hitzig, but was soon abandoned by the former), and he admitted frankly that there is not a word to be said *a priori* against the abstract possibility, and even probability, that Paul may have written such brief personal notes to private friends, which would remain for a time in their possession, and later on, coming into the hands of our second-century Paulinist, might have been used by him as a welcome basis for the composition of new apostolic letters. He admitted further, and indeed showed in detail, that each separate item, taken by itself, is capable of being fitted into one moment or another in Paul's known life. But what seemed to him decisive against this, as the true explanation of the facts before us, was the utter impossibility of finding any one situation into which they can all be fitted. Convincing enough as they are when taken singly, he shows how, as a whole and collectively, they contradict each other at point after point. From this he draws the inference that they cannot be authentic messages from the real Paul, but must be regarded as belonging to the Pauline mask assumed by the *auctor ad Timotheum.*

'This mere imitation soon gets itself involved in internal contradictions, and so betrays itself for what it is. Thus we read here in rapid succession, 2 Tim. iv. 11, 16, "only Luke is with me", and "at my first defence no one stood by me", and between stands, iv. 12, "Tychicus I sent to Ephesus", with no connecting link between these sentences. We are to suppose that "all" have forsaken the captive. Yet, as Alexander is an opponent, only Demas is actually named, v. 10. For the με ἐγκατέλιπεν does not refer to Crescens and Titus, as does the ἐπορεύθη. These seem rather to have been sent, like Tychicus, in the interests of the Mission. And if "all" have deserted the Apostle, and only Luke is with him, what about the companions named in verse 21 ? Such *lapsus memoriae et calami* readily befall one who is thinking himself into a strange situation, but not one who really is lying forsaken in prison' (ib.).

Holtzmann and others before and after him have in fact made out an unanswerable case for their thesis, that there is no single moment in Paul's life, as known to us from Acts and the ten epistles, into which these personal references as a whole can by any ingenuity be inserted. There is no need to labour this point, for it is one of the very few on which all parties are now agreed. Isolated details might at need be explained away. We might say that Luke was the only companion still sharing Paul's imprisonment, and yet a few leading members of the Roman Church might have found courage and opportunity to visit him and send greetings to Timothy. But the whole picture is simply riddled with inconsistencies. It is like a jig-saw puzzle, or rather, several, of which the separate pieces, once mixed together, defy all efforts to make them fit one another so as to form one complete picture within the required frame.

But that the inference drawn by Holtzmann from this undeniable fact was nevertheless a mistaken inference, is common ground to practically all present-day scholars. A necessary inference it certainly is not. For there are at least two other alternatives, one of which, it is now agreed, he dismissed too lightly—though it is by no means agreed which of the two this is. To these alternative explanations, and the choice between them, we shall return presently. Meanwhile, it may be taken as agreed further that Holtzmann's conclusion is not only needless, but is also, to say the least, extremely improbable. It does not do justice to the extraordinary realism which its advocates, from Baur onwards, could not help seeing in these personal details, but of which they failed to grasp the true significance. These are too vivid, individual, concrete, and altogether too life-like to be dismissed as mere fiction—at any rate until every other possibility has been exhausted. We have no right, it is true, to deny dogmatically and *a priori* the possibility of a second-century Christian possessing a grain of historic imagination; nor does the mere fact that some of his contemporaries seem to have been singularly lacking in this respect justify us in setting any arbitrary or narrow limits to his gifts in this direction. Fiction is often more realistic than the report of an eyewitness. But as fiction these details would be not only good, but incomparably and incredibly true to life. The most inimitable features of the most inimitable style in all literature are too faithfully reproduced. They have the genuine Pauline stamp. They ring true.

In order to satisfy ourselves that this is no merely subjective impression, but is based on objective and concrete facts, let us now inquire what happens when these alleged Pauline fragments are isolated from their present context and subjected to the same linguistic tests as we have applied to the epistles as a whole. Do they, or do they not survive the ordeal? The answer is in the affirmative. Of all that has been said in Part II about the far-reaching and deeply underlying divergences of the Pastorals from the normal Pauline type, hardly a line applies to the paragraphs of which we are now speaking. They keep well inside the normal Pauline number of *Hapax Legomena* and of other words not found elsewhere in the ten Paulines. And such as there are, in no way suggest a second-century origin, nor raise a doubt of their Pauline authorship. Phrases which might have been borrowed from the ten Paulines are conspicuous by their absence, or at least their rarity. For the rest we have Pauline words used in a perfectly Pauline way. And of these (to clinch all) a really extraordinary number, 40 or more to the page (practically every significant word), make here their solitary appearance in the Pastorals.

(i) Apart from the first and last pages of 2 Tim., the lowest number of non-Pauline words in any complete page in the Pastorals, counting repetitions, is 22, the highest 46, and the average 35·1. On the first page of 2 Tim. which is largely a mosaic of phrases from the ten Paulines, there are 16, on the last 11. The average throughout the ten Paulines is 13·2, the range from 8 to 17·3. (See Diagram III, p. 25.)

The lowest number of N. T. *Hapax Legomena* in any other complete page in the Pastorals is 13, the highest 23, the average 17·4. On the first page of 2 Tim. there are 11, on the last 4. In the Paulines they range from 3·3 to 6·2, the average being 4·5 (or, including repetitions, from 4, 2 Thess.–Philem., to 7·7, 2 Cor.)

Of these four, two, $\mu\epsilon\mu\beta\rho\acute{a}\nu a$ and $\phi a\iota\lambda\acute{o}\nu\eta s$, are Latin words and do not occur in Goodspeed ; $\dot{a}\nu\acute{a}\lambda\upsilon\sigma\iota s$ only once, in 1 Clem. ;

PAULINE ELEMENTS

χαλκεύς once each in Hermas and the *Ep. ad Diognetum*. In Titus iii. 12 f. there are no *Hapax Legomena*.

Of the other non-Pauline words in these paragraphs, νομικός does not occur in Goodspeed, λέων is a quotation from Ps. xxii. 22, ἀπολείπω occurs in both groups, but in a different sense from that which it bears here. If Paul does not happen to use λίαν, δρόμος, or χείμων, he has at any rate ὑπερλίαν, ἔδραμον, and παραχειμάζω; and no one would think of calling either of these words, nor yet κριτής nor λείπομαι, a link with the vocabulary of second-century Christendom. They fall, every one of them, under the category referred to on p. 51 f. (iii). Their absence from Paul's other epistles and their presence here is simply and adequately explained by the remark, that he had no occasion to use them elsewhere, and now that he has the occasion, they were the natural words for him to use.

(ii) On the other hand we find, in these short paragraphs, the following long list of words which do occur in Paul's epistles, but are not found elsewhere in the Pastorals—in Titus iii. 12 ff., πέμπω, ἐκεῖ, κέκρικα, παραχειμάζω, σπουδαίως, προπέμπω, ἀναγκαῖος, χρεία, ἄκαρπος, ἀσπάζομαι (*bis*), φιλέω.

In 2 Tim. iv. 6-22—σπένδομαι, ἐφίστημι, τελέω, λοιπόν (adv.), ἀπόκειμαι, στέφανος, ἀγαπάω (*bis*), βασιλεία (*bis*), ἐγκαταλείπω (*bis*), ἀποστέλλω, βιβλίον, ἀσθενέω, ἀπολογία, παραγίνομαι, λογίζομαι, ῥύομαι (*bis*), ἐπουράνιος, στόμα, ἀσπάζομαι (*bis*); while ἀναλαμβάνω, μένω, παρίστημι are used in different senses from those which they carry elsewhere in the Pastorals.

In the remaining verses in the body of 2 Tim. which we, in common with many others, regard as genuine, the following Pauline words make their only appearance in the Pastorals— πολλάκις, ἅλυσις, σπουδαίως, ζητέω, εὑρίσκω (*bis*), παρὰ-κυρίου, διωγμός (*bis*), πάθημα, οἶος (*bis*), ὑποφέρω, ῥύομαι (*bis*), κρίνω, βασιλεία, ἐφίστημι, εὐαγγελιστής: and the following, if unique in Paul, are at least equally so in the writer of these epistles (the first five are also missing in the Apostolic Fathers)—νομικός (subs.), φαιλόνης, μεμβράνα, εὐκαίρως, ἀκαίρως, χειμών, χαλκεύς, λίαν, λέων, ἀναψύχω, βέλτιον, ἀγωγή, ἀνάλυσις, δρόμος, κριτής.

(iii) It is precisely in these passages that we find those examples of the characteristic Pauline *Anacolutha* and *Oratio Variata* (2 Tim. iii. 11, iv. 1, 17), of the familiar play on words (εὗρέν με ... εὑρεῖν ἔλεος 2 Tim. i. 17 f., ἐπίστηθι ... ἐφέστηκεν iv. 2, 6, εὐκαίρως ... ἀκαίρως ... ὁ καιρός ib., πληροφόρησον ... σπένδομαι iv. 5 f., εὔχρηστος iv. 11, cf. pp. 112 f., 122 f.), and the parentheses (2 Tim. i. 18, iv. 8, 14, 16), which have sometimes been used, too hastily, to prove the 'genuineness' of the Pastorals as a whole.

(iv) When submitted to the same acid tests which have led us to deny the Pauline authorship of these epistles in their present form, the passages now in question thus emerge with their authenticity more than ever confirmed. They stand side by side with the more certainly genuine of Paul's epistles, and are separated from the bulk of the Pastorals by the same gulf which divides these from the genuine epistles.

But still further, not only can the diction of these passages be truly described as identical with that of the ten Paulines generally. In each separate instance, we find on examination special points of resemblance, clear, definite, and unmistakable, with the Paulines of precisely that period to which the subject-matter of the fragment in question has led us to assign it. See pp. 118 ff.

This fact stands in striking and significant contrast with that other fact, to which we have already drawn attention (pp. 24, 48 f.), that when treated as a homogeneous unit, the Pastorals can neither by any ingenuity be made to fit any single situation in the known life of Paul, nor do they show any special linguistic affinity with the later epistles, such as we should reasonably have expected to find, on the hypothesis that they were written last of all, during a period of release and a second Roman imprisonment.

And yet again, all these observations together cast into high relief one other fact, which emerged in the course of our previous investigations, viz. that 2 Tim., when treated as an integral whole, consistently stands much nearer to the genuine Paulines than do the other two Pastorals. (Diagrams I and II, pp. 21, 23.)

This is due, as we now see, simply and solely to the page and a half of admittedly genuine Pauline matter included in this epistle. When this is eliminated, and the suspected paragraphs are examined by themselves, they are found to contain just as large a proportion of non-Pauline words as the other two Pastorals. In fact the record page in all these epistles is 2 Tim. ii. 15–iii. 6, with 46 such words.[1] This is followed first by half a page or so of composite matter, in which first- and second-century elements alternate, and then by that page of personal references the authenticity of which we have seen no reason to doubt, but every reason to affirm. See Diagram III, p. 25.

We have now brought into juxtaposition a whole series of undeniable facts which, even when regarded in their separate groups, all seem to tell strongly against the traditional opinion and in favour of the view advocated in these pages. Their combined effect seems to us quite irresistible in its cogency. It clinches and completes our linguistic argument. If there be an explanation of these various results, by which they can all be made to seem consistent with either (1) the Pauline authorship of these epistles as a whole, or (2) the non-Pauline authorship of these Personalia, we must confess that it has hitherto entirely escaped us.

Again, no adequate explanation has ever yet been given by Baur, Holtzmann, or their followers, of the curiously uneven way in which these Personalia are distributed among our three epistles. Why should 2 Tim. have the lion's share, and 1 Tim. little or nothing? On Holtzmann's principles our author was just as much 'bound to do what he could to give an appearance of probability to his fiction' in the one case as in the other. And if bound to try, able also to succeed. For the author who was, *ex hypothesi*, capable of inventing such life-like imitations of Paul's manner once, and twice, was surely equally capable of doing the same again for the third time. Practice makes perfect. We should have expected to find the circumstances and personalities of the Ephesian church reproduced with a touch no less sure and convincing. But nothing of the kind. After the half-hearted beginning 1 Tim. i. 3, he breaks off in the middle of his sentence; qualifies in ii. 15 any too definite expectations raised by the half promise in vs. 14; and hardly seems to make another effort, unless we are to regard the apostolic panacea (1 Tim. v. 23) as a last experiment in this direction. Granting that he had already used up the most interesting moment in Paul's life—the eve of

[1] Further, the elimination of these admittedly Pauline passages involves a reduction in the total number (542) of words common to the vocabularies of this writer and of Paul, by between fifty and sixty, and the addition of these to the number of characteristic Pauline terms not used by this writer on his own account.

his martyrdom, when, if ever, a man's utterances will be received as prophetic—there was still something more than this to be made of that dramatic crisis which compelled him to turn his back for the last time on the scene of so many labours, and drove him from the midst of so many friends to enter on a new stage of his life-journey.

Besides, the writer who was gifted enough to invent touches like the σπένδομαι, &c., in verse 6, the εὔχρηστος in verse 11, the φαιλόνης, &c., in verse 13, and in fact the whole section 2 Tim. iv. 6-22, would surely have been capable of avoiding some of its more glaring inconsistencies and discrepancies. He would not have made Paul follow up the noble and impressive announcement of his immediate 'departure' by a series of commissions, which, if he meant what he said and said what was true, it would have been a physical impossibility for Timothy to receive and carry out till long after it was too late. He would not have made the Apostle waste his last moments in telling Timothy what must have been stale news—like the mission of Tychicus to Ephesus, the detention of Erastus at Corinth, and of Trophimus at Miletus, and the result of that defence which Timothy himself had been sent to Philippi on purpose to report to their friends there.

Nor is it easy to assign any really satisfactory motive for such details as e.g. the cloak and parchments. If they were intended to deceive us into the belief that Paul himself really did write this passage, they have certainly achieved a marvellous success—in spite of Baur's warnings. But in that case, what becomes of Holtzmann's theory of a perfectly naïve and innocent pseudonymity? It would then be difficult to avoid the crude commonplace verdict of a fraud and a forgery, deliberate, and, we should have to admit, almost diabolically clever. It would be difficult to sustain Holtzmann's antithesis between our author, with his high purpose, pure conscience, and exalted motives, and 'the real *falsarius*, more interested in his mask' than in the ideas he wished to introduce beneath it. But failing that, what other motive can we assign? Is it purely an artistic touch? If so, it is the most consummate art, amounting to positive genius; and we wonder why there are not more 'happy thoughts' of the same kind scattered through these epistles. But convincing as this detail is in itself, the same can hardly be said of its present setting. Holtzmann is sure that our Paulinist 'never thought of a second imprisonment.

In 2 Timothy there hovered before his mind the situation Acts xxviii. 30 f'. (H. *PB.* p. 51.) So far we may agree. But then there must also have hovered before his mind in this connexion the situation Acts xx 13 f., when Paul was last at Troas. On that occasion the Apostle set out alone towards the end of April (Ramsay, *Paul the Traveller*, p. 289), to walk to Assos, where he joined the ship in which his companions had meanwhile sailed from Troas. Now, about the previous midsummer, when he left Troas in the opposite direction (2 Cor. ii. 12 f., cf. 1 Cor. xvi. 8), it was as natural for him to leave his heavy cloak behind, as it was for him to claim it again before the winter storms began (p. 117 ff.). But on Holtzmann's theory the inventor of this realistic touch spoiled it by requiring his readers to suppose (*a*) that Paul let slip the natural and obvious opportunity to send his property by the ship in charge of Luke or another, and (*b*) that he then allowed it to lie unclaimed at the house of Carpus through *four* long winters, only to send for it now in his last hours against that *fifth* winter which he knew he would not live to see. Considered as fiction, our Personalia would seem to lose more than they gain in verisimilitude from the necessity for such assumptions.

No, Holtzmann's view shares at this point with the Traditional opinion a certain *prima facie* simplicity, which, however, proves on closer examination to be illusory, and involves us more and more deeply, the further we follow it, in hopeless entanglements. We are prepared for the inevitable blunders of the ordinary dull secondary writer, who tries in vain to put himself into another man's place, and betrays himself at every turn by ineptitudes, inconsistencies, and contradictions. Nor have we any rooted prejudice against the hypothesis of a second-century Christian possessing very high gifts of creative imagination. But two such persons rolled into one, and then identified with the author of the rest of the Pastorals, make too complex a personality altogether. The mental agility which needed no second imprisonment theory to provide time for a certain development in style, diction, &c., but could leap at a moment's notice, between one dip of the pen and another, from the very tone, speech, and accents of the Apostle to the current phraseology of the early second century and back again—taxes our credulity beyond the breaking-point. If five years were not enough for such a change, still less five minutes!

We conclude therefore that modern scholarship is right in refusing with one voice, though for a variety of reasons, to regard these Personalia as pure fiction invented by the *auctor ad Timotheum et Titum* in order to lend verisimilitude to the rest of his handiwork.

And we turn back accordingly to consider those remaining alternatives one of which Holtzmann dismissed, as we have seen, too lightly. We speak of alternatives. But according to many scholars there is only one remaining alternative. If Paul wrote these personal references himself, and if there is no single moment in his known life at which he could have written them, they argue, then it must follow, as the night the day, that he must have written them at some later period than that known to us from Acts and the other Paulines. In other words, these verses presuppose, and are a primary witness for, that very release, eastern journey, and second imprisonment on which, as is now agreed with almost complete unanimity among 'conservative' scholars, the 'authenticity' of these epistles depends.

The objections to this solution in either of its forms—whether as involving the genuineness of the entire three Pastorals, or only that of these Personalia—are as follows:

2. *The Second Imprisonment Theory and the Personalia in the Pastorals.*

(i) *The Evidence of Eusebius.*

Our earliest explicit reference to such a second Roman imprisonment following a period of release, occurs in Eusebius, some 260 years after an event, or series of events, which, if they really took place, were of the very first importance and deepest interest to the Christian Church as a whole, and must, especially on the modern hypothesis, have been widely known both in the East and in the West, and of course in Rome itself. That our knowledge of Peter's last years is equally hazy[1] is true enough, but hardly removes the difficulty. However, 'all things come to him who waits,' and at last in A.D. 324 we find the statement (*H. E.* ii. 22), following a reference to the close of Acts: 'At that time, then, after making his defence, he is said (λόγος ἔχει) to have

---

[1] Harnack, *AC. L.* i, p. 240.

been sent again on the ministry of preaching, and having entered the same city (Rome) a second time, to have ended his life with martyrdom. While a prisoner in bonds he writes the Second Epistle to Timothy, in which he mentions both his former defence and his imminent end. Receive his own testimony on these points.' Then follows a quotation and exposition of 2 Tim. iv. 16 f., 6, 11, in which it is argued that the 'first defence' implies a previous captivity. 'Thus much we have said to show that the Apostle's martyrdom was not accomplished during that sojourn of his at Rome in which Luke wrote.'

There is thus no doubt that by the end of the first quarter of the fourth century 'it was said', and Eusebius believed it, and argued for it, that Paul entered on a new lease of life, and a new stage of preaching activity, after the imprisonment recorded in Acts xxviii.

Now Eusebius has preserved many a priceless record of historic fact which would otherwise have been lost to us—but also many a baseless legend. The question is, to which category the statement before us belongs. For, judged by modern standards, it is clear that 'his judgement was decidedly inferior to his erudition'.[1]

We look to see whether in this instance, as in so many others, he is able to support his own statement by a quotation from, or at least a reference to, some earlier authority. But there is nothing of the kind here. The only evidence that he can, or at any rate does, produce, is a bit of more than questionable exegesis from one of the very epistles whose authenticity is now supported in turn by reference to his statement. The allusion to a 'first defence' 2 Tim. iv. 18 clearly implies a 'second defence'. We shall show in due course where and when and in what circumstances both first and second defences were made (p. 121 f.). But that it also implies an acquittal by Caesar, release, and second Roman imprisonment, with an interval of from three to five years between, crowded with apostolic activities, journeys to Spain, Greece, Macedonia, Asia, and Crete, is hardly a tenable proposition.

But if Eusebius and those who follow him in this matter are utterly wrong in their exegesis here, we are thrown back for the rest upon the phrase λόγος ἔχει, with which he introduces the

[1] Bright, *Intr. to the H. E.* 1872, p. xlvi.

whole story. What exactly does this phrase cover? How much can we legitimately infer from it? As the words are in themselves so elastic and capable etymologically of such varied shades of meaning, it seems worth while to inquire in what other passages they recur. The result is not very encouraging for those who wish to lay any stress on the historicity of this particular incident. Eusebius uses the same formula to introduce (*a*) the legend that Philo had familiar conversation with St. Peter in Rome during the days of Claudius (*H. E.* ii. 17); (*b*) the tradition that the body of Ignatius was devoured by wild beasts (*H. E.* iii. 36)—the only evidence produced, in this case also, being that of Ignatius himself (in Rom. 4 f.); (*c*) the opinion that Tatian was the founder of the Encratite heresy (*H. E.* iv. 28)—' a sect which existed before his time' (Harnack, *Enc. Brit.*, s. v. Tatian); (*d*) the legend of the Thundering Legion (*H. E.* v. 5, twice over in this connexion); (*e*) the story that Pantaenus found in India the Gospel of Matthew in Hebrew, which had been brought thither by the Apostle Barnabas (*H. E.* v. 10).

(ii) Once this extension of Paul's life on the strength of 2 Tim. iv. 16 f. had thus won a place in 'history', it was only natural that later writers should perpetuate the same error. So Jerome, *de Vir. Ill.* v, who also repeats the story about Philo and Peter, ib. 11; Theodoret, *Hist. Eccl.* ii. 22 and *Comment. ad comma* 17 *alterius ad Tim. epist.*; Epiphanius, *Contra Carp. Haer.* vii. 6; Chrysostom, Euthalius (interval of ten years between the two imprisonments! Zacagni, 532, Zahn, *Einl.* i. 453), Nicephorus Callisti, *Eccl. Hist.* ii. 33 f., who incorporates large sections of the text of Eusebius, and places not only 1 Tim. and Titus but also the epistles to the Corinthians, Galatians, Colossians, Philippians, Thessalonians, as well as πρὸς Ἰουδαίους (=Heb.) and Romans in the later period thus gained in Paul's life.

Of course these additional links add nothing whatever to the strength of the chain as a whole.

(iii) We have now therefore to turn back and examine the series of highly debatable inferences and deductions upon which this hypothesis of a second imprisonment really depends, in the absence of any definite statement or explicit reference to it in any Church writer prior to Eusebius.

The principal elements in this series are:

PAULINE ELEMENTS

A. The argument from the Chronology of Paul's life.
B. The evidence of Clement and of the Muratorian canonist.
C. The evidence of the Personalia in the Pastorals.

A. *Chronology.* First and foremost comes the argument from chronology, or rather, from two rival and mutually contradictory chronologies—the usual conservative scheme, which brings Paul to Rome for the first time in A. D. 60/61, and fixes his death as late as 66/7, and Harnack's own scheme [1] which brings Paul to Rome as early as 56/7 and fixes his death in 64.

The one point in common between these two schemes is that both leave an interval of five or six years between the close of Acts and the death of Paul, to be filled up somehow.

For the rest, all the weight of learning and force of conviction brought to bear in defence of either theory must needs go to weaken the other, making it the more difficult for us to regard an inference drawn from either of them as being, in the present state of our knowledge, 'an assured fact of history'. The truth is that the chronology of Paul's life is an enormously difficult and intricate subject, covering an immense amount of ground, and one on which experts are still far from having arrived at an agreement.[2] A minute examination of the relevant data would carry us far beyond the scope of the present work; but one or two vital points can and must be mentioned here.

It is not by any means an agreed matter among competent authorities that Paul's death should be set as late even as the year 64. After describing, in the famous passage to which we shall return presently, the martyrdoms of Peter and Paul, Clement goes on in his next chapter to tell how 'to these there was gathered a great multitude of the elect, who suffered many and dire torments and set us the noblest of examples'. It certainly looks as if Clement were here referring to the Neronic persecution of A. D. 64 as something that happened *after* the deaths of Peter and Paul. (So e.g. Moffatt, *I. N. T.*, p. 417.) This would, indeed, as Moffatt says, clinch the matter.

But apart from any such consideration, even supposing that Paul did live on for several years after the 'two years' of un-

---

[1] *Chronologie der altchristlichen Litteratur*, 1897, i, p. 240 n.
[2] See the very learned and thorough article by C. H. Turner in Hastings, *D. B.*, for a strong criticism of Harnack's dates.

hindered preaching and teaching in the hired lodging at Rome (Acts xxviii. 30), it would not by any means follow that he must have been released, still less that he must have gone on to Spain or back to the Aegean. We are aware of no valid objection to the view, that the actual sequel to the ἀκωλύτως with which Acts closes, was a period of closer confinement, in which the Apostle was no longer allowed the same freedom to preach, but had to be content with the thought that others were doing so, and that the Word at any rate was still 'not bound'. While holding that this was in all probability the actual course of events for a short period, at the end of which Paul met his death, we see no reason for setting any narrow or rigid limit to this final period of real imprisonment. Whether the term of Paul's life after the close of Acts was long or short, it is easier to understand our lack of information about it, if he was immured in some Roman prison cell, than on the assumption that he was at large, travelling to and fro, revisiting old churches, founding new ones, introducing new methods of Church organization, engaging in new controversies, and adding fresh and important chapters to the story of his apostolic labours—chapters that, by a cruel fate, were never written down with pen and ink, or if so written were forthwith lost beyond recall.

Then there is the fact, which Harnack himself admits is at least 'worth mentioning', that in his Farewell to the Ephesian elders at Miletus (Acts xx. 25, 38), Paul is reported to have said, 'I know that ye all ... shall behold my face no more'. The usual conservative explanation of this passage is that Paul's foreboding was not bound to be realized. But in that case, it seems strange that the author of Acts, writing after the event, should have failed to convey the least hint that Paul's forecast, and the sorrow and tears which it caused, had a happier sequel than he anticipated at the time. Zahn sees this difficulty, but sees also a way of escape. οὐκέτι, he assures us, does not imply 'never again', but only 'not for a while'. It does not exclude the possibility that a time may yet come when the Apostle will resume his intercourse with the churches of Asia (*Einl.* i, p. 448). But surely the passionate grief of Paul's friends, and the way in which the whole pathos of the story is centred in this hard word, forbid any such softening interpretation.

B. Next we have the statement by Clement of Rome that Paul, having taught the whole world righteousness, came to the τέρμα τῆς δύσεως and having borne witness (μαρτυρήσας) before the rulers, so found his release from this world, and departed to the holy place (v. 5–7). This phrase τὸ τέρμα τῆς δύσεως is translated 'boundary of the West', or of the Western world, as regarded from the point of view of a Roman, i. e. Spain. But while τέρματα in the plural might conceivably bear this unusual meaning, the natural, proper, and usual meaning of this word is rather the starting-point or winning-post of a race, or the end of a journey, especially the race of life.[1] And that this is the meaning here is rendered all the more likely by the fact that the whole context is full of the figure of the apostolic athlete running his great race for the immortal prize in the stadium of the world. Note the ἀθλητάς v. 1, ἤθλησαν v. 2, βραβεῖον v. 5, κῆρυξ v. 6, κλέος v. 6, δρόμον ... γέρας vi. 2, and finally the ἐν γὰρ τῷ αὐτῷ ἐσμεν σκάμματι, καὶ ὁ αὐτὸς ἡμῖν ἀγὼν ἐπίκειται vii. 1. Now the goal of this race was certainly not Spain, but Rome, from whatever point in the world-stadium one happened to be regarding it. τῆς δύσεως is a defining Genitive, Western goal, or, goal in the West as opposed to its starting-point in the East. There is no need to understand αὐτοῦ, though we think with Schmiedel (*E. B.* 4600) and others that it would have been perfectly good Greek to omit it here. Nor was there any need to add τοῦ δρόμου, nor any other explanatory words, which would have made an awkward double Genitive. The meaning is clear enough without any such addition.

If the phrase and its general context favour this interpretation, the immediate continuation of the sentence seems to demand it. For in spite of anything that can be urged to the contrary,[2] it plainly suggests that Paul reached his final goal, bore his martyr-witness, and so (οὕτως) found his release from this world, all at

---

[1] e. g. Pindar, *Pyth.* ix. 202, Soph. *El.* 686 f. δρόμου τὰ τέρματα. Cf. Stephanus, *Thes.* s. v. '. . . quamvis aliquid inter τέρμα et καμπτήρ esse discriminis videatur; ita scribente Polluce 3, c. 30 [§ 147] περὶ δὲ ὁ κάμπτουσι, νύσσα κ. καμπτήρ· ἵνα δὲ παύονται, τέλος κ. τέρμα κτλ.' Eur. *Hipp.* 140 τέρμα νίκης ... = metam qua victoria terminata est. Pind. *Isthm.* iii. 85 τέρμ' ἀέθλων, Simonides, βιότου ποτὶ τέρμα, Aesch. *Prom.* 284 τέρμα κελεύθου, Soph. *Aj.* 48, &c. Soph. *O. C.* 725 τέρμα τῆς σωτηρίας, Eur. *Andr.* 1081 γήρως πρὸς τέρμασιν, *Hipp.* 140 θανάτου τέρμα.

[2] Zahn, *Einl.* i. 452.

the same place. The evident parallel between the two martyrdoms, Peter's (v. 4 οὕτω μαρτυρήσας ἐπορεύθη εἰς τὸν τόπον . . .), and now Paul's (v. 7 καὶ μαρτυρήσας . . . οὕτως . . . καὶ ἐπορεύθη εἰς τὸν τόπον . . .) forbids us to make this second μαρτυρήσας refer to witness borne by the Apostle before some tribunal or other in Spain. There is not the shadow of a hint that between the ἐλθών and the μαρτυρήσας, or between that and the ἀπηλλάγη, there lay a whole long and important period of missionary journeyings East and West, fresh perils and escapes, new developments of doctrine and of polity, &c.

No ancient writer interprets Clement in the manner required by the modern conservative argument, nor quotes him in support of the release in general, or of the Spanish journey in particular.

So, as Bartlet says,[1] ' Clement goes over bodily to the other side '.

Failing Clement, far more weight than it will carry is now thrown on the corrupt passage in the Muratorian fragment, with its reference in crabbed Latin to 'a departure of Paul from the City, when he departed for Spain'. This in turn is based, according to Zahn (*Einl.* i, p. 452), on the legendary Gnostic Acts of Peter (A.D. *c.* 160–170). Nor is the origin of this Gnostic legend itself far to seek. In Romans xv. 24, 28 Paul had written of his intention to go on from Rome to Spain. For the type of mind with which we have here to do, nothing more was needed in the way of materials. The mythopoeic imagination could be trusted to do the rest.

This does not exclude the possibility that others may have found their way, independently of heretical inventions, from the same starting-point to the same conclusion. Take, for instance, the remark of Athanasius that Paul 'did not shrink from going to Rome, nor from proceeding to Spain '[2] or the similar expression in Cyril of Jerusalem.[3] From either of these sentences it would be a very short step to the belief that the Apostle had actually done that which he aspired to do, or did not shrink from doing, especially as it is in each case coupled with an aspiration which was undoubtedly realized.

C. One thing at least is absolutely certain—neither Clement

---

[1] *A. A.* 1907, p. 202.   [2] *Ep. ad Dracontium*, 4.
[3] *Catech.* xvii. 13 κατηχήσαντα δὲ καὶ τὴν Ῥώμην καὶ μέχρι Σπανίας τὴν προθυμίαν τοῦ κηρύγματος ἐκτείναντα.

nor the Fragmentist nor any other ancient writer has a word to say about any eastern journey of the Apostle subsequent to his 'first' Roman imprisonment. Yet apart from such a journey neither a Spanish journey nor a second imprisonment avail in the least to provide room for these Personalia, let alone the whole three epistles. The *sole* evidence for that eastern journey consists in an inference drawn by Harnack, Zahn, and their followers from the two premises (*a*) that the Personalia in 2 Tim. and Titus are genuine, and (*b*) that Paul cannot have written them at any one moment in his earlier life. Apart from that inference it is safe to say that the whole theory of a release, eastern journey, and second imprisonment would not for very long remain standing on the other two feet of Harnack's tripod, the arguments from (1) chronology and (2) Clement's τέρμα τῆς δύσεως and the Fragmentist's Spanish visit.

But granting these premises (*a*) and (*b*), does any such conclusion really follow? On what grounds are we obliged to suppose that these disjointed sentences were all written at the same time or from the same place? Why should they not have been written indeed by Paul, but at different times? This is the alternative possibility to which Holtzmann and Harnack and Zahn, with their respective followers, hardly seem to have given adequate attention. And it is precisely this omission which vitiates alike the pure-fiction theory and the second imprisonment theory, and with this, incidentally, the whole modern case for the 'authenticity' of the Pastorals.

For it is just here, so the great majority of 'liberal' critics believe, that the true solution of our problem is to be found. Several brief personal notes addressed by the Apostle at various times to one or another of his friends, are preserved by them, and are still in existence half a century or so after his death. These are eventually copied out from the scattered scraps of papyrus on to a single sheet, either by our author himself or by some other scribe, and so incorporated at the end of his first two epistles. They would, presumably, come into his hands without explanatory notes or headings of any kind to show the actual circumstances of their birth. How was he to discover, what has escaped the notice of devout readers for eighteen centuries, including many scholars ancient and modern? It would have needed a method of study quite foreign to the early second century, to have deduced from a minute comparison of the internal evidence with the data provided by Acts and the other Paulines, that we have here references not to any one situation, but to several, at intervals varying from a few weeks to some years.

We have now reached the very crux of our argument, in so far as the Pauline authorship of these epistles can be said to stand or fall with the success or otherwise of the attempt to find a place for them within the lifetime of the Apostle. And we shall find that this 'argumentum Achilleum ... chronologicum', as Ginella called it (1865, p. 109) does indeed lay bare a vulnerable heel to the shafts of criticism.

We shall see (pp. 115 ff.) that for every personal reference in the paragraphs with which we have just been dealing, there is at least one moment in Paul's life as known to us from Acts and the other Paulines, which fits it like a glove. Some of these items simply corroborate what we knew already. Others add to our knowledge some extremely interesting detail which no ingenuity could ever have deduced from our other sources, but which, now that we have it, harmonizes admirably with all the rest of our information.

Yet on the second imprisonment theory in either of its forms all this is mere coincidence—a somewhat lengthy and complicated string of accidents, but nothing more. Not one of these notes, it seems, refers to the occasion which suits it so perfectly; but they one and all refer really to similar occasions which recurred during this alleged extension of Paul's life—for all of which they are in turn the principal evidence, and, for a large and crucial part of it, the only evidence. That is to say, the judgement that they cannot be fitted into Paul's earlier life is the only positive ground for asserting that Paul ever visited Nicopolis, Corinth, Troas, Miletus, or the shores of the Aegean, after he had once reached Rome. But that judgement is now shown to be erroneous. They can be fitted into the earlier life, provided only that we give up the vain and needless attempt to force them all into the same situation.

That being so, what becomes of the inference drawn from this erroneous judgement? As an inference it falls to the ground.

But it may still be maintained as an independent hypothesis!

We do not know, say its advocates, that Paul died at the end of the first Roman imprisonment.[1] The onus of proof rests, they claim, on those who deny his release. This denial is itself ' mere hypothesis' (so Zahn, *Einl. N. T.* i. 439). In the absence of positive proof that Paul did not, subsequently to his arrival in Rome, visit Macedonia, Corinth, Troas, Miletus, Crete, and Nicopolis, who shall forbid us to assume that he did, and so provide a new framework into which all these Personalia can then be fitted without further difficulty ? Given these extra pages, blank pages, at the end of Paul's life-story, why not write on them the required journeys, labours, and incidents?

But before taking this step, let us at least see clearly what follows. In that case history must have repeated itself with a vengeance!

1. On this new eastern journey also, Erastus remains for some reason at Corinth. Once again Paul visits Troas with Timothy and Trophimus as his companions. Once more he leaves Troas if not alone and on foot in summer, at least again in circumstances which make it natural for him to leave his heavy cloak and other impedimenta behind. Only now we must suppose that months, instead of weeks, elapse before he claims them again. Once more they touch at Miletus.

2. Coming to more recent memories, in this imprisonment, as in the first, mischief has been made by Jews from Asia, led apparently by the same Jew from Asia. Alexander has been nursing his old grudge year in, year out, and not content with having used his influence with his fellow Jews at Ephesus and at Jerusalem to Paul's detriment, has dogged his steps to Rome, and has been successful in pulling the strings not only of Jewish but of Roman justice, in the imperial city itself, and before the supreme tribunal. Not only Ananias, but Nero has lent an ear to this Jewish coppersmith, and become the tool of his spite.

A second time Paul has had as his recent prison-companions Luke, Mark, Tychicus, Timothy, and Demas. Once again he has sent Tychicus to Ephesus. Mark, whose arrival the Colossians are told to expect, Col. iv. 10, and who has already dis-

---

[1] 'It is true that the Pastoral Epistles imply a period of activity in Paul's life of which we have no other evidence: but neither is there any evidence against it, our ignorance being here complete.' Hort, *Jud. Christianity*, p. 130 f.

appeared from Paul's company in Phil., is now recalled apparently from the same neighbourhood. And the epithet εὔχρηστος which Paul applied in that first imprisonment to another renegade who had lived down his defection (Philem. 11), is now applied in this second imprisonment to Mark, not, as we think, shortly afterwards while the phrase (with its somewhat subtle association of ideas) was still fresh in his mind, but from three to five years later. Timothy who was to be sent away at the end of the first imprisonment, now near the end of the second, is again at a distance, and just as Paul had then intended that Timothy should soon return with comforting tidings (Phil. ii. 18), so now we find him recalled to the Apostle's side. Luke 'the beloved physician' (Col. iv. 14) is still faithful to the last.

Nor is the parallel confined to the outward circumstances of the Apostle. It extends to the very changes in his frame of mind, his alternating moods of buoyant hopefulness and dark forebodings (not for himself, but for the loyalty of his friends). The feeling of loneliness and isolation expressed in Phil. ii. 20 f., and the lack of any mention of the names of companions as still with him, has its counterpart here in the statements 'only Luke is with me', 'Demas has forsaken me', &c. Once again Paul exults that while he is bound, the Word of God runs free. Once again, as the end draws near, Paul is conscious of a change for the worse in his situation; his once numerous band of comrades dwindles, and only one or two can be utterly trusted. The rest, those whom he has not sent away on missions, show signs of uneasiness and concern for their own safety, Phil. ii. 23, 2 Tim. iv. 9.

In Phil. ii. 17 he sees his own life being poured out as a libation on the altar of sacrifice—either[1] as a sequel so certain, or a hypothesis so 'vividly before his eyes' as to seem a present fact, or else[2] as a process actually begun in the 'drain of vitality' resulting from the privations of his long imprisonment and the drawn out strain of suspense.—In either case it suggests a process whose final consummation is still in the future, and (should all go well, as it may, at his trial) in the indefinite future. He is 'not yet' made perfect, 'not yet' within reach of the prize (οὐχ ὅτι ἤδη ἔλαβον, ἢ ἤδη τετελείωμαι, iii. 12).

But now he says ἤδη σπένδομαι, and this time it is clear that

---

[1] Lightfoot, ad loc.   [2] C. H. Dodd in a letter to the present writer.

in his mind the process is as good as finished. The last drops of that red wine are being spilled. In the continuing metaphors we have one perfect tense after another. This really is the end. The die is cast. No 'hypothesis', but grim, glorious certainty. The issue no longer hangs in the balance. The long expected opportunity of opportunities has come,—is at the door (ἐφέστηκεν, cf. the ἐπίσταται αἰφνίδιος in 1 Thess. v. 3). Then he was longing for the time to come when he should receive the summons to weigh anchor, and put out to sea on that last voyage, when he should see his Pilot face to face, Phil. i. 23 τὴν ἐπιθυμίαν ἔχων εἰς τὸ ἀναλῦσαι καὶ σὺν Χριστῷ εἶναι. Now the call has come, the anchor is weighed, and the moment of his departure has arrived—ὁ καιρὸς τῆς ἀναλύσεώς μου ἐφέστηκεν. Then he was still running his unfinished race for the prize, with eyes set on the mark (Phil. iii. 11 ff., iv. 1), now the race is over, and all that remains is for an Umpire more just than Caesar to confer the crown of victory. In Col. i. 5 he had spoken of the hope stored up (ἀποκειμένην) in heaven, and now he knows that the reward of faithfulness is indeed stored up for him (ἀπόκειται).

Now assuming that all this was really written by Paul shortly after he wrote Philippians, nothing would be more natural than this repetition of the figures which had then been foremost in his mind—with just the very difference which we find, that what was there a future possibility is now a present or accomplished fact. But on the second imprisonment theory we have to believe that Paul kept firmly fixed in his mind this whole series of figures, some of them very rare (we might say, unique), for several years on end, crowded years, of intense activity and of marked development both in outlook and vocabulary, and that his last word at the end of this second captivity was just a repetition of the same sentiments in the same words as he had used in his letter to the Philippians at the end of the first. It does not seem very likely. As Bacon says: 'To the martyr also there sometimes comes an unexpected reprieve. Years after he may utter a second time his last farewells. But that which, under such circumstances, he will *not* do, is to return to his former leave-taking, and, with no reference to having used the figure before, borrow thence the phraseology for his parting legacy' (*N. T. I.*, p. 134).

Some conservatives have inclined in recent years to minimize this impression of a close resemblance between the two captivities. According to Spitta (1893, p. 106), 'the two imprisonments are in fact as unlike to one another as the epistle to the Philippians and 2 Timothy, and as like as one imprisonment generally is to another'. We confess our total inability to square this verdict with the facts just pointed out. The truth is rather that Paul's second Roman imprisonment, if he ever had a second, must have been in an astounding number of details an exact duplicate of the first.

This was recognized even by orthodox scholars in days when the admission was not known to be so dangerous as it is to the traditional opinion. 'How remarkable it is', exclaims good Paul Anton in the year 1727, commenting on 2 Tim. ii. 9, 'that when Paul was brought to Rome for the first time... he was chained, but the Gospel was not chained (Acts xxviii. 16-31)... in this second imprisonment also, when he is again bound,... he could again say here the same thing.' It is indeed remarkable! And the resemblance goes, as we have seen, far beyond anything that he pointed out. One, two, half a dozen points of contact between the two imprisonments we might have accepted without a word. But as the number of them increases, the odds against the recurrence of them all increase also in something more than a geometrical progression. The total number of these points of contact is between thirty and forty. It is in fact hardly less than the entire series. It may be too much to say that such a thing is impossible. But it is, to say the least, wildly improbable.

But even so, does it save us? On the contrary, this last desperate expedient proves on examination to be no way of escape from all our difficulties. It only leads us into yet further entanglements. 'Only Luke' is with the Apostle, yet 'Eubulus, Linus, Pudens, Claudia, and all the brethren' send greetings. Paul is already being offered, and the time of his departure has arrived. Nothing remains for him but the crown of righteousness. Yet, with the light of that great Hereafter on his face, and its glory already dawning on his soul, he stops to pen a message to Timothy somewhere in the heart of Asia Minor, bidding him first make careful arrangements for the preservation of the genuine apostolic teaching from generation to generation. He is to appoint as officers charged with this duty, faithful men who shall be capable of teaching others also (i. 2); he must take care that these are themselves thoroughly grounded in the Truth, warning them against certain doctrinal errors which will spread after Paul is gone, and preparing them to recognize and resist these when the time comes. After he has done all this, Timothy is to set off on his journey to Rome, pick up Mark, presumably at Colossae (Col. iv. 10), call at Troas for cloak, &c., and make haste to bring them all along before the winter.

If we are to take that noble and impressive farewell seriously, he must have known that it was a physical impossibility for Timothy to carry out these commissions until too late. And if we are to take the commissions seriously, they compel us to suppose that in that farewell Paul exercised a mental reservation which would rob it of half its impressiveness and pathos. Paul could perfectly well have written both—Farewell (2 Tim. iv. 5 ff.) and twofold Summons (iv. 9, 21)—but not at the same time, nor as parts of the same letter.

Not even with the help of a second imprisonment, then,—not even if we assume, without a shred of evidence, that Paul returned from Rome to the Aegean,—do we get rid of the inner contradictions between one personal detail and another in 2 Timothy. Those contradictions are inherent in the supposition that these details were originally all of a piece and belong to one set of circumstances. But this supposition is vital to the second imprisonment theory.

That theory therefore, it would seem, must fall to the ground; and the possibility that Paul might have written every word of the Personalia, at different times and places, though not at any one time or place, is the heel of that Achilles.

3. *The Five Genuine Notes, their Several Dates, Birthplaces, and Occasions.*[1]

(i) Titus iii. 12–15. Paul writes from Western Macedonia, several months after 2 Cor. x–xiii, and before 2 Cor. i–ix, bidding Titus, who is at Corinth, be ready to join him in Epirus.

---

[1] For an account of previous 'Partition Theories' see Moffatt, *H. N. T.* pp. 700 ff., *I. N. T.*, pp. 403 ff.

When I shall send Artemas unto thee, or Tychicus, give diligence to come unto me to Nicopolis: for there I have determined to winter. Set forward Zenas the lawyer and Apollos on their journey diligently, that nothing be wanting unto them. And let our people also learn to maintain good works for necessary uses, that they be not unfruitful. . . .
All that are with me salute thee. Salute them that love us in faith. Grace be with you all.

Some months before Paul left Ephesus for the last time, he explained to the Corinthians[1] his intention to pay them an extended visit, and possibly spend the winter among them, after first passing through Macedonia. Apparently they were expecting him to take Corinth first, on his way to Macedonia, and then again on his way to Jerusalem. But, gladly as he would have given them the double 'benefit' (2 Cor. i. 15), that plan would involve, in the first instance, a hasty visit (ἐν παρόδῳ), which, at the present critical juncture (ἄρτι), he was anxious to avoid. Meanwhile Timothy might be coming, with others, and if so, they must not let any one 'despise' him. Paul had done his utmost to persuade Apollos to join this company; but Apollos declined. He would come, however, on the next convenient opportunity. It was soon made only too clear that the disaffection at Corinth was even more serious than Paul had realized. Certain persons had taken full advantage of their opportunities, while his back was turned, to disparage his work and undermine his influence. Much against his will, and to the detriment of urgent claims at Ephesus, he was forced to pay a flying visit to Corinth,[2] only to find that he might as well have spared himself the trouble. The time was too short, and the mischief had gone too far. His enemies had not struck without first making sure of support. Remarks like those quoted in 2 Cor. x. 10 left him nothing to say, and nothing to do but withdraw. Deeply humiliated, and in great distress of mind, he returned to Ephesus, and wrote the letter mentioned in 2 Cor. ii. 4, 9, vii. 8. With the severity of injured love, it vindicated his good faith and authority. There are strong reasons for believing, with Moffatt (*I. N. T.*, pp. 116 ff.) and many others, that this 'intermediate letter' is preserved in the last four chapters of our 2 Cor. The

---
[1] 1 Cor. xvi. 6–12.
[2] 2 Cor. xii. 14, xiii. 1 f. (τρίτον τοῦτο) . . . ὡς παρὼν τὸ δεύτερον.

jubilant assurance of his restored confidence (vii. 16) could hardly have been followed, in one and the same letter, by such expressions of profound mistrust as we find, e.g., in xii. 20 f. It was now the turn of Titus to try whether he could succeed, where Timothy and Paul himself had failed. Soon afterwards Paul left Ephesus. For the reason stated in 2 Cor. ii. 1, he took the long northern route, resolved to enter Corinth for the third time, as soon as he could do so happily,—i.e., on hearing from Titus of the success of his efforts,—but not before ($\mu\grave{\eta}$ $\pi\acute{a}\lambda\iota\nu$ $\grave{\epsilon}\nu$ $\lambda\acute{\upsilon}\pi\eta$). He had some hope of finding Titus at Troas (2 Cor. ii. 12 f.); but this zealous friend had not yet had time to carry out his difficult task; so he missed that conditional appointment. Restless and distraught, Paul could not stay to take the opportunities opening up at Troas, but pushed on into Macedonia. There too he found no relief, but afflictions on every side, fightings without and forebodings within (vii. 5). This period of suspense must have lasted longer than is sometimes realized. For (a) in 2 Cor. ix. 2 Paul has boasted that Achaia had been ready with its collection 'for a year past' ($\grave{a}\pi\grave{o}$ $\pi\acute{\epsilon}\rho\upsilon\sigma\iota$). Achaia was certainly not ready when he wrote 1 Cor. xvi. 1 f. (b) He left Ephesus about Pentecost (1 Cor. xvi. 8), and reached Jerusalem about Pentecost in the following year (Acts xx. 16). That voyage took some seven weeks,[1] and was preceded by the three months in Greece (Acts xx. 3), during which he arrived at Corinth, finished the collection, and wrote his Epistle to the Romans (xv. 25 f.), and the note to Ephesus (Rom. xvi).[2] Allowing a month for the journey into Macedonia, we are left with at least six months during which his activities are summarized in Acts xx. 2. He made his way right across Macedonia, presumably by the Via Egnatia, pressing on that collection for the poor at Jerusalem, and proclaiming his gospel of divine comfort and immortal hope. At Dyrrachium we picture him looking out over the Adriatic towards where, beyond the western horizon, Rome beckoned. It was now only a step to Illyricum. Thus was realized his dream of 2 Cor. x. 15. While that faith, or fidelity, which had

---

[1] Ramsay, *Paul the Traveller*, pp. 289 ff.
[2] With greetings to Prisca and Aquila and the Church at their house, 3 ff. Cf. 1 Cor. xvi. 19, and note (v) pp. 127, 134. On Rom. xvi. see Moffatt, *I.N.T.* p. 136.

waned, was waxing again, he did in fact sow the good seed on virgin soil in 'regions beyond'. That he did not then simply retrace his steps, is already suggested by the κύκλῳ (Rom. xv. 19); and this is confirmed, on our view, by the note before us, written about this time. How Titus kept this appointment, and was able to bring such good news as made up for many things, we read in 2 Cor. i–ix, written, perhaps at Nicopolis, under the great reaction of joy which followed his coming. We now learn that Apollos had found his convenient opportunity, and was at Corinth, on his way to some destination which we have no means of defining more closely. If now, notwithstanding the κέκρικα (Titus iii. 12), Paul did after all spend part at least of that winter at Corinth, he would not this time be accused of having changed his mind too 'lightly' (2 Cor. i. 17).

The diction of this note coincides with that of 1 Cor. xvi at too many points to leave room for doubt that it must have been written after no great interval. ὅταν, πέμψω, πρός σε, (ὑμᾶς), ἤ, ἐλθεῖν πρός με, παραχειμάσαι, Ἀπολλώ, πρόπεμψον, ἵνα, μή, ἀσπάζονταί σε (ὑμᾶς), ... οἱ πάντες, ἄσπασαι τοὺς φιλοῦντας (φιλεῖ), ἡ χάρις μετὰ πάντων ὑμῶν together make a series which can hardly be dismissed as merely accidental. See further, for ἐκεῖ Rom. xvi. 24, κέκρικα 1 Cor. vii. 37, v. 3, ii. 2, σπουδάσον 2 Cor. viii. 16 f. (σπουδήν ... σπουδαιότερος of Titus), ἀναγκαῖος 1 Cor. xii. 22, 2 Cor. ix. 5, χρείας 1 Cor. xii. 1, &c., Rom. xii. 13, ἄκαρπος 1 Cor. xiv. 14.

(ii) 2 Tim. iv. 13–15, 20, 21a, Paul writes from Macedonia, after the visit to Troas mentioned in 2 Cor. ii. 12 f., bidding Timothy, who has returned to Ephesus, join him before winter.

The cloke that I left at Troas with Carpus, bring when thou comest, and the books, especially the parchments. Alexander the coppersmith did me much evil: the Lord will render to him according to his works: of whom be thou ware also; for he greatly withstood our words. . . .

Erastus abode at Corinth: but Trophimus I left at Miletus sick. Do thy diligence to come before winter.

Shortly before Paul left Ephesus, he sent Timothy and Erastus into Macedonia (Acts xix. 22). Erastus must have gone on to Corinth, where Paul found him, on his own arrival from Nicopolis, holding a civic appointment such as fell to few Christians in those days, but not forgetful of his old friends at Ephesus (Rom. xvi. 23).

In Acts xix. 23 ff., we read how Demetrius the silversmith gathered together the members of his own and allied guilds of metal-workers, and organized a protest against the interference with 'our trade'. At this meeting Alexander is put forward by the Jews to explain that he and his friends have no sort of connexion with these Christians—quite the reverse! ($ἀπολογεῖσθαι$)— but is shouted down by the angry crowd, to whom Jews and Christians were all one. This incident was not likely to diminish the hostility of Alexander and his party towards Paul and his friends, and they seem to have lost no time in making further trouble. Paul now in a few words informs Timothy of what happened in his absence, and warns him against this dangerous man, who is sure to take any chance that offers of proving his zeal at the expense of any friend of Paul.

Not that Alexander would have confessed to any feeling so personal as a grudge. With the cold inhumanity of his kind, he would have protested that his action was dictated solely by 'principle', and was not directed against Paul and Timothy as men, but against their pernicious teaching (verse 15 $λίαν\ γὰρ\ ἀντέστη\ τοῖς\ ἡμετέροις\ λόγοις$). Any suffering inflicted on the misguided individuals who were responsible for that teaching was of course not his fault. He only did his duty. Paul understands this perfectly. Was not he too once self-betrayed by the same sophistry? But he has learned to believe in a Justice which will not be deterred, by any protestations of lofty motive, from visiting on evil deeds their appropriate punishment. To that unerring justice he leaves this typical bigot, and meanwhile bids Timothy be on his guard.

The only occasion on which Paul is actually recorded to have been at Miletus; was on the journey to Jerusalem. If it were necessary on that account to assume that he had never been there before, and that it was then that Trophimus fell ill, then verse 20, 21a must have been written at Patara, where Paul changed ships (Acts xxi. 1), and his last port of call on the Asiatic mainland. This would leave just time for Trophimus to recover and join the Apostle before, or soon after, his arrival in Jerusalem Acts xxi. 29).

For Luke tells us that Paul spent seven days at Tyre, one at Ptolemais, and several (πλείους) at Caesarea, not to mention the seven days at Jerusalem, during which, at the latest, Trophimus must have arrived. This fragment, 20, 21a, would thus stand alone, unless verses 12, 13 belonged to the same note. After the seven days at Troas (Acts xx. 4 ff.), Luke and others go round by sea, while Paul crosses by road to join them at Assos. Timothy, like Trophimus, was of the party that sailed to Troas; but he is not named after this in Acts. Erastus stayed at Corinth, as Timothy must have known. It is possible, though not quite likely, that Paul forgot to send his cloak &c., in the ship.

But it seems much more probable that he left that heavy winter-garment behind when setting out from Troas about midsummer, the previous year, and that he sent for it from Northwest Macedon about the same time as his note (1) to Titus, when thoughts of the coming winter were, as we know, in his mind.

It is generally assumed that Paul sailed from Ephesus to Troas. But this is not stated in our sources, and is less likely than it seems at first sight. For, a year later, anxious as he was to see his friends at Ephesus once more, he decided (κεκρίκει, Acts xx. 16 f.) against putting in there, on the ground that, if he was to reach Jerusalem by Pentecost, he must not waste precious time (χρονοτριβῆσαι). Instead, he sent for the Ephesian elders to meet him at Miletus. This meant for them a journey of about 35 miles each way, by the shortest route, and for him a corresponding delay. It certainly would seem a curious method of saving time,[1] but for a fact which is sometimes overlooked in this connexion. The port of Ephesus was always subject to one great natural drawback, which in the end proved its ruin. The channel between it and the sea was liable to become choked with silt brought down by the river Caÿster.[2] In Strabo's time (xiv. 24. p. 641) a breakwater, built in the reign of Attalus II, had aggravated this tendency. The resulting obstruction of traffic must have been almost at its worst when Paul sailed for Syria. For it was only a few years later (A.D. 61–62) that Soranus, the energetic proconsul of Asia, cleared the channel and opened the

---

[1] Ramsay, *Paul the Traveller*, p. 295. [2] Ramsay, in *D. B.* i. p. 721 f.

harbour.[1] This explains Paul's choice of Miletus as the most convenient—or least inconvenient—port for communication with Ephesus from the sea, and makes it highly probable that, on leaving Ephesus, eleven months earlier, he went first to Miletus, taking with him the Ephesian Trophimus. Down to the last moment he was hoping for some messenger (?Erastus) to arrive with good news from Corinth. In that case he would gladly have crossed the Aegean forthwith. But it was not to be. In this instance 'no news' was 'bad news'. With a heavy heart he left Trophimus to recover from his illness, and sailed to Troas. In the meanwhile Timothy will have returned to Ephesus. He was again in Paul's company when 2 Cor. i–ix was written (i. 1), and must therefore have received some message calling him to the Apostle's side. That message, if we are not mistaken, is now before us. Thus we may reasonably suppose that Paul got his warm cloak before that winter, and that, in writing 2 Cor. i–ix and Rom., he was able to use those very books and parchments which had lain for some few weeks at the house of Carpus. If the brief lines referring to Erastus and Trophimus were added as a postscript, either on the *verso*, or otherwise distinct from the rest of the note, this would explain their separation from it, and their insertion, with similar fragments, at the end of 2 Timothy.

The following words are shared with Titus iii. 12 ff., 2 Cor. i–ix, and Rom., the nearest epistles in time, if our reconstruction be correct,—σπούδασον ἐλθεῖν (Titus iii. 12), πρὸ χειμῶνος (cf. Titus iii. 12 παραχειμάσαι), ἡμέτερος (cf. Titus iii. 14, Rom. xv. 4), μένω, ἀσθενέω, ἔρχομαι, πολλά, κακά, all *passim*, τοῖς (ἡμ.) λόγοις cf. Rom. iii. 4, 2 Cor. i. 18, ἐνδείκνυμαι Rom. ii. 15, 2 Cor. viii. 24, λίαν (cf. 2 Cor. xi. 5, xii. 12 ὑπερλίαν) ἀποδώσει κτλ. quoted Rom. ii. 6, φυλάσσω Rom. ix. 19, &c., ἀνθίστημι Rom. ix. 19, &c.

(iii) 2 Tim. iv. 16–18a (?18b). Paul writes from Caesarea, soon after his arrival under escort from Jerusalem:

At my first defence no one took my part, but all forsook me: may it not be laid to their account. But the Lord stood by me, and strengthened me; that through me the message might be fully proclaimed, and that all the Gentiles might hear: and I was delivered out

---

[1] Tacitus, *Ann.* xvi. 23 'portui Ephesiorum aperiendo curam insumpserat'. See Furneaux's note, ad loc., and Waddington, *Fastes des prov. asiat.* pp. 134–40, on the date of this proconsulate.

of the mouth of the lion. The Lord will deliver me from every evil work, and will save me unto his heavenly kingdom : (? to whom &c.).

The 'first defence' refers to no Roman *prima actio*,—this was all still in the future—but simply to the events described in Acts xxii. 1 ff. (ἀκούσατέ μου τῆς πρὸς ὑμᾶς νυνὶ ἀπολογίας). Luke's story entirely, if tacitly, bears out Paul's present statement, that of the brethren at Jerusalem none stood up for him on this occasion. At the second defence (xxiii. 1) they apparently had no opportunity of doing so, even if they had wished or dared (xxii. 30). But, as Luke too tells us, the Lord stood by him in this time of peril, and assured him that his work on earth was not yet done. He need have no doubt that he will yet win through to the goal of his race, and the crowning opportunity to preach his gospel, at Rome (xxiii. 11 ἐπιστὰς αὐτῷ ὁ Κύριος εἶπε κτλ.).

Verse 14 f., the reference to Alexander, might possibly belong to this note. For when Paul arrived at Jerusalem he was soon attacked by 'Jews from Asia' (Acts xxi. 27). Even without Paul's help we might perhaps have thought we could guess from what town in Asia this party hailed, and the name and trade of their leader!

If verse 18 belongs to this note, then Acts xxiii. 12 sq., the futile vow of the forty Jews, was a case in point of the sort of 'evil work' through which Paul was brought safely in fulfilment of his destiny. But as the deliverance which he there expects, is to set him 'in the heavenly kingdom', it may be better possibly to include that verse in the letter written more than four years after this, on the eve of his martyrdom. See (v) pp. 126 ff.

Paul may perhaps have written πληρωθῇ here, and in verse 5, as in Rom. viii. 4, not πληροφορηθῇ, which in his epistles bears a different meaning (Rom. iv. 21, xiv. 5, Col. iv. 12).

The language of this note, like the situation, is much nearer to Romans than to any other epistle. We find ἀπολογία 2 Cor. vii. 11, ἀπολογέομαι Rom. ii. 15, ἐγκαταλείπω ix. 29, λογίζομαι iv. 3, 22, παρέστη xvi. 2, ἐνδυναμόω iv. 20, δι' ἐμοῦ xv. 18, τὸ κήρυγμα xvi. 25, ἵνα πληρωθῇ viii. 4, cf. xv. 19, ἀκούσωσιν x. 14, πάντα τὰ ἔθνη xvi. 26, ἐρύσθην xv. 31 (ἵνα ῥυσθῶ ἀπὸ τῶν ἀπειθούντων ἐν τῇ Ἰουδαίᾳ ... Ἰερουσαλήμ), στόμα iii. 14, &c.

(iv) 2 Tim. iv. 9-12, 22b. Timothy is recalled to Rome, *c.* A. D. 62.

Do thy diligence to come shortly unto me: for Demas forsook me, having loved this present world, and went to Thessalonica; Crescens to Galatia, Titus to Dalmatia. Only Luke is with me. Take Mark, and bring him with thee: for he is useful to me for ministering. But Tychicus I sent to Ephesus. ... Grace be with you.

Timothy has presumably been to Philippi, as promised in Phil. ii. 19, 23, but instead of returning at once, has taken first the opportunity to visit his old home at Lystra. He now learns that his presence in Rome is urgently needed. Of all the little devoted band who were with the Apostle when he wrote Eph.-Col.-Philem., Luke 'the beloved physician' alone remains. The rest are scattered. Demas (Philem. 24, Col. iv. 14) has broken down under the strain of imminent danger, and has gone to Thessalonica, the home of Aristarchus (Acts xx. 4). Mark, we gather, is at some place known to Timothy, through which Timothy would pass on his return journey. He must therefore have been sent thither during the interval between the dispatch of Col.-Philem. and Timothy's own departure from Rome. Now in Col. iv. 10 Paul mentions the fact that the Colossians were at that time already prepared for Mark to arrive in the near future. He confirms this expectation, and bespeaks for the nephew of Barnabas a kindly reception. There is no need then to look any farther for the place at which Timothy was to 'pick up Mark' on his way to Rome. Like Onesimus, Mark has lived down his former defection (Acts xiii. 13, xv. 37 ff.), and having been once ἄχρηστος, is now εὔχρηστος ... ἵνα μοι διακονῇ ἐν τοῖς δεσμοῖς τοῦ εὐαγγελίου (Philem. 11 f.). Titus, of whom we last heard as having been summoned to Nicopolis (Titus iii. 12 f.), has evidently been across the Adriatic to visit Paul, and has now returned to continue his labours on the same coast (cf. p. 117 f.).[1] We know, and so did Timothy (Col. i. 1), that Tychicus was sent to Ephesus (Col. iv. 7, Eph. vi. 21). He is now reminded of this fact in order to complete the enumeration of Paul's recent companions, and so to illustrate the Apostle's loneliness and need for the fellowship and ministrations of the few on whose loyalty to the last he can still rely.

---

[1] Cf. Tacitus, *Ann.* ii. 53 'honorem (consulatus) Germanicus iniit apud urbem Achaiae Nicopolim, quo venerat per Illyricam oram, viso fratre Druso in Dalmatia agente' (W. J. Woodhouse, s. v. 'Dalmatia' in *Enc. Bib.*).

There remain only Epaphras, Jesus Justus, and Aristarchus (Philem. 23 f., Col. iv. 10-13) to be accounted for. We have Paul's word for the intense anxiety which the first of these had been feeling as to the welfare of his own converts at Colossae, Laodicea, and Hierapolis, and in view of the complete confidence expressed by the Apostle in all three, it is difficult to believe that they were any of them with him when he wrote Phil. ii. 20 f. There is thus no need for us to fall back on the possible, though hardly probable, identity of Epaphras with the Epaphroditus who was sent to Philippi (ii. 25 f.), nor on the suggestion that the name of Aristarchus may have been omitted by some accident from the end of the present note. As it stands, this note in no way contradicts our previous information, but at various points confirms it, and at others supplements it with new and altogether convincing details.

The diction of this note like the next, but unlike the first three, shows clear and special points of contact with the epistles of the Roman imprisonment. For σπούδασον cf. Eph. iv. 3, for ταχέως Phil. ii. 19 (of Timothy), ἀγαπάω Eph. vi. 6, &c., Col. iii. 12, &c., τ. νῦν αἰῶνα Eph. i. 21, ii. 2 (ἐν τ. αἰῶνι τούτῳ), ἀναλαμβάνω Eph. vi. 13, 16, μόνος Col. iv. 11, Phil. iv. 15, and especially εὔχρηστος εἰς διακονίαν Philem. 11 ff. (εὔχρηστος ... ἵνα μοι διακονῇ), Col. iv. 17, Eph. iv. 12, and finally the benediction ἡ χάρις μεθ' ὑμῶν = Col. iv. 18.

This message reached Timothy too late. Soon after its dispatch, Paul made his final appearance before the Roman tribunal, and was condemned by an unjust judge to die. On the eve of his martyrdom, or perhaps on the very day, he wrote,—

(v) his noble last letter and farewell to Timothy, in which he assures him of his complete confidence, bids him carry through to the end his task, as he, Paul, has now done; and so breaks to him the news that they two will not meet in this world again. The references to Paul's early sufferings and persecutions 'at Antioch, at Iconium, and at Lystra', recall memories which will have been renewed by Timothy's recent visit to those familiar scenes. Hurrying back, as we may be sure the real Timothy would, on receipt of the summons (iv), and picking up Mark at Colossae, as instructed, he was met at Ephesus by this last message, which cancelled its predecessor, filled his heart with sorrow, and his eyes once more with tears, and gave him that commission, to the fulfilment of which the rest of his own life was devoted.

Our 2 Tim. consists of this last letter edited and brought up to date by the *auctor ad Timotheum*, for the benefit of the less heroic Timothys of his own day, with the three earlier notes (ii, iii, and iv) tacked on at the end—perhaps under the genuine impression that they were postscripts to (v)—a mistake for which he, if it was he, need not be blamed, seeing that (1) it has been shared for eighteen centuries by Christian readers, who have seen no incongruity between these Personalia and the situation envisaged in the bulk of the letter, (2) there were no explanatory notes on the documents before him, (3) his mistake, made in good faith, has led at least to the preservation of these priceless relics.

In attempting to reconstruct this Farewell Letter, we are obviously confronted with still greater difficulties, and must proceed with the added caution and reserve which they demand. For our task is no longer, as in the previous notes, confined to the comparatively simple business of separating one genuine fragment from another, and assigning each to its appropriate set of circumstances. The situation here is clear enough. But we have now to disentangle the words and sentences of an original letter from additions and amplifications made by one who had prepared himself for his task by prolonged study of the Apostle's writings. That the letter before us consists of these diverse elements we are convinced, for the reasons already stated. But it would be idle to pretend that we can feel at all points the same confidence, that we do at certain points, of our ability to draw with precision the line between the real Paul and his editor.

We have, for instance, not the slightest hesitation in believing the Onesiphorus paragraph (i. 16-18), and the glorious climax (iv. 6-8), to be as certainly the utterance of Paul himself as anything that has come down to us under his name. And we are equally confident that he never wrote, nor dictated, nor authorized, nor conceived, such a passage as ii. 23—iii. 9 (see Text, Appendix IV). A good deal of chapter i seems to be clearly a cento of phrases culled from the ten Paulines. But we must frankly admit our inability to feel quite the same assurance, when it comes to deciding:

PAULINE ELEMENTS

(*a*) How much, if any, of the introductory greeting i. 1 f. was written by Paul on this occasion. That he had previously used every word of it, is obvious, especially if we may adopt the marginal reading of W. H. (κυρίου 'Ιησοῦ Χριστοῦ). He calls Timothy his beloved child in 1 Cor. iv. 17, but in Philem. refers to his comrade of so many years as 'the brother'. At this moment of tender parting he might perhaps have reverted to the old affectionate description. We find κατ' ἐπαγγελίαν Gal. iii. 29 (cf. Acts xiii. 23), but never before in the present sort of connexion.

(*b*) The reference to Lois and Eunice (i. 5) might easily have been derived from contemporary traditions. Yet the language of this verse is free from phrases which could be traced to our genuine Paulines (unless we except χαρᾶς πληρωθῶ, cf. Phil. ii. 2 πληρώσατέ μου τ. χαράν). The only non-Pauline words are μάμμη, which presents no difficulty, and ὑπόμνησις (elsewhere in the N. T. only in 2 Peter, twice). We have omitted the verse mainly because we can find no satisfactory way of connecting it with the certainly genuine paragraphs.

(*c*) Other verses which come near the border-line are ii. 1, iv. 2b.

PAUL'S LAST LETTER

The Lord grant mercy unto the house of Onesiphorus: for he oft refreshed me, and was not ashamed of my chain; but, when he was in Rome, he sought me diligently, and found me (the Lord grant unto him to find mercy of the Lord in that day); and in how many things he ministered at Ephesus, thou knowest very well.

But thou didst follow my teaching, conduct, purpose, faith, long-suffering, love, patience, persecutions, sufferings; what things befell me at Antioch, at Iconium, at Lystra; what persecutions I endured: and out of them all the Lord delivered me.

I charge thee in the sight of God, and of Christ Jesus, who shall judge the quick and the dead, and by his appearing and his kingdom; preach the word; be instant in season, out of season . . .

Do the work of an evangelist, fulfil thy ministry.

For I am already being offered, and the time of my departure is come. I have fought the good fight, I have finished the course, I have kept the faith: henceforth there is laid up for me the crown of righteousness, which the Lord, the righteous judge, shall give to me at that day: and

PAULINE ELEMENTS

not only to me, but also to all them that have loved his appearing . . . to whom be the glory for ever and ever. Amen.

Salute Prisca and Aquila, and the house of Onesiphorus. . . . Eubulus saluteth thee, and Pudens, and Linus, and Claudia, and all the brethren. The Lord Jesus be with thy spirit.

Written at Rome *c.* A. D. 62, on the eve of Paul's martyrdom, to meet Timothy at Ephesus on his way back from Lystra.

The letter falls into four parts:

I. Onesiphorus and his labour of love, i. 16–18.

II. Timothy's own comradeship over a longer period. Divine protection in past perils, iii. 10 f.

III. A last charge laid on Timothy to carry on the great work, and finish his task, as Paul has finished his, iv. 1, 2a, 5b.

IV. The sure reward of faithful service, iv. 6–8. Doxology, last greetings, and benediction, iv. 18b, 19, 21b, 22a.

1.

The letter begins with a grateful reference to services rendered, in Timothy's absence, by a friend from Ephesus, who had made it his business to seek out the prisoner of Tigellinus (Tac. *Ann.* xv. 51. 5)—not the easiest task in the world, nor the safest—and had found him in that closer confinement, to which he must have been transferred during or before his trial, from the hired lodging of Acts xxviii. 30.

There is a great story behind Paul's brief but suggestive record of that search through Rome. We seem to catch glimpses of one purposeful face in a drifting crowd, and follow with quickening interest this stranger from far coasts of the Aegean, as he threads the maze of unfamiliar streets, knocking at many doors, following up every clue, warned of the risks he is taking but not to be turned from his quest; till in some obscure prison-house a known voice greets him, and he discovers Paul chained to a Roman soldier.

Having once found the way, Onesiphorus is not content with

a single visit, but true to his name, proves unwearied in his ministrations. Others have flinched from the menace and ignominy of that chain: but this visitor counts it the supreme privilege of his life to share with such a criminal the reproach of the Cross. One series of turnings in the vast labyrinth he comes to know as if it were his own Ephesus.

We can partly divine what these visits must have meant to one whose bodily powers, spent and broken by much privation, were in urgent need of such material comforts as Onesiphorus would not fail to bring. Still more as tokens of that love which 'never faileth', must they have refreshed a spirit jaded by suspense, disappointed and saddened by recent experience of cynical injustice and of craven disloyalty.

For in those days his Roman citizenship had proved to be a worthless thing, and Roman justice a mockery. Once, when he was on his trial at Jerusalem, leading members of the Church there had not lifted a finger to help him. He had borne them no grudge for that.[1] Now members of the Church at Rome, where he lay in graver peril, had been active in making of the very gospel a tool to injure his case. In that he had contrived to find reason for rejoicing.[2] But that was not all, nor the worst. Some on whom he had thought he could rely to the uttermost, had failed him in these last critical days. Alarmed by ominous signs of coming storm, they had fled to a safe distance, proving only too conclusively that in their minds, after all, their own interests came first, and 'the things of Jesus Christ' second. So Paul was left almost if not quite alone.[3] For he had felt it right to send some others, besides Timothy, on errands of vital importance, setting the requirements of the kingdom, as ever, before his own necessities (e.g. Mark, Col. iv. 11, and Epaphroditus, Phil. ii. 25). Lonely and tired and ill, he would not have been human if these desertions had not cut him to the quick. Yet of all this he now says not a word, but only speaks with passionate gratitude of the relief brought by this faithful friend.

But Onesiphorus has paid his last visit. Paul does not say what has become of him. For others' sakes, as well as his own, the prisoner must be careful what he writes. Some things must

---

[1] p. 120 f.   [2] Phil. i. 16, 18.   [3] 2 Tim. iv. 10; Phil. ii. 20 f., p. 123.

always be left for a trusty messenger to tell by word of mouth.[1] That he had taken many and great risks for Paul, and for the work of Christ, is certain. He who so risks his life, has given it, whether or not he receive it again. The impression conveyed to most readers is that Onesiphorus had ventured into this dangerous quarter once too often, and paid, or was likely to pay, the penalty with his life.

Paul's prayer for him is that in the Hereafter he may be repaid in his own coin by One, whose promise stands, 'Blessed are the merciful, for they shall obtain mercy'. As he had persevered till he found Paul in this dark cell, so in that bright Day when he reaches the goal of his life's quest, may he find a still truer Friend, and better welcome, awaiting him There. Meanwhile in one household at Ephesus they will be needing that same mercy to comfort them, when they hear the news that will accompany this letter. He prays that they may find it; and sends them such an account of those last weeks at Rome, as would at least mingle a just pride with their sorrow. So he discharges this debt of gratitude as best he can—pays an immortal tribute to the memory of his friend, rescues his name from oblivion, and links it for ever with his own, as one of those who held not their lives of any account, so that they might accomplish the ministry which they received from the Lord Jesus (Acts xx. 24).

That Onesiphorus should have proved himself worthy of such a tribute would be no surprise to those who had known the man long and well enough to recognize his real character. It was like him, they would say, recalling one instance after another of his thoughtful self-effacing ministry. There was one time in particular, five to seven years earlier, when he and Paul and Timothy were all in Ephesus together. Doubtless Timothy had every reason to realize then, and to remember now, how well this true disciple had learned the lesson taught in those 'words of the Lord Jesus'—'It is more blessed to give than to receive' (Acts xx. 35).

A comparison of this passage with that in which Paul tells the Philippians (ii. 25 ff.) of similar services rendered, and risks taken, by Epaphroditus, leaves no room for doubt that he who wrote

---

[1] Col. iv. 7, Eph. vi. 21 f., Phil. ii. 23.

the one, wrote also the other, and after no long interval. Each helps us to understand how it was, that so many were willing to put their lives in jeopardy for his sake.

II.

But Paul was not one to keep all his gratitude for the dead, and forget what he owed to the living friend, whose services and comradeship reached back over a still longer period.

For himself the thought of what is coming has no terrors. For Love and Faith have transfigured Death, and banished Fear. But he realizes none the less what the news of his death must mean to Timothy. With infinite care and delicacy he chooses his words to break the shock of those tidings, and comfort the sad heart of his friend. First he will rob inevitable grief at least of its sting, by meeting beforehand all bitter thoughts of vain regret or needless self-reproach, that Timothy was not in his place by Paul's side at the last. He will set What-has-been to silence What-might-have-been. Then he will show him the brighter side of this sorrow.

Nothing that any one else may have done, and nothing that has happened, or can happen now, will ever be able to eclipse the unwavering devotion of this man after Paul's own heart, this kindred spirit (ἰσόψυχον, Phil. ii. 20), who has followed like his faithful shadow over more miles than either of them could count. Long before ever they set foot in Ephesus as heralds of the Gospel, Timothy had responded with youthful enthusiasm to Paul's invitation, and had left all, to join him on what was then already a perilous mission. He knows, none better, what happened to Paul before that, at Antioch, at Iconium, and at Lystra. No need to write out the much longer list of places where they two together have since then carried their lives in their hands, as they flung in the face of an unbelieving world the eternal challenge of the Cross. Uphill and down, through storm and sunshine, leaving the old home very far behind, they have tramped side by side, learning to know and understand each other, as only they can, who have seen one another in many different lights and changing moods, and under very varied circumstances. In the fierce furnace of tribulation, and in the crucible of pain, they have proved each the other's fidelity, and have found it pure gold.

It does not seem too much to say that Timothy must indeed have 'followed' Paul's teaching, alike in its detail and in its large outlines, as no other ever did or ever will. For when Paul was writing his early letters to the Thessalonians, as in his varied correspondence with the Corinthian Church, Timothy was there by his side. When he dictated his masterpiece to the Romans, Timothy was there, while Tertius wrote. More recently in Rome, as he wove the rich many-coloured fabric of those charges to the churches of Asia, or revealed in the note to Philemon more of the real Paul than any but an intimate might see; and last of all, only a little while ago, when he opened his inmost heart to those loyal friends at Philippi, Timothy was there—not as an absolutely silent and impassive bystander, but venturing perhaps now and then to offer a suggestion. In each of these, except the circular which we know as Ephesians, he is named either as a trusted colleague[1] or as joint-sender along with Paul; and this can hardly have been a mere idle compliment.

He knew therefore the actual circumstances under which each of these immortal letters was written. He could recall the very look, tone, and gesture with which many of those thoughts were first uttered, that have changed so many lives. There would be other letters too, doubtless, known to Timothy, but lost to us (e.g. to the Laodiceans, Col. iv. 16).

He has had unique opportunities of following not only the written, but also the spoken words of the Apostle—sermons on great occasions, discourses in school and synagogue, fierce debates, conversations in street or market or upper room—personal applications of one divine remedy to the infinite variety of human need.

Meanwhile his youth has hardened into manhood, and the disciple (or Chela, as they might say in India), has become the honoured and trusted comrade, and the 'son', 'the brother' (Philem. 1, cf. 1 Cor. iv. 17). Sharing the vision of a Kingdom, they have shared also the travail which makes that Kingdom come. They have learned to be silent together without embarrassment, or speak without reserve, as men may, who

---

[1] 1 Cor. iv. 17, xvi. 10 f., Rom. xvi. 21.

have passed through deep waters together. And this old fisher of men might have repeated what that other old fisherman, in Theocritus, says to his mate, as they lie in their hut by the sea, wakeful through the long, dark hour before dawn :

ὡς καὶ τὰν ἄγραν τὠνείρατα πάντα μερίζευ.[1]

So it has come to pass that Timothy has been initiated into the inner secrets of Paul's mind, has marked the drift of his great arguments and the connexion between diverse elements in his teaching—has entered into his aims and ideals, his hopes and fears, his dreams and disappointments, and shared with him the ventures of that faith which stakes all on the present power, and final victory, of 'things not seen'. He has come very near to the great heart of Paul, has caught the glow of its passion, felt the throb of its desire, and marvelled at the inexhaustible reserves of its calm fortitude.

He knows too, as hardly another, what it has all cost— amid what difficulties, in what sheer physical weakness, weariness, and pain, and in the teeth of what relentless opposition, open and underhand, Paul has carried out his life-purpose through the years. It was a hunted man, with a price set on his head, as well as a sick man, tortured and hampered by some incurable complaint, who built up that mighty edifice, to withstand the shocks of time, and become one of the permanent factors shaping the thoughts and moulding the destinies of men. Yes, Timothy knows, though he cannot understand, the hatred which has dogged the steps of his friend—by what awful vows men with pious phrases on their lips have bound themselves to kill him—and by how very little they have failed. But one thing more he knows, that hitherto the Unseen Deliverer has brought him safely through all.

Therefore he has the right to share Paul's confidence that in this direst assault of evil powers the same Divine Helper will stand by him to the end. Not that Paul has any illusions, or is blind to the desperate nature, humanly speaking, of his present situation. When he wrote to the Philippians, there still seemed quite a good hope of his being set free to revisit his churches, and continue his work on earth. But now that is all over, and there is not the remotest chance of his escaping alive from the

---

[1] *Idyll* xxi. 31 : 'Be partner of my dreams, as of my fishing'.—A. C. Benson, *Upton Letters*, p. 282.

hands of his enemies. From Caesar's verdict there is in this world no further appeal.

Yet even so he is safe! Through this most perilous pass the Lord will be his Helper; and the same Hand which long ago rescued him from 'wild beasts at Ephesus', and from 'the lion's mouth' at Jerusalem, will bring him unharmed through the very jaws of death, and set him in the heavenly kingdom.[1] And now in this sublime confidence, which finds its climax in the doxology, iv. 18,—

III.

The Apostle lays on Timothy the last solemn charge, in the witnessing presence of mighty Invisible Powers, binding him to his duty by vows more strait than ever Arthur laid upon his knights. Come what may, he is to herald the Word. Let his message ring out inevitable as the Day of Judgement, and his preaching catch from his theme some of its tremendous urgency. Keep close at the appointed task ($\epsilon\pi\acute{\iota}\sigma\tau\eta\theta\iota$), as one whose Taskmaster is close at hand ($\epsilon\phi\acute{\epsilon}\sigma\tau\eta\kappa\epsilon\nu$, cf. 1 Thess. v. 2 f. $\epsilon\pi\acute{\iota}\sigma\tau\alpha\tau\alpha\iota$). This he must do, not waiting for the convenient season, like some excellent persons and brilliant preachers (1 Cor. xvi. 12 ὅταν εὐκαιρήσῃ), but sowing the good seed in all weathers and beside all waters. 'In season', yes, watching always for the best opportunity, missing no heaven-sent chance, buying up the right moment, though it cost all he has. But also, 'out of season'— daring the apparently hopeless venture, holding on when all seems lost, preaching to deaf ears, knocking still at fast-bolted doors, finding in opposition and peril only an added incentive to go forward (1 Cor. xvi. 8 f.). Timothy is to do the work, not of an ecclesiastic (honourable and necessary as later experience may prove such service to be), but of an evangelist. His to take up the torch and wave it; to carry the light of a great Hope into the dark places of sorrow, sin, and despair; and so labouring, to fill up his cup of human service.

IV.

For Paul's own cup is full to the brim, nay, is already being poured out (see p. 112 f.). At last he has received the summons so

---

[1] p. 121 f. In any case, Paul was of this mind to the last.

long and eagerly awaited. For him the midnight is past. He stands watching the day break. His hour of destiny has come. The anchor is weighed, the vessel ready. A wind from heaven is filling her sails. And the voyager is ready too. It is high time for him to put out to sea. There will be no shipwreck this time!

So in Paul's spirit broods the deep content of one who has played his part like a man in the great game of life. He has run his race. He has kept the faith, not like some zealous custodian of traditions received, at second-hand, from a mightier Past, but as a pioneer guards the gate of a land he helped to discover; as a seeker stands for the Truth revealed to his eyes by no mortal's showing, but by a light from heaven.

All that remains for him now is to go and receive the victor's crown, laid up in store for him in some safe treasure-house of the great Unseen. This a Judge more just than Caesar will give him on that Day whose promised coming is the refrain of Paul's triumph-song. But not Paul only—there would be no joy for him in any reward, which he could not look forward to sharing with others—all who have loved the Lord's appearing, shall have their part in the glory of that marvellous dawn.

That is all. There is indeed nothing more to be said. A last greeting to Paul's chief friends at Ephesus, Prisca and Aquila, who risked their lives for him long ago (Rom. xvi. 3 f.), and would do it again, if occasion offered; and the family of Onesiphorus. Then greetings to Timothy from four members of the Roman Church by name, and from the brethren generally. The letter closes with the simple benediction.

Of this last message Bengel's golden phrase tells the whole truth, and nothing but the truth:

' Testamentum Pauli et cygnea cantio est haec epistula '.[1]

To these five notes the oracular remark of Erasmus may be applied, without a trace of that irony which seems to lurk in the words, as often as they are quoted with reference to these epistles as a whole:

' Non est cuiusvis Paulinum effingere pectus.'[2]

---

[1] 'This letter is Paul's testament and swan-song.'
[2] Not every one can feign the heart of Paul.'

PAULINE ELEMENTS

There is a saying attributed to Averrhoes, the Arab philosopher:

'Bonum est cribrare modium sabuli ut quis inveniat unam margaritam'.[1]

It has been necessary for us to sift many bushels of the dryest sand that ever drifted—collecting Particles, Prepositions, *Hapax Legomena*, passing these through index after index as through a sieve—calculating percentages, poring over diagrams, and striving to wrest from arid pages of statistics their lost secret. Now at the end, if our argument holds, we find not one pearl only, but a cluster of five, and see them restored, each to its own place on the shining thread of Paul's life-story.

[1] 'It is good to sift a measure of sand, and find one pearl.'—E. C. Gardner, *Dante's Ten Heavens*, p. 3.

EPILOGUE

It only remains to indicate very briefly some of the more important results for New Testament study and Church History which would follow, in the event of the conclusions drawn in this essay being confirmed by the verdict of scholarship.

1. In the first place, the non-Pauline elements would no longer form the basis of what would in that case be recognized as mistaken conceptions of the personal development of the Apostle, and of the general development of the Church during his lifetime. But these elements would remain as an important factor in the materials for a historic reconstruction of actual developments in Christian ideals, doctrine, and polity during the reigns of Trajan and Hadrian.

2. Our reasons for regarding the other ten epistles as genuine would be strongly reinforced (*a*) by the external evidence of this new witness who, in the early years of the second century knew, revered, and quoted, all or most of them, as the very words of Paul, (*b*) by the internal evidence of our statistical tables and other linguistic tests in which they are seen to form so consistently a close series.

3. The genuine notes would gain a new and greatly enhanced value and interest by being thus restored to their true context and historical setting in the actual life of the Apostle.

4. Our conception of that life would be shorn of the old legend of a release and second Roman imprisonment, with all the network of mistaken inferences which have for so many years derived from it their plausibility.

5. But for the rest, the historicity of the heroic figure and personality of Paul, as delineated in the Acts and in the genuine epistles, would receive new and striking confirmation.

APPENDIX I

A. *Words found in the Pastorals, but not in the ten Paulines.*
306 (including repetitions 437).

+ Apostolic Fathers only.
* In Apostolic Fathers and also in Apologists.
× In Apologists only.
• In neither.
c Only in quotations from the LXX.

The figure after a word indicates the number of times it occurs. Where there is no figure, the word occurs only once.

A 1. 'Pastoral *Hapax Legomena*'. Not elsewhere in the N. T., 175 (incl. reps. 220).

(i) 1 TIMOTHY only, 75 (incl. reps. 86).

+ 11 ἁγνεία 2, βλαβερός, δίλογος, διώκτης, ἑτεροδιδασκαλέω 2, ματαιολογία, ὁμολογουμένως, πραϋπαθία, πρόσκλισις, τεκνογονέω, ὑπερπλεονάζω.
* 8 ἄλλως, ἀνεπίλημπτος 3, ἀπέραντος, ἀπόδεκτος 2, ἔλαττον (adv.), ἔντευξις 2, θεοσέβεια, φιλαργυρία.
× 19 αἰδώς, ἀμοιβή, ἀνδροφόνος, ἀποδοχή 2, ἀπρόσιτος, διατροφή, ἔκγονος, ἐντρέφομαι, ἐπίορκος, ἐπιπλήσσω, ἤρεμος, καταλέγομαι, κόσμιος 2, μετάλημψις, μονόομαι, νοσέω, ῥητῶς, ὑπόνοια, ψευδολόγος.
• 37 ἀδηλότης, ἀνδραποδιστής, ἀντίθεσις, ἀντίλυτρον, ἀπόβλητος, ἀποθησαυρίζω, αὐθεντέω, βάθμος, γραώδης, γυμνασία, διαπαρατριβή, ἑδραίωμα, ἐκζήτησις, ἐπαρκέω 3, εὐμετάδοτος, καταστολή, καταστρηνιάω, καυστηριάζομαι, κοινωνικός, λογομαχία, μητραλῴης, νεόφυτος, ξενοδοχέω, οἰκοδεσποτέω, πατραλῴης, περιπείρω, πλέγμα, πορισμός 2, πρόκριμα, σκέπασμα, στόμαχος, τεκνογονία, τεκνοτροφέω, ὑδροποτέω, ὑψηλοφρονέω, φλύαρος, ψευδώνυμος.
[? also • κοσμίως ii. 9 W. H.ᵐ, v. S.ᵐ. • πυκνός adj. v. 23 (as adv. Luke v. 33, Acts xxiv. 26), cf. A 2 (i). × ὕστερος (Matt. xxi. 31 W. H., not v. S.), cf. A 2 (i). • ἀγαθοεργέω vi. 18 = ἀγαθουργέω Acts xiv. 17, cf. A 2 (i).]

(ii) 2 TIMOTHY only, 48 (incl. reps. 50).

+ 11 ἀγωγή, ἀναζωπυρέω, ἀνάλυσις, ἀνανήφω, ἀναψύχω, ἀπαίδευτος, δειλία, ἐπισωρεύω, καταστροφή, νεωτερικός, χαλκεύς.

* 9 ἀθλέω 2, βέλτιον, γόης, ἐνδύνω, καταφθείρομαι, μηδέποτε, πιστόομαι, πραγματία, χρήσιμος.
× 7 ἀκρατής, ἀνεξίκακος, ἀνήμερος, ἀποτρέπομαι, φίλαυτος, φιλήδονος, φιλόθεος.
• 21 ἀκαίρως, ἀνεπαίσχυντος, ἀντιδιατίθεμαι, ἄρτιος, ἄσπονδος, ἀφιλάγαθος, γάγγραινα, γυναικάριον, ἔκδηλος, ἔλεγμος, ἐπανόρθωσις, θεόπνευστος, κνήθομαι, λογομαχέω, μάμμη, μεμβράνα, ὀρθοτομέω, στρατολογέω, συνκακοπαθέω 2, σωφρονισμός, φελόνης.

(iii) Titus only, 30 (incl. reps. 30).

+ 6 βδελυκτός, ἐγκρατής, κατάστημα, περιούσιος c, στυγητός, φιλότεκνος.
* 6 ἀψευδής, ἐκστρέφομαι, ὀργίλος, πρεσβῦτις, σωτήριος, φροντίζω.
× 3 ἰουδαϊκός, σωφρονίζω, σωφρόνως.
• 15 αἱρετικός, ἀκατάγνωστος, αὐτοκατάκριτος, ἀφθορία, ἐπιδιορθόω, ἐπιστομίζω, ἱεροπρεπής, καλοδιδάσκαλος, ματαιολόγος, νομικός adj., οἰκουργός, περιφρονέω, φιλάγαθος, φίλανδρος, φρεναπάτης.

(iv) 1 and 2 Timothy, 9 (incl. reps. 1 Tim. 11, 2 Tim. 10).

+ 2 ἀστοχέω 3, παρα(κατα)θήκη 3.
* 1 ἀνόσιος 2.
× 2 πρόγονος 2, τυφόομαι 3.
• 4 διδακτικός 2, κενοφωνία 2, νομίμως 2, ὑποτύπωσις 2.

(v) 1 Timothy and Titus, 10 (incl. reps. 1 Tim. 12, Tit. 12).

* 4 διαβεβαιόομαι 2, διάγω 2, σεμνότης 3, σώφρων 4.
× 1 πλήκτης 2.
• 5 αἰσχροκερδής 2, ἄμαχος 2, γενεαλογία 2, νηφάλιος 3, πάροινος 2.

(vi) 2 Timothy and Titus, 1 (incl. reps. 2 Tim. 1, Tit. 1).

+ 1 εὐσεβῶς 2.
[? also × ἀνατρέπω 2 Tim. ii. 18, Titus i. 11 (Jo. ii. 15 W. H., not W. H.^{m} v. S.), cf. A 2 (vi).]

(vii) 1 and 2 Timothy and Titus, 2 (incl. reps. 1 Tim. 3, 2 Tim. 2, Tit. 2).

+ 1 διάβολος adj. 3.
* 1 ὠφέλιμος 4.

A 2. In the Pastorals and other N.T. books, not in the ten Pauline Epistles. 131 (incl. reps. 217).

(i) 1 Timothy only, 52 (incl. reps. 61).

+ 11 ἀφιλάργυρος, βραδύνω, βυθίζω, γυμνάζω, μαργαρίτης, περιποιέομαι, πολυτελής, πρεσβυτέριον, πρόδηλος 2, σπαταλάω, σωματικός.

APPENDIX I 139

* 28 ἀμελέω, ἀντιλαμβάνομαι, ἀπόλαυσις, ἀποπλανάω, ἄσπιλος, δίπλοος, εἰσφέρω, ἐκφέρω, ἐμπίπτω 3, ἐπακολουθέω 2, ἐπιλαμβάνομαι 2, ἐπισκοπή, ἐπίσταμαι, ἐπιτίθημι, εὐεργεσία, ἡσύχιος, θνήσκω, ἱματισμός, κτίσμα, λοιδορία, μελετάω, νεότης, παραδέχομαι, περίεργος, προάγω 2, προσέρχομαι, σωφροσύνη 2, ὑβρίζω.
× 7 δυνάστης, ἐπιμελέομαι, εὐσεβέω, ζωογονέω, ὀρέγομαι 2, προσμένω 2, ὕστερος.
• 6 ἀγαθοεργέω, ἑξήκοντα, νίπτω, νομοδιδάσκαλος, περιέρχομαι, πυκνός.

(ii) 2 Timothy only, 33 (incl. reps. 34).

+ 7 ἀργύρεος, ἐμπλέκω, κακοπαθέω 2, νομή, προδότης, προπετής, ὑπόμνησις.
* 17 ἄνοια, βρέφος, δρόμος, κριτής, λέων, λίαν, μάχομαι, μέντοι, μεταλαμβάνω, μήποτε, σοφίζω, στερεός, στεφανόω, φιλάργυρος, χαλεπός, χειμών, χρύσεος.
× 7 ἀχάριστος, γεωργός, ἐπιτιμάω, ζωγρέω, κακοῦργος, ξύλινος, στρατιώτης.
• 2 ἐξαρτίζω, εὐκαίρως.

(iii) Titus only, 15 (incl. reps. 17).

+ 4 αὐθάδης, ἐπιφαίνω 2, νοσφίζομαι, παλιγγενεσία.
* 10 ἀνωφελής, ἡδονή, θηρίον, κοσμικός, λείπω 2, λυτρόομαι, μιαίνω, πειθαρχέω, ὑγιής, φιλανθρωπία.
• 1 νομικός (subs.).

(iv) 1 and 2 Timothy, 8 (incl. reps. 1 Tim. 12, 2 Tim. 8).

* 6 βίος 2, βλάσφημος 2, ἐκτρέπω 4, κῆρυξ 2, παρακολουθέω 2, χείρων 2.
× 1 βέβηλος 4.
• 1 ἐπίθεσις 2.

(v) 1 Timothy and Titus, 10 (incl. reps. 1 Tim. 20, Tit. 11).

+ 1 φιλόξενος 2.
* 7 ἀργός 3, κοσμέω 2, μαρτυρία 2, νεώτερος 5, ὅσιος 2, πρεσβύτερος 5 προσέχω 5.
× 1 κατηγορία 2.
• 1 ἀνυπότακτος 3.

(vi) 2 Timothy and Titus, 6 (incl. reps. 2 Tim. 8, Tit. 6).

* 4 αἰτία 3, ἀπολείπω 3, ποικίλος 2, ὑπομιμνήσκω 2.
× 1 ἀνατρέπω 2.
• 1 περιΐστημι 2.

(vii) 1 and 2 Timothy and Titus, 7 (incl. reps. 1 Tim. 18, 2 Tim. 11, Tit. 11).

* 5 ἀρνέομαι 7, δεσπότης 4, εὐσέβεια 10, μῦθος 4, παραιτέομαι 4.
× 1 ζήτησις 3.
• 1 ὑγιαίνω 8.

	1 Tim.		2 Tim.		Titus.		Total.	
	A 1.	A 2.	A 1.	A 2.	A 1.	A 2.	A 1.	A 2
+	14	12	15	7	8	5	32	23
*	14	46	11	32	11	26	29	77
×	22	10	9	10	4	3	32	18
•	46	9	25	5	20	4	82	13
	96	77	60	54	43	38	175	131
	173		114		81		306	

Words found in one Pauline Epistle.

(i) Romans, 261 (including repetitions, 336).

B 1. Also in the Pastorals, but in no other N. T. book. 10 (incl. reps. 10).

+ 3 ἀδιάλειπτος, ἀλαζών, ἀνακαίνωσις.
* 2 πλάσσω, ὑποτίθημι.
• 5 ἄστοργος, μόρφωσις, ὀδύνη, σωρεύω c, ὑβριστής.

B 2. In the Pastorals, and elsewhere in the N. T. 23 (incl. reps. 37).

+ 2 ἐπαισχύνομαι 2, παγίς c.
* 20 ἀπειθής, ἀπιστέω, ἀπιστία 4, ἀπωθέομαι 2 c, ἀσέβεια 2, ἀσεβής 2, ἐκεῖ 2, ἡμέτερος, καθαρός, καθίστημι 2, κοινός 2, ὁμολογέω 2, [? × ὀνειδίζω, 1 Tim. iv. 10 W. H.ᵐ, v. S., not W. H., cf. c 2], ῥίζα 4, τάχος, ὑπερήφανος, φέρω, ψεύστης. ἀντιλέγω c, ἀποστρέφω c, ἐκχέω c.
• 1 ὀνειδισμός c.

C 1. Not in the Pastorals, nor elsewhere in the N. T. 103 (incl. reps. 127).

+ 12 ἀνοχή 2, ἐπαναμιμνήσκω, ἱλαρότης, καινότης 2, κατάλαλος, προδίδωμι c, προηγέομαι, σκληρότης, συνδοξάζω, συντέμνω c, χρηματισμός, ψεῦσμα.

APPENDIX I 141

* 14 ἀφικνέομαι, ἀχρεόομαι c, ἐκκαίομαι, ἐκπετάννυμι c, ἐπικαλύπτω c, κακοήθεια, κατασκάπτω c, νῶτος c, πλάσμα, προγίνομαι, προέχομαι, σύμβουλος c, ὑπολείπομαι c, χρῆσις 2.

× 24 ἀναλογία, ἀναπολόγητος 2, ἄνθραξ c, ἀποστυγέω, ἀσπίς c, γραπτός, δολιόω c, ἐπονομάζομαι, ἑπτακισχίλιοι c, ἤτοι, θειότης, θεοστυγής, καθοράω, λάρυγξ c, νομοθεσία, ὄρεξις, παράκειμαι 2, προπάτωρ, σεβάζομαι, συναγωνίζομαι, σύντριμμα c, σύνφημι, ὑπερφρονέω, ὑπόλιμμα c.

• 53 ἀγριέλαιος 2, ἀλάλητος, ἀμετανόητος, ἀνελεήμων, ἀνεξεραύνητος, ἀνόμως 2, ἀντιστρατεύομαι, ἀποτολμάω, ἀποτομία 2, ἀρά c, ἀσθένημα, ἀσύνθετος, δικαιοκρισία, δικαίωσις 2, ἐγγύτερον, ἑκατονταετής, ἐκκλάομαι 3, ἐνκεντρίζω 6, ἐπιποθία, ἐφευρετής, θήρα c, ἱεροσυλέω, ἱερουργέω, καλλιέλαιος, κατάκριμα 3, κατάνυξις c, λίμμα, ματαιόομαι, μεταλλάσσω 2, οἰκτείρω c, παλαιότης, πάρεσις, πιότης, προαιτιάομαι, πρόσλημψις, προστάτις, σύμφυτος, συναναπαύομαι, συνήδομαι, συνκάμπτω c, συνμαρτυρέω 3, συνπαρακαλέομαι, συνστενάζω, συνωδίνω, τολμηροτέρως, ὕπανδρος, ὑπερεντυγχάνω, ὑπερνικάω, ὑπόδικος, φιλόστοργος, φρόνημα 4, χρηστολογία, ψιθυριστής.

C 2. Not in the Pastorals, but elsewhere in the N. T. 125 (incl. reps. 162).

+ 13 ἀντιτάσσομαι, ἀπέναντι c, ἀσχημοσύνη, γνωστός, δώρημα, ἐπαναπαύομαι, ἐπιπίπτω c, καθήκω, πταίω, στεναγμός, φιλοξενία. Twice — κοιτή, σκοτίζομαι.

* 81 ἄβυσσος c, ἀΐδιος, αἰνέω c, ἄκακος, ἀκροατής, ἄμμος c, ἀνάγω, ἀνταπόδομα c, ἀριθμός c, ἀφαιρέω c, βούλημα, γέμω c, δεῦρο, διαγγέλλω c, διαπορεύομαι, διαταγή, διάφορος, ἐκζητέω c, ἐκχύννομαι, ἐλάσσων c (adj.), ἐμπίμπλημι, ἐπίσημος, ἐπιτυγχάνω, ἐπιφέρω, ἑρπετόν, ἥκω c, θεάομαι, ἰός c, κατάγω, κατανοέω, καταράομαι, κατηγορέω, κεραμεύς, κύκλῳ, λειτουργέω, λόγιον, μέμφομαι, μεταξύ, μήπω, οἰκέτης, οἰκουμένη c, ὁμοθυμαδόν, ὁμοιόω c, ὁρίζω, πέρας c, πετεινόν, πηλός, πιπράσκω, πού, πρόβατον c, πρόθυμος, πρόνοια, προφητικός, σκληρύνω, συντελέω c, συντρίβω, σφαγή c, ταλαιπωρία c, ταλαίπωρος, τάφος c, τράχηλος, τυφλός, φονεύω c, φόνος, ὡραῖος c, ὡσεί. Twice— ἀδύνατος, ἀτιμάζω, ἐκκλίνω, λατρεία, μεστός, μοιχεύω, προγινώσκω, προσκόπτω, ὑψηλός. 3 times—ἀσύνετος, ἐντυγχάνω, νικάω. 5 times—ἀπειθέω, δικαίωμα, κλάδος.

× 24 ἀνταποκρίνομαι, ἀποβολή, ἐγκαλέω, ἐμφανής c, ζέω, λάχανον, λογικός, μήτρα, ὁδηγός, ὀνειδίζω c, ὀξύς c, παιδευτής, ποιητής, συνσχηματίζομαι, τετράπους, ὕπνος, φάσκω, χρηματίζω, ὠφελία. Twice—ἐλαία, μοιχαλίς, φόρος, φυσικός. 4 times—συγγενής.

• 7 ἀναζάω, ἔνδικος, ἱλαστήριον, μόλις, ὀφείλημα, συναντιλαμβάνομαι, κατακαυχάομαι 2.

APPENDIX I

(ii) 1 CORINTHIANS, 266 (incl. reps. 415).

B 1. 7 (incl. reps. 9).
+ 1 ἀρσενοκοίτης.
* 4 ἀθανασία 2, ἱερός, συμβασιλεύω, ὑπεροχή.
× 1 ἐκκαθαίρω.
• 1 ἀλοάω 2 (1 c).

B 2. 22 (incl. reps. 51).
* 20 ἀποστερέω 3, βοῦς 2 (1 c), γαμέω 9, δαιμόνιον 4, δείκνυμι, εἶτα 3, ἐπιτρέπω 2, ἔσχατος 5, μάταιος 2, μιμνήσκομαι, μωρός 4, νομίζω 2, παραγίνομαι, παρατίθημι, τυγχάνω 3, ὑποφέρω, φεύγω 2, φιλέω, χήρα, χρυσίον.
• 2 παραχειμάζω, φιμόω c.

C 1. 98 (incl. reps. 127).
+ 19 ἄκων, ἀνδρίζομαι, ἀπελεύθερος, ἔκτρωμα, ἐνέργημα 2, ἐντροπή 2, θηριομαχέω, ἴαμα 3, κατακαλύπτομαι 3, καταστρώννυμαι, μαρὰν-ἀθά, μωρία 5, παρεδρεύω, πάροδος, περίψημα, συνζητητής, τάγμα, φιλόνεικος, χρηστεύομαι.
* 15 ἀνάξιος, ἄψυχος, διαίρεσις 3, ἐγκρατεύομαι 2, ἐξαίρω c, ἐπιθυμητής, ἐπισπάομαι, ἑρμηνία 2, ἦθος, μέθυσος 2, ὁμιλία, παίζω c, σύμφορος 2, σύμφωνος, συνγνώμη.
× 20 ἄγαμος 4, ἀγενής, ἀντίλημψις, ἀπόδειξις, ἀσχημονέω 2, αὐλός, διόπερ 2, δουλαγωγέω, δράσσομαι c ?, δυσφημέω, ἐκνήφω, ἑορτάζω, καλάμη, καταχράομαι 2, κόμη, λύσις, μήτιγε, πτηνός, πυκτεύω, φρήν 2.
• 44 ἀδάπανος, ἀδήλως, αἴνιγμα, ἀκατακάλυπτος 2, ἀμετακίνητος, ἀναξίως, ἀπερισπάστως, ἀρχιτέκτων, ἀστατέω, ἀσχήμων, ἄτομος, βρόχος, γεώργιον, γυμνιτεύω(?), διερμηνευτής, εἰδώλιον, ἐνκοπή, ἐπιθανάτιος, ἑτερόγλωσσος c, εὐπάρεδρος, εὔσημος, εὐσχημοσύνη, ἠχέω, ἱερόθυτος, κομάω 2, κυβέρνησις, κύμβαλον, λογία 2, λοίδορος 2, μάκελλον, νή, νηπιάζω, ὁλοθρευτής, ὄσφρησις, παραμυθία, πιθός, περικάθαρμα, περπερεύομαι, ῥιπή, συνμερίζομαι, τυπικῶς, ὑπέρακμος, χοϊκός 3, ὡσπερεί.

C 2. 139 (incl. reps. 228).
+ 19 ἀγνωσία, ἀμέριμνος, ἀργύριον, δειπνέω, ἐκπειράζω, κατάκειμαι, κινδυνεύω, κόκκος, κυριακός, μαλακός, περιάγω, πνευματικῶς, συνκεράννυμι, σχολάζω. Twice—βιωτικός, κλάω, ποίμνη. 3 times—ἀγοράζω. 10 times—ἀνακρίνω.
* 78 ἄδηλος, ἀκολουθέω, ἀκρασία, ἀμπελών, ἀπάγω, ἀποφέρω, αὔριον c, δή, διαιρέω, δώδεκα, ἐάω, εἴκοσι, εἰσακούω c, ἔνοχος, ἐπάνω, ἐπιβάλλω, ἐπίκειμαι, ἰχθύς, καίω, κατακαίω, κιθάρα, κτῆνος, λοιδορέω, μηνύω, μοιχός, οὐαί, οὐδέποτε, ὄφελος, παιδίον, πανταχοῦ, παράγω, πάσχα, πεντακόσιοι, πέντε, περιτίθημι, πλεῖστος, ποιμαίνω, πόλεμος, πόμα,

APPENDIX I

προσκυνέω, ῥάβδος, σελήνη, σῖτος, στάδιος, συμβαίνω, συνάγω, συνετός c, τίμιος, τοίνυν, τύπτω, ὑπηρέτης, χαλκός, χιλιάς. Twice—ἀνά, ἀνάμνησις, ἄτιμος, ἄφωνος, γάλα, δεῖπνον, ἐκδέχομαι, θύω, κείρω, μέλει, μυρίος, πορνεύω, πόρνη, συνήθεια. 3 times—ἅρπαξ, ἀστήρ, νῖκος c, ὅλως, σχίσμα. 4 times—φυτεύω. 5 times—εἰδωλόθυτος, μετέχω. 7 times—συνέρχομαι. 8 times—ποτήριον. 11 times—προφητεύω.

× 20 ἀλαλάζω, ἀπολούω, γραμματεύς, ἔννομος, εὐγενής, θάπτω, θέατρον, ἱερόν, μαίνομαι, παροξύνομαι, πεντηκοστή, πωλέω, χόρτος, ψευδομάρτυς. Twice—ἄζυμος, κέντρον, κριτήριον, ξυράομαι, ὁσάκις. 4 times—ψυχικός.

• 22 ἀροτριάω, ἄρρωστος, αὐλέομαι, ἔκβασις, ἐλεεινός, εὐκαιρέω, καταμένω, κιθαρίζω, κορέννυμαι, μολύνω, περιβόλαιον, σαλπίζω, συνεῖδον, συνστέλλω, τήρησις, ὑπωπιάζω. Twice—γαμίζω, γογγύζω, διδακτός, εὐσχήμων. 3 times—ἐξουσιάζω. 4 times—διερμηνεύω.

(iii) 2 CORINTHIANS, 197 (incl. reps. 264).

B 1. 5 (incl. reps. 5).
+ 1 ὀστράκινος.
* 1 αὐτάρκεια.
• 3 ἀποτόμως, ναυαγέω, στρατεία.

B 2. 15 (incl. reps. 20).
+ 1 ἀνάγνωσις.
* 9 ἀρκέω, ἀφίστημι, βαρέομαι 2, διαφθείρω, ἐπαίρω 2, ἕτοιμος 3. βασιλεύς. ἀεί 2, ἔξωθεν.
× 5 δάκρυ, μάχη, ὁμολογία, πλάνος, συναποθνήσκω.

C 1. 92 (incl. reps. 128).
+ 11 ἁγνότης 2, ἀγρυπνία 2, βυθός, δόλιος, εἰσδέχομαι c, καταβαρέω, κατάκρισις 2, πέρυσι 2, πτωχεύω, στενοχωρέομαι 3, ψιθυρισμός.
* 9 ἀνεκδιήγητος, ἁρμόζομαι, ἐπακούω c, ἡνίκα 2, ἱλαρός c, πανοῦργος, πένης c, προαιρέομαι, σπουδαῖος 3.
× 17 ἄμετρος 2, ἄρρητος, αὐθαίρετος 2, ἐκδαπανάομαι, ἐκφοβέω, ἐπιτιμία, ἥδιστα 2, παραυτίκα, παραφρονέω, προαμαρτάνω 2, προσαναπληρόω 2, συλάω, συνκατάθεσις, συνπέμπω 2, φωτισμός 2, ψευδαπόστολος, πεντάκις [πεντακισχίλιοι Jus.].
• 55 ἀβαρής, ἀγανάκτησις, ἁδρότης, ἀνακαλύπτω 2, ἀπαρασκεύαστος, ἀπεῖπον, ἀπόκριμα, αὐγάζω, δίψος, δολόω, δότης c, δυσφημία, ἐθνάρχης, ἐκδημέω 3, ἐλαττονέω c, ἐλαφρία, ἐνδημέω 3, ἐνκρίνω, ἐνπεριπατέω c, ἐντυπόω, ἐξαπορέομαι 2, ἐπενδύομαι 2, ἐπιπόθησις 2, ἐπισκηνόω, ἑτεροζυγέω, εὐφημία, ἐφικνέομαι 2, ἱκανότης, καθαίρεσις 3, κάλυμ-

μα 4, καπηλεύω, καταναρκάω 3, κατάρτισις, κατοπτρίζομαι, μετοχή, μολυσμός, μωμάομαι 2, νυχθήμερον, ὀχύρωμα, προενάρχομαι 2, προκαταρτίζω, προσκοπή, σαργάνη, σκῆνος 2, σκόλοψ, συμφώνησις, συναποστέλλω, συνυπουργέω, συστατικός, ὑπερβαλλόντως, ὑπερέκεινα, ὑπερεκτείνω, ὑπερλίαν 2, φειδομένως, φυσίωσις.

C 2. 85 (incl. reps. 111).

+ 14 ἐκδύω, ἐλαφρός, ἐπιεικία, θαῦμα, καταλαλία, λιθάζω, μέριμνα, παρεκτός, συνοχή, χορηγέω. Twice—ἀτενίζω, καλύπτω, πλάξ. 4 times—προθυμία.

* 49 ἀποτάσσομαι, ἀριστερός, ἀρχαῖος, βαρύς, βοηθέω c, γένημα, δαπανάω, ἐξίστημι, ἔσωθεν, ἡδέως, θυγάτηρ c, καθαιρέω, λῃστής, λίθινος, μέλας, μετανοέω, μετρέω, ὀπτασία, πάλαι, παντοκράτωρ, παράδεισος, παρέρχομαι, πληθύνω, ποταμός, προέρχομαι, πρόκειμαι, πρόσκαιρος, σπόρος, τεῖχος, τεσσαράκοντα, τηλικοῦτος, ὕβρις, ὑψόω, χειροτονέω, χρίω, χωρέω. Twice—βουλεύομαι, ἐγγράφομαι, λάμπω, μήτι, μίκρον, νηστεία, πλατύνω, πληγή, ὑπόστασις, φυλακή. 3 times—ἀφροσύνη, τρίς. 5 times—θαρρέω.

× 14 ἐπίστασις, ἐρημία, ἑτοίμως, ἡττάομαι, θυρίς, καταβάλλω, μεταμέλομαι, ὀδυρμός, οἰκητήριον, περιαιρέω, πιάζω, σκορπίζω c, τυφλόω, χαλάω.

• 8 ἁγιότης, ἔσοπτρον, ὁδοιπορία, ῥαβδίζω, συνέκδημος, ψύχος. Twice—περίσσευμα, πτωχεία.

(iv) GALATIANS, 85 (incl. reps. 100).

B 1. 0.

B 2. 5 (incl. reps. 6).

+ 1 ὑπόκρισις.
* 3 βιβλίον c, ζυγός, στύλος.
• 1 μεσίτης 2.

C 1. (incl. reps. 35).

+ 5 βασκαίνω, ἰουδαΐζω, ἰουδαϊσμός 2, κενόδοξος, μυκτηρίζομαι.
* 6 δάκνω, εἴκω, ἐπικατάρατος 2 c, ἱστορέω, πεισμονή, φθονέω.
× 4 ἀλληγορέω, μορφόομαι, πατρικός, προκαλέομαι.
• 17 ἐθνικῶς, ἐκπτύω, ἐπιδιατάσσομαι, εὐπροσωπέω, ἰουδαϊκῶς, κατασκοπέω, ὀρθοποδέω, παρείσακτος, προευαγγελίζομαι, προθεσμία, προκυρόομαι, προσανατίθεμαι 2, στίγμα, συνηλικιώτης, συνστοιχέω, συνυποκρίνομαι, φρεναπατάω.

C 2. 48 (incl. reps. 59).

+ 1 ἐκλύομαι.
* 31 ἀνατίθεμαι, ἄνωθεν, ἀποκόπτω, ἆρα, βοάω c, διαμένω, ἐγκράτεια,

APPENDIX I

ἐκβάλλω c, ἐμμένω c, ἐνιαυτός, ἐξαιρέω, ἐπίτροπος, εὐθέως, καταγινώσκω, κρεμάννυμι c, μετατίθημι, μήν c, ὅμοιος, προστίθημι, ῥήγνυμι c, στεῖρος c, τίκτω c, τριάκοντα, ὑποστρέφω, φαρμακία, φορτίον. Twice—ἐξαποστέλλω, ταράσσω, ὠδίνω. 3 times—κατάρα. 5 times—παιδίσκη.

× 8 ἀναστατόω, δεκαπέντε, ἐνευλογέομαι c, μεταστρέφω, συνπαραλαμβάνω, τετρακόσιοι, ὑποστέλλω. Twice—ἀνέρχομαι.

• 8 ἀκυρόω, ἐξορύσσω, ἴδε, παρατηρέω, πηλίκος, προεῖδον, τεκνίον. Twice—πορθέω.

(v) EPHESIANS 93 (incl. reps. 106).

B 1. 1.
× 1 λουτρόν.

B 2. 8 (incl. reps. 10).
✱ 5 ἀναλαμβάνω 2, ἀπατάω, διάβολος (subs.) 2, παιδεία c, τιμάω c.
× 1 ἀσωτία.
• 2 ἅλυσις, εὐαγγελιστής.

C 1. 40 (incl. reps. 45).
+ 5 ἀνανεόομαι, ἑτοιμασία, εὔνοια, κληρόομαι, συνοικοδομέω.
✱ 5 ἄθεος, ἄσοφος, ἐκτρέφω 2, ἑνότης 2, μέγεθος.
× 4 βέλος, κατώτερος, πάλη, συνμέτοχος 2.
• 26 αἰσχρότης, ἄνοιξις, ἀπαλγέομαι, ἐλαχιστότερος, ἐξισχύω, ἐπιδύω, ἐπιφαύσκω, εὐτραπελία, θυρεός, καταρτισμός, κλυδωνίζομαι, κοσμοκράτωρ, κρυφῇ, κυβία, μακροχρόνιος c, μεθοδία 2, μεσότοιχον, μωρολογία, παροργισμός, πολυποίκιλος, προελπίζω, προσκαρτέρησις, ῥυτίς, συναρμολογέω 2, συνπολίτης, σύνσωμος.

C 2. 44 (incl. reps. 50).
+ 11 ἀπειλή, κατοικητήριον, μῆκος, ὁσιότης, πάροικος, σαπρός, σκοτόομαι, σπίλος, φραγμός, χαριτόω. Twice—πανοπλία.
✱ 26 ἄγνοια, ἀγρυπνέω, αἰχμαλωσία c, ἀκρογωνιαῖος, ἄνεμος, δῶρον, ἐκπορεύομαι, ἐπέρχομαι, ἐργασία, εὖ c, εὔσπλαγχνος, ἡλικία, καταβολή, κραυγή, ὀργίζομαι c, ὀσφύς, περιζώννυμαι, πλάτος, ποιμήν, πολιτεία, σωτήριον, ὕδωρ, φρόνησις. Twice—μακράν, ὕψος. 3 times—ἀμφότεροι.
× 4 ἀνίημι, πατριά, χειροποίητος. Twice—ὑπεράνω.
• 3 προσκολλάομαι c, συνκαθίζω, ὑποδέομαι.

(vi) PHILIPPIANS 76 (incl. reps. 81).

B 1. 4 (incl. reps. 6).
✱ 2 κέρδος 2, σεμνός.
• 2 προκοπή 2, σπένδομαι.

APPENDIX I

B 2. 5 (incl. reps. 5).
+ 1 ἐπίσκοπος.
* 2 ἐπιεικής, ὀπίσω.
× 2 ἐπέχω, σπουδαίως [-οτέρως].

C 1. 37 (incl. reps. 38).
+ 10 ἀγνῶς, ἀκαιρέομαι, ἀναθάλλω, ἐπιπόθητος, εὐψυχέω, λῆμψις, μεγάλως, παραπλήσιον, συναθλέω 2, ὑπερυψόω.
* 4 αἴσθησις, κενοδοξία, προσφιλής, σκοπός.
× 5 ἄλυπος, αὐτάρκης, ἑτέρως, μυέομαι, πολίτευμα.
• 18 ἀπουσία, ἁρπαγμός, γνησίως, ἐξανάστασις, ἐπεκτείνομαι, εὔφημος, ἰσόψυχος, κατατομή, καταχθόνιος, ὀκταήμερος, παραβολεύομαι, παραμύθιον, πτύρομαι, σκύβαλον, συμμορφίζομαι, σύνζυγος, συνμιμητής, σύνψυχος.

C 2. 30 (incl. reps. 32).
+ 5 αἴτημα, ἐξαυτῆς, τελειόω, ὑστέρησις, χορτάζω.
* 18 ἀρετή, ἀσφαλής, βίβλος, γογγυσμός, διαστρέφω, εἰλικρινής, ἔντιμος, ἐπιλανθάνομαι, ἴσος, καίπερ, κύων, οἶμαι, πολιτεύομαι, σκολιός, συνλαμβάνω, ταπείνωσις. Twice—ζημία, μορφή.
× 3 ἀναλύω, ἀποβαίνω, φωστήρ.
• 4 ἀδημονέω, ἀφοράω, βεβαίωσις, πραιτώριον.

(vii) COLOSSIANS 58 (incl. reps. 60).
B 1. 0.
B 2. 3 (incl. reps. 3).
+ 1 πλουσίως.
* 1 κρύπτω.
× 1 ἀπόκειμαι.

C 1. 33 (incl. reps. 34).
+ 2 αἰσχρολογία, προσηλόω.
* 6 ἀνταπόδοσις, δογματίζομαι, θεότης, νεομηνία, ὁρατός, στερέωμα.
× 5 ἀθυμέω, εὐχάριστος, πλησμονή, συλαγωγέω, φιλοσοφία.
• 20 ἀνέψιος, ἀνταναπληρόω, ἀπεκδύομαι 2, ἀπέκδυσις, ἀπόχρησις, ἀρεσκία, ἀφειδία, βραβεύω, ἐθελοθρησκία, εἰρηνοποιέω, ἐμβατεύω, καταβραβεύω, μετακινέω, μομφή, παρηγορία, πιθανολογία, προακούω, πρωτεύω, σωματικῶς, χειρόγραφον.

C 2. 22 (incl. reps. 23).
+ 6 γεύομαι, δυναμόω, παραλογίζομαι, πικραίνω, τελειότης. Twice—σύνδουλος.
* 10 ἀποκρίνομαι, ἀπόκρυφος, ἔνταλμα, ἐξαλείφω, ἑορτή, θρησκεία, θρόνος, ἰατρός, κλῆρος, πόνος.

APPENDIX I

× 2 σκιά, ὑπεναντίος.
• 4 ἅλας, ἀρτύω, δειγματίζω, θιγγάνω.

(viii) 1 THESSALONIANS 41 (incl. reps. 47).
B 1. 1.
× 1 ἤπιος.
B 2. 7 (incl. reps. 8).
+ 2 νήφω 2, παραγγελία.
✱ 4 ἀντέχομαι, γαστήρ, ἐναντίος, ἐφίστημι.
× 1 διαμαρτύρομαι.
C 1. 20 (incl. reps. 23).
+ 1 ὁλοτελής.
✱ 5 ἀμέμπτως 3, ἀναμένω, ἄτακτος, θεοδίδακτος, ὁσίως.
× 4 ἐκδιώκω, ὀλιγόψυχος, περιλείπομαι 2, τρόφος.
• 10 ἀπορφανίζω, ἐνορκίζω, ἐξηχέομαι, κέλευσμα, κολακία, ὀμείρομαι, προπάσχω, σαίνομαι, συμφυλέτης, ὑπερβαίνω.
C 2. 13 (incl. reps. 15).
+ 1 ἀσφάλεια.
✱ 9 αἰφνίδιος, ἀληθινός, ἀληθῶς, ἡσυχάζω, κτάομαι, ὁλόκληρος, τοιγαροῦν, ὠδίν, εἴσοδος 2.
• 3 ἀπάντησις, ἀρχάγγελος, παραμυθέομαι 2.

(ix) 2 THESSALONIANS 26 (incl. reps. 31).
B 1. 1.
✱ 1 ἐπιφάνεια.
B 2. 4 (incl. reps. 6).
✱ 4 ἀξιόω, ἡσυχία, κρίσις, μήτε 3.
C 1. 10 (incl. reps. 12).
+ 4 ἀτάκτως 2, ἐνκαυχάομαι, περιεργάζομαι, σημειόομαι.
✱ 1 τίνω.
• 5 ἀτακτέω, ἔνδειγμα, ἐνδοξάζομαι 2, καλοποιέω, ὑπεραυξάνω.
C 2. 11 (incl. reps. 12).
✱ 7 ἀναιρέω, ἄτοπος, δίκη, καταξιόομαι, μιμέομαι 2, σαλεύω, φλόξ.
× 2 ἀποστασία, σέβασμα.
• 2 ἐπισυναγωγή, θροέομαι.

(x) PHILEMON 10 (incl. reps. 10).
B 1. 1.
+ 1 εὔχρηστος.
B 2. 1.
✱ 1 πρεσβύτης.

148 APPENDIX I

C 1. 5 (incl. reps. 5).
+ 1 ἑκούσιος (Mar. 1).
* 2 ἄχρηστος, ὀνίναμαι.
• 2 ἀποτίνω, προσοφείλω.

C 2. 3 (incl. reps. 3).
* 2 ἀναπέμπω, ἐπιτάσσω.
× 1 ξενία.

D.

A 2. 131 *Non-Pauline words shared by the Pastorals with the individual books of the N. T.*
(Words underlined, and numbers bracketed, in one N. T. book only.)

(i) = 1 Tim. only.   (iv) = 1 and 2 Tim.
(ii) = 2 Tim. only.   (v) = 1 Tim. and Titus.
(iii) = Titus only.   (vi) = 2 Tim. and Titus.
(vii) = 1 and 2 Tim. and Titus.

(1) Matthew. (i) ἀμελέω, διπλόος, εἰσφέρω, ἐμπίπτω, ἐξήκοντα, ἐπιλαμβάνομαι, ἐπιτίθημι, θνῄσκω, μαργαρίτης, νίπτω, προάγω, προσέρχομαι, προσμένω, ὑβρίζω, ὕστερος: (ii) γεωργός, ἐπιτιμάω, κριτής, λίαν, μήποτε, στρατιώτης, χαλεπός, χειμών: (iii) νομικός (subs.), παλιγγενεσία, ὑγιής: (iv) χείρων: (v) ἀργός, κοσμέω, πρεσβύτερος, προσέχω: (vi) αἰτία, ποικίλος: (vii) ἀρνέομαι.   34 (3)

(2) Mark. (i) ἀποπλανάω, ἐκφέρω, ἐξήκοντα, [ἐπακολουθέω], ἐπιλαμβάνομαι, ἐπίσταμαι, ἐπιτίθημι, θνῄσκω, νεότης, νίπτω, παραδέχομαι, πολυτελής, προάγω, προσέρχομαι, προσμένω, πυκνός(?): (ii) γεωργός, ἐπιτιμάω, εὐκαίρως, λίαν, μήποτε, στρατιώτης, χειμών: (iii) θηρίον, ὑγιής: (iv) βίος, [παρακολουθέω], χείρων: (v) πρεσβύτερος, μαρτυρία: (vi) αἰτία, ποικίλος: (vii) ἀρνέομαι, παραιτέομαι.   3[4]/32 (2)

(3) Luke (not Acts). (i) βυθίζω, ἐμπίπτω, ἐξήκοντα, ἐπιμελέομαι, σωματικός: (ii) ἄνοια, ἀχάριστος, γεωργός, ἐπιτιμάω, ζωγρέω, κακοῦργος, λίαν, φιλάργυρος: (iii) ἡδονή, λείπω, λυτρόομαι, νομικός (subs.): (iv) βίος, παρακολουθέω [+? Mark], χείρων: (v) κοσμέω: (vi) ποικίλος, ὑπομιμνῄσκω, (vii) ὑγιαίνω.   24 (9)+ 32 (8) Luke and Acts = 56 (17)

(4) John. (i) ἐπιτίθημι, θνῄσκω, ἱματισμός, νίπτω, προσέρχομαι: (ii) γεωργός, μάχομαι, μέντοι, μήποτε, νομή, στρατιώτης, χειμών: (iii) μιαίνω, ὑγιής: (iv) χείρων: (v) κατηγορία, μαρτυρία, νεώτερος, πρεσβύτερος (?): (vi) αἰτία, ἀνατρέπω (?), περιΐστημι, ὑπομιμνῄσκω: (vii) ἀρνέομαι, ζήτησις.

25 (3)

APPENDIX I 149

(5) Acts (not Luke). (i) ἀγαθοεργέω, ἐπίσταμαι, εὐεργεσία, εὐσεβέω, μελετάω, παραδέχομαι, περίεργος, περιέρχομαι, προσμένω, σωφροσύνη: (ii) ἀργύρεος, δρόμος, ἐξαρτίζω, μάχομαι, μεταλαμβάνω, προπετής, χειμών: (iii) θηρίον, νοσφίζομαι, πειθαρχέω, ὑγιής, φιλανθρωπία: (iv) βλάσφημος, ἐπίθεσις: (v) ὅσιος: (vi) περιΐστημι: (vii) εὐσέβεια, ζήτησις.
28 (12) + 32 (8) Luke and Acts = 60 (20)

(6) Luke and Acts. (i) ἀντιλαμβάνομαι, δυνάστης, εἰσφέρω, ἐκφέρω, ἐπισκοπή, ζωογονέω, ἐπιτίθημι, θνήσκω, ἱματισμός, νεότης, ἐπιλαμβάνομαι, νομοδιδάσκαλος, περιποιέομαι, πρεσβυτέριον, προάγω, προσέρχομαι, πυκνός, ὑβρίζω: (ii) βρέφος, κριτής, μήποτε, προδότης, στρατιώτης: (iii) ἐπιφαίνω: (v) μαρτυρία, νεώτερος, πρεσβύτερος, προσέχω: (vi) αἰτία: (vii) ἀρνέομαι, δεσπότης, παραιτέομαι.   32 (8) + 24 (9) Luke + 28 (12) Acts = 84 (29)

(7) Hebrews. (i) ἀμελέω, ἀπόλαυσις, ἀφιλάργυρος, γυμνάζω, εἰσφέρω, ἐκφέρω, ἐμπίπτω, ἐπιλαμβάνομαι, ἐπίσταμαι, ὀρέγομαι, παραδέχομαι, περιέρχομαι, προάγω, πρόδηλος, προσέρχομαι: (ii) κριτής, λέων, μεταλαμβάνω, μήποτε, στερεός, στεφανόω, χρύσεος: (iii) ἀνωφελής, θηρίον, κοσμικός, μιαίνω: (iv) βέβηλος, ἐκτρέπομαι, ἐπίθεσις, χείρων: (v) ἀνυπότακτος, ὅσιος, πρεσβύτερος, προσέχω: (vi) αἰτία, ἀπολείπω, ποικίλος: (vii) ἀρνέομαι, παραιτέομαι.   39 (10)

(8) 1 Peter. (i) ἄσπιλος, ἐπακολουθέω [+ ? Mark], ἐπισκοπή, ἡσύχιος, λοιδορία, πολυτελής, προσέρχομαι: (ii) βρέφος, λέων, στερεός: (iii) λυτρόομαι: (v) κοσμέω, νεώτερος, πρεσβύτερος, φιλόξενος: (vi) ποικίλος: (vii) δεσπότης.   17 (4)

(9) 2 Peter. (i) ἄσπιλος, βραδύνω, γυμνάζω: (ii) ἐμπλέκω, σοφίζω, ὑπόμνησις: (iii) αὐθάδης, ἡδονή: (iv) βλάσφημος, κῆρυξ, χείρων: (v) ἀργός, προσέχω: (vi) ὑπομιμνήσκω: (vii) ἀρνέομαι, δεσπότης, εὐσέβεια, μῦθος. [+? καταστροφή, καταφθείρομαι].   18 (7)

(10) James. (i) ἄσπιλος, ἐπίσταμαι, κτίσμα, σπαταλάω: (ii) γεωργός, κακοπαθέω, κριτής, μάχομαι, μέντοι: (iii) ἡδονή, θηρίον, λείπω: (v) ἀργός, πρεσβύτερος: (vi) ποικίλος.   15 (2)

(11) 1, 2, 3 John. (i) προάγω: (ii) λίαν: (iv) βίος: (v) μαρτυρία, πρεσβύτερος: (vi) ὑπομιμνήσκω: (vii) ἀρνέομαι, ὑγιαίνω.   8

(12) Jude. (i) ἐπίσταμαι: (ii) ἐπιτιμάω, μέντοι: (iii) μιαίνω: (vi) ἀπολείπω, ὑπομιμνήσκω: (vii) ἀρνέομαι, δεσπότης.   8

(13) Revelation. (i) διπλόος, ἑξήκοντα, ἐπιτίθημι, κτίσμα, μαργαρίτης: (ii) ἀργύρεος, λέων, ξύλινος, χρύσεος: (iii) θηρίον: (v) κοσμέω, μαρτυρία, ὅσιος, πρεσβύτερος: (vii) ἀρνέομαι, δεσπότης.   16 (1)

E.

(A 1) *Hapax Legomena and* (A 2) *other Non-Pauline words shared by the Pastorals with Apostolic Fathers and Apologists.* 211.

(1) 1 Clem.: A 1. 21. (i) ἁγνεία, ἀπέραντος, ἔντευξις, πρόσκλισις: (ii) ἀγωγή, ἀθλέω, ἀναζωπυρέω, ἀνάλυσις, ἀπαίδευτος, ἐνδύνω, καταστροφή, πιστόομαι: (iii) βδελυκτός, περιούσιον, στυγητός, σωτήριος: (iv) ἀνόσιος: (v) σεμνότης, σώφρων: (vi) εὐσεβῶς: (vii) ὠφέλιμος.

A 2. 42. (i) ἀπόλαυσις, βυθίζω, ἐκφέρω, ἐμπίπτω, ἐπακολουθέω, ἐπισκοπή, ἐπίσταμαι, εὐεργεσία, ἡσύχιος, νεότης, παραδέχομαι, περιποιέομαι, πρόδηλος, προσέρχομαι, σωφροσύνη: (ii) δρόμος, κριτής, λέων, λίαν, μεταλαμβάνω, μήποτε, νομή, προπετής: (iii) αὐθάδης, ἐπιφαίνω, θηρίον, λυτρόομαι, παλιγγενεσία: (iv) βίος, κῆρυξ: (v) ἀργός, κοσμέω, μαρτυρία, ὅσιος, πρεσβύτερος, προυέχω, φιλόξενος: (vi) αἰτία, ἀπολείπω, ὑπομιμνήσκω: (vii) δεσπότης, εὐσέβεια. 63

(2) 2 Clem.: A 1. 7. (i) ἔντευξις, θεοσέβεια, φιλαργυρία: (ii) ἀθλέω, βέλτιον: (iii) ἐγκρατής: (iv) ἀστοχέω.

A 2. 21. (i) ἀπόλαυσις, ἄσπιλος, γυμνάζω, παραδέχομαι, προσέρχομαι: (ii) ἄνοια, κακοπαθέω, κριτής, μεταλαμβάνω, στεφανόω: (iii) ἡδονή, κοσμικός, λυτρόομαι: (iv) βίος: (v) ὅσιος, πρεσβύτερος, προσέχω: (vi) αἰτία: (vii) ἀρνέομαι, εὐσέβεια, μῦθος. 28

(3) Ignatius: A 1. 13. (i) ἁγνεία, ἑτεροδιδασκαλέω, πραϋπάθεια, [πρεσβυτέριον = Christian Presbytery]: (ii) ἀναζωπυρέω, ἀνανήφω, ἀναψύχω, ἐνδύνω, νεωτερικός, χρήσιμος: (iii) ἀψευδής, κατάστημα, φροντίζω: (v) διάγω.

A 2. 26. (i) ἀμελέω, ἐμπίπτω, ἐπακολουθέω, ἐπισκοπή, μαργαρίτης, μελετάω, παραδέχομαι, πρεσβυτέριον, προάγω, σωφροσύνη: (ii) δρόμος, λίαν, μήποτε, σοφίζω: (iii) ἀνωφελής, ἡδονή, θηρίον, λείπω, λυτρόομαι: (iv) βίος, ἐκτρέπω, χείρων: (v) κοσμέω, πρεσβύτερος, προσέχω: (vii) ἀρνέομαι. 39

(4) Polycarp: A 1. 6. (i) ἁγνεία, δίλογος, ματαιολογία, φιλαργυρία: (iii) ἐγκρατής: (vii) διάβολος (adj.).

A 2. 14. (i) ἀμελέω, ἀποπλανάω, ἀφιλάργυρος, εἰσφέρω, ἐκφέρω, ἐπακολουθέω, λοιδορία, προάγω: (ii) κριτής, χαλεπός: (iii) πειθαρχέω: (v) νεώτερος, πρεσβύτερος: (vi) ἀπολείπω. 20

(5) Martyrdom of Polycarp: A 1. 4. (i) ἀνεπίλημπτος: (ii) δειλία, μηδέποτε: (iii) ἀψευδής.

A 2. 18. (i) ἀντιλαμβάνομαι, βραδύνω, πολυτελής, προάγω, προσέρχομαι: (ii) λέων, στεφανόω, χαλεπός: (iii) θηρίον, κοσμικός: (iv) βίος, κῆρυξ, χείρων: (v) κοσμέω, μαρτυρία, προσέχω: (vi) ποικίλος: (vii) ἀρνέομαι. 22

APPENDIX I

(6) Didache: A 1. 3. (i) διώκτης: (iii) ὀργίλος: (iv) ἀστοχέω.

A 2. 18. (i) ἀπόλαυσις, ἀφιλάργυρος, εἰσφέρω, ἡσύχιος, ἱματισμός, νεότης, προσέρχομαι, σωματικός: (ii) κριτής, λίαν, μάχομαι, φιλάργυρος, μήποτε: (iii) αὐθάδης, κοσμικός, λυτρόομαι: (v) ἀργός, προσέχω: (vii) δεσπότης.   21

(7) Barnabas: A 1. 4. (i) διώκτης: (ii) ἐνδύνω, ἐπισωρεύω, μηδέποτε.

A 2. 24. (i) ἐπίσταμαι, ἐπιτίθημι, ἡσύχιος, ἱματισμός, μελετάω, νεότης, πολυτελής, σπαταλάω: (ii) κριτής, μάχομαι, μήποτε, νομή, σοφίζω, στερεός, στεφανόω: (iii) θηρίον, λυτρόομαι: (v) ἀργός, μαρτυρία, νεώτερος, πρεσβύτερος, προσέχω: (vi) ὑπομιμνήσκω: (vii) δεσπότης.   28

(8) Hermas: A 1. 21. (i) ἁγνεία, ἄλλως, βλαβερός, ἔλαττον (adv.), ἔντευξις, ὑπερπλεονάζω: (ii) βέλτιον, δειλία, ἐνδύνω, καταφθείρομαι, μηδέποτε, πραγματεία, χαλκεύς, χρήσιμος: (iii) ἐγκρατής, ἐκστρέφω, πρεσβῦτις, φιλότεκνος: (iv) παρακαταθήκη: (v) σεμνότης: (vii) ὠφέλιμος.

A 2. 54. (i) ἀντιλαμβάνομαι, ἀποπλανάω, ἄσπιλος, βραδύνω, δίπλοος, εἰσφέρω, ἐμπίπτω, ἐπιλαμβάνομαι, ἐπίσταμαι, ἐπιτίθημι, ἡσύχιος, θνήσκω, ἱματισμός, κτίσμα, παραδέχομαι, περίεργος, περιποιέομαι, πολυτελής, προσέρχομαι, σπαταλάω: (ii) βρέφος, ἐμπλέκομαι, κριτής, λίαν, μεταλαμβάνω, μέντοι, μήποτε, προδότης, στεφανόω, ὑπόμνησις, χαλεπός, χειμών, χρύσεος: (iii) ἀνωφελής, αὐθάδης, ἡδονή, θηρίον, λείπω, λυτρόομαι, μιαίνω, νοσφίζομαι, ὑγιής: (iv) βλάσφημος, χείρων: (v) ἀργός, κοσμέω, μαρτυρία, νεώτερος, πρεσβύτερος, φιλόξενος: (vi) αἰτία, ποικίλος: (vii) ἀρνέομαι, δεσπότης.   75

(9) Ep. ad Diognetum: A 1. 7. (i) ἀπόδεκτος, θεοσέβεια, ὁμολογουμένως, τεκνογονέω: (ii) γόης, χαλκεύς: (iii) σωτήριος.

A 2. 20. (i) ἀμελέω, ἐπίσταμαι, εὐεργεσία, κτίσμα, παραδέχομαι: (ii) ἀργύρεος, δρόμος, μεταλαμβάνω, χρύσεος: (iii) ἡδονή, θηρίον, πειθαρχέω, φιλανθρωπία: (iv) βίος: (v) κοσμέω: (vi) αἰτία, ποικίλος: (vii) ἀρνέομαι, δεσπότης, παραιτέομαι.   27

(10) Papias: A 1. 1. (v) διαβεβαιόομαι.

A 2. 3. (ii) μέντοι: (iv) παρακολουθέω: (v) πρεσβύτερος.   4

(12) Aristeides: A 1. 1. (iii) ὀργίλος.

A 2. 6. (ii) ἄνοια, χειμών: (iii) ἀνωφελής, μιαίνω: (iv) χείρων: (vi) μῦθος.   7

(13) Tatian: A 1. 19. (i) ἄλλως, ἀμοιβή, ἀπρόσιτος, θεοσέβεια, μονόομαι, νοσέω, ὕστερος, φιλαργυρία, ψευδολόγος: (ii) ἀθλέω, ἀκρατής, γόης, πραγματεία, χρήσιμος: (iii) πρεσβῦτις: (v) πλήκτης, σεμνότης, σώφρων: (vii) ὠφέλιμος.

A 2. 42. (i) ἀπόλαυσις, ἐκφέρω, ἐπιτίθημι, εὐεργεσία, ζωογονέω, θνήσκω, λοιδορία, μελετάω, ὀρέγομαι, προάγω, προσέρχομαι: (ii) ἀχάριστος, βρέφος, δρόμος, ζωγρέω, κριτής, λέων, λίαν, μεταλαμβάνω, στεφανόω, φιλάργυρος, χαλεπός, χειμών, χρύσεος: (iii) ἡδονή, κοσμικός: (iv) βέβηλος, βίος, κήρυξ, παρακολουθέω: (v) μαρτυρία, νεώτερος, ὅσιος, πρεσβύτερος, προσέχω: (vi) αἰτία, ποικίλος: (vii) ἀρνέομαι, δεσπότης, ζήτησις, μῦθος, παραιτέομαι.   61

(14) Justin: A 1. 40. (i) ἄλλως, ἀμοιβή, ἀνδροφόνος, ἀπέραντος, ἀπόδεκτος, ἀποδοχή, διατροφή, ἔντευξις, ἐπίορκος, θεοσέβεια, καταλέγομαι, κόσμιος, μετάλημψις, ῥητῶς, ψευδολόγος: (ii) ἀκρατής, ἀνεξίκακος, ἀποτρέπομαι, βέλτιον, ἐνδύνω, καταφθείρω, μηδέποτε, φίλαυτος, φιλήδονος, φιλόθεος, χρήσιμος: (iii) ἐκστρέφομαι, ἰουδαϊκός, σωτήριος, σωφρονίζω, σωφρόνως, φροντίζω: (iv) ἀνόσιος, πρόγονοι, τυφόομαι: (v) διαβεβαιόομαι, διάγω, σώφρων: (vi) ἀνατρέπω: (vii) ὠφέλιμος.

A 2. 76. (i) ἀμελέω, ἀντιλαμβάνομαι, ἀποπλανάω, ἄσπιλος, διπλόος, δυνάστης, εἰσφέρω, ἐκφέρω, ἐμπίπτω, ἐπακολουθέω, ἐπιλαμβάνομαι, ἐπιτίθημι, ἐπιμέλομαι, ἐπισκοπή, ἐπίσταμαι, εὐσεβέω, θνήσκω, ἱματισμός, κτίσμα, μελετάω, νεότης, ὀρέγομαι, παραδέχομαι, περίεργος, προάγω, προσέρχομαι, προσμένω, σωφροσύνη: (ii) ἄνοια, ἀχάριστος, γεωργός, ἐπιτιμάω, κακοῦργος, κριτής, λέων, μάχομαι, μεταλαμβάνω, μέντοι, μήποτε, ξύλινος, σοφίζομαι, στερεός, στρατιώτης, χαλεπός, χρύσεος: (iii) ἀνωφελής, ἡδονή, θηρίον, λείπω, λυτρόομαι, μιαίνω, πειθαρχέω, ὑγιής, φιλανθρωπία: (iv) βίος, βλάσφημος, ἐκτρέπομαι, κήρυξ, παρακολουθέω, χείρων: (v) κατηγορία, κοσμέω, μαρτυρία, νεώτερος, ὅσιος, πρεσβύτερος, προσέχω: (vi) αἰτία, ἀπολείπω, ποικίλος: (vii) ἀρνέομαι, δεσπότης, εὐσέβεια, ζήτησις, μῦθος, παραιτέομαι.   116

(15) Athenagoras: A 1. 22. (i) αἰδώς, ἄλλως, ἀνδροφόνος, ἀνεπίλημπτος, ἀπρόσιτος, ἔκγονος, ἐντρέφομαι, ἤρεμος, θεοσέβεια, καταλέγομαι, νοσέω, ὑπόνοια: (ii) ἀνεξίκακος, ἀνήμερος, πιστόομαι, πραγματεία, φιλόθεος: (iii) ἀψευδής: (iv) ἀνόσιος, πρόγονοι: (v) διάγω: (vi) σώφρων.

A 2. 37. (i) ἀμελέω, ἐμπίπτω, ἐπιμέλομαι, εὐεργεσία, ἡσύχιος, θνήσκω, λοιδορία, παραδέχομαι, περίεργος, προάγω, προσέρχομαι: (ii) γεωργός, λέων, μέντοι, ξύλινος, στεφανόω, χαλεπός: (iii) ἡδονή, θηρίον, κοσμικός, φιλανθρωπία: (iv) βίος, παρακολουθέω, χείρων: (v) κατηγορία, κοσμέω, νεώτεροι, ὅσιος, πρεσβύτερος, προσέχω: (vi) αἰτία, ὑπομιμνήσκω: (vii) δεσπότης, εὐσέβεια, μῦθος, παραιτέομαι.   59

(16) Melito: A 1. 2. (i) ἐπιπλήσσω: (iv) πρόγονοι.

A 2. 3. (i) ἐμπίπτω, ἐπίσταμαι: (vii) ζήτησις.   5

(17) Dionysius Cor.: A 1. (ii) ἀναψύχω: (v) διάγω.   2

APPENDIX I

F.

132 *Words found in more than one Pauline Epistle, but not in the Apostolic Fathers.*

Only nine of these occur in the Pastorals (B 1. 3, B 2. 6).

• 73 of these are wanting also in the Apologists, and of these only one ἀνυπόκριτος (Rom., 2 Cor., 1 and 2 Tim.) occurs in the Pastorals.

The number after each word indicates the number of Pauline epistles in which it occurs. Where no number is given, the word is in two Paulines only.

(1) Rom. 68 (• 38).

B 1. 2. (i) προνοέω : (ii) ἐνοικέω 3.

B 2. 3. (i) παράκλησις 7 : (ii) ἀπολογία 3 : (iv) • (ἀνυπόκριτος .

C 1. 28 (• 19) ἁγιωσύνη 3, διαστολή, ἔκδικος, κρέας, παραζηλόω, παρεισέρχομαι, τάχα, ποίημα, φθόγγος, • (ἀποκαραδοκία, δοκιμή, δυνατέω, ἐλλογάω, ἔνδειξις 3, εὐσχημόνως 3, ἥττημα, καταλλαγή, καταλλάσσω 3, προεπαγγέλλομαι, προσαγωγή, σύμμορφος, συναιχμάλωτος 3, συνθάπτομαι, υἱοθεσία 3, ὑπερπερισσεύω, ὕψωμα, φιλοτιμέομαι 3, φύραμα 3).

C 2. 35 (• 18) ἐκπίπτω, κράζω, μωραίνω, νεκρόω, πόσις, συνκλείω, φράσσω, κάθο, ἀνταποδίδωμι 3, ἀποστολή 3, ἀφορίζω 3, ἐνκόπτω 3, θησαυρίζω 3, ἀπολύτρωσις 4, φθάνω 4, φίλημα 4, κοινωνία 6, • (ἀββά, γυμνότης, κῶμος, ὀκνηρός, παραβάτης, περισσεία, πώρωσις, συναπάγομαι, συνσταυρόω, ἐφάπαξ, οὗ, ἀνάθεμα 3, ἐκδίκησις 3, προερῶ 3, ἀπεκδέχομαι 4, εὐδοκία 4, στήκω 6, συνεργός 7).

(2) 1 Cor. 49 (• 20).

B 1. 1. (v) ἀνέγκλητος.

B 2. 4. (i) παράκλησις 7 : (ii) ἀπολογία 3, ὀνομάζω 3, φωτίζω.

C 1. 15 (• 8) διαστολή, κρέας, παραζηλόω, συναναμίγνυμαι, συνκρίνω, φανέρωσις, φθόγγος, • (εἰλικρινία, ἥττημα, παιδαγωγός, στέγω, φύραμα, εὐσχημόνως 3, καταλλάσσω 3, μετασχηματίζω 3).

C 2. 29 (• 12) ἐνεργής, ἰδιώτης, καθεύδω, καταπίνω, μεθύω, μωραίνω, παρασκευάζω, καθό, ὅμως, ἀποστολή 3, θησαυρίζω 3, συμβιβάζω 3, ψαλμός 3, πλήν 3, ἀπολύτρωσις 4, φίλημα 4, κοινωνία 6, • (ἀπρόσκοπος, ζυμόω,

APPENDIX I

κραταιόομαι, ἐφάπαξ, οὗ, ἀνάθεμα 3, ἀσπασμός 3, πανουργία 3, ἔνι 3, ἀπεκδέχομαι 4, στήκω 6, συνεργός 7).

(3) 2 Cor. 48 (• 29).

B 1. 2. (i) προνοέω : (ii) ἐνοικέω 3.

B 2. 3. (i) παράκλησις 7 : (ii) ἀπολογία 3 : (iv) • (ἀνυπόκριτος).

C 1. 25 (• 19) ἁγιωσύνη 3, θριαμβεύω, νόημα 3, συνκρίνω, ὑπεραίρομαι, φανέρωσις, • (ἀνακρίνω, δοκιμή 3, δυνατέω, εἰλικρινία, ἔνδειξις, ἐπιβαρέω 3, ἐρεθίζω, ἱκανόω, ἰσότης, καταλλαγή, καταδουλόω, καταλλάσσω 3, κυρόω, μετασχηματίζω 3, προεπαγγέλλομαι, στέλλομαι, ὑπερπερισσεύω, ὕψωμα, φιλοτιμέομαι 3).

C 2. 18 (• 9) ἰδιώτης, καταπίνω, παρασκευάζω, φράσσω, ἀφορίζω 3, θησαυρίζω 3, φθάνω 4, φίλημα 4, κοινωνία 6, • (ἀχειροποίητος, γυμνότης, δεκατέσσαρες, περισσεία, ἐκδίκησις 3, πανουργία 3, προερῶ 3, περισσοτέρως 4, συνεργός 7).

(4) Gal. 33 (• 21).

B 1. 0.

B 2. 1. (i) ἀναστροφή.

C 1. 8 (• 7) ἀληθεύω, • (ἐνάρχομαι, καταδουλόω, κυρόω, παιδαγωγός, παρεισέρχομαι, υἱοθεσία 3, φύραμα 3).

C 2. 24 (• 14) ἀναλίσκω, ἐκπίπτω, ἐνέχω, κράζω, συνκλείω, ὅμως, ἀποστολή 3, ἀφορίζω 3, ἐνκόπτω 3, κοινωνία 6, • (ἀββά, δεκατέσσαρες, ζυμόω, κῶμος, παραβάτης, προεῖπον, συναπάγομαι, συνσταυρόω, ἀνάθεμα 3, προερῶ 3, ἔνι 3, ἀπεκδέχομαι 4, περισσοτέρως 4, στήκω 6).

(5) Eph. 31 (• 16).

B 1. 0.

B 2. 3. (i) ἀναστροφή : (ii) ὀνομάζω 3, φωτίζω.

C 1. 14 (• 10) ἀληθεύω, αὔξησις, ποίημα, ὕμνος, • (ἀποκαταλλάσσω, ἁφή, ἐπιχορηγία, θάλπω, ὀφθαλμοδουλία, προσαγωγή, ῥιζόομαι, συνζωοποιέω, υἱοθεσία 3, ὑπερεκπερισσοῦ).

C 2. 14 (• 6) δόμα, θώραξ, σβέννυμι, ᾠδή, συνβιβάζω 3, ψαλμός 3, πλήν 3, ἀπολύτρωσις 4, • (κραταιόομαι, μεθύσκομαι, πώρωσις, πανουργία 3, περιποίησις 3, εὐδοκία 4).

(6) Phil. 24 (• 16).

B 1. 0.

B 2. 2. (i) παράκλησις 7 : (ii) ἀπολογία 3.

C 1. 10 (• 9) νόημα, • (ἀποκαραδοκία, δοκιμή 3, ἐλλογάω, ἐνάρξομαι, ἔνδειξις, ἐπιχορηγία, μετασχηματίζω 3, σύμμορφος, συνστρατιώτης).

C 2. 12 (• 7) δόμα, πρόφασις, πλήν 3, φθάνω 4, κοινωνία 6, •(ἀπρόσκοπος, ὀκνηρός, ἀπεκδέχομαι 4, εὐδοκία 4, περισσοτέρως 4, στήκω 6, συνεργός 7).
(7) Col. 27 (• 16).
B 1. 2. (ii) ἐνοικέω 3 ; (v) ἀνέγκλητος.
B 2. o.
C 1. 14 (• 12) θριαμβεύω, ὕμνος, •(ἀνακαινόω, ἀποκαταλλάσσω, αὔξησις, ἀφή, ἐρεθίζω, ἱκανόω, ἰσότης, ὀφθαλμοδουλία, ῥιζόομαι, συναιχμάλωτος 3, συνζωοποιέω, συνθάπτομαι).
C 2. 11 (• 4) καθεύδω, νεκρόω, πόσις, ᾠδή, συνβιβάζω 3, ψαλμός 3, ἀπολύτρωσις 4, •(ἀχειροποίητος, ἀσπασμός 3, ἔνι 3, συνεργός 7).
(8) 1 Thess. 23 (• 12).
B 1. o.
B 2. 1. (i) παράκλησις 7.
C 1. 8 (• 6) ἁγιωσύνη 3, ἔκδικος, •(ἐπιβαρέω 3, εὐσχημόνως 3, θάλπω, στέγω, ὑπερεκπερισσοῦ, φιλοτιμέομαι 3).
C 2. 14 (• 6) θώραξ, μεθύω, πρόφασις, σβέννυμι, ἀνταποδίδωμι 3, ἐνκόπτω 3, φθάνω 4, φίλημα 4, •(μεθύσκομαι, προεῖπον, περιποίησις 3, περισσοτέρως 4, στήκω 6, συνεργός 7).
(9) 2 Thess. 13 (• 7).
B 1. o.
B 2. 1. (i) παράκλησις 7
C 1. 4 (• 2) συναναμίγνυμαι, ὑπεραίρομαι, •(ἐπιβαρέω 3, στέλλομαι).
C 2. 8 (• 5) ἀναλίσκω, ἐνέχω, ἀνταποδίδωμι, •(ἀσπασμός 3, ἐκδίκησις 3, περιποίησις 3, εὐδοκία 4, στήκω 6).
(10) Philem. 7 (• 3).
B 1. o.
B 2. 1. (i) παράκλησις 7.
C 1. 3 (• 2) τάχα, •(συναιχμάλωτος 3, συνστρατιώτης).
C 2. 3 (• 1) ἐνεργής, κοινωνία 6, •(συνεργός 7).

G.
Compounds with a-privative.

(1) Rom. 48 } B 1. 4. ἀδιάλειπτος, ἄστοργος, ἀτιμία, ἀφθαρσία.
a. p. p. 1·8 } B 2. 17. ἀγνοέω, ἀόρατος, ἀπιστία, ἀσεβής, ἀσθένεια, ἄφθαρτος,—ἀδικία, ἀπιστέω, ἀσθενέω, ἀληθής, ἀνομία, ἀνυπόκριτος, ἀνόητος, ἀδόκιμος, ἀπειθής, ἀσέβεια, ἀλήθεια.

C 1. 12. ἀλάλητος, ἀμετανόητος, ἀναπολόγητος, ἀνελεήμων, ἀνεξεραύνητος, ἀνόμως, ἀσθένημα, ἀσύνθετος, ἀχρεόομαι,—ἀδιαλείπτως, ἀμεταμέλητος, ἀνεξιχνίαστος.

C 2. 15. ἄβυσσος, ἀΐδιος, ἄκακος, ἀσχημοσύνη, ἀδύνατος, ἀτιμάζω, ἀσύνετος, ἀπειθέω,—ἀκέραιος,—ἄδικος, ἀκαθαρσία, ἀπείθεια, ἀσέλγεια, ἀσθενής, ἄφρων.

(2) 1 Cor. 47 } B 1. 4. ἀθανασία, ἀτιμία, ἀφθαρσία, ἀνέγκλητος.
a. p. p. 2 } B 2. 11. ἀγνοέω, ἀθετέω, ἄνομος, ἀσθένεια, ἄφθαρτος, ἀδικία, ἀσθενέω, ἄκαρπος, ἄπιστος, ἀδόκιμος, ἀλήθεια.

C 1. 15. ἄγαμος, ἀγενής, ἀδάπανος, ἀδήλως, ἀκατακάλυπτος, ἄκων, ἀμετακίνητος, ἀνάξιος, ἀναξίως, ἀπερισπάστως, ἀστατέω, ἀσχημονέω, ἀσχημόνων, ἄτομος, ἄψυχος.

C 2. 17. ἀγνωσία, ἄδηλος, ἄζυμος, ἀκρασία, ἀμέριμνος, ἄρρωστος, ἄτιμος,—ἀκαταστασία, ἀπρόσκοπος, ἀφόβως,—ἀδικέω, ἄδικος, ἀκαθαρσία, ἀκαθαρτός, ἀσθενής, ἄφρων, ἄφωνος.

(3) 2 Cor. 27 } B 1. 1. ἀτιμία.
a. p. p. 1·6 } B 2. 10. ἀγνοέω, ἀσθένεια, ἀδικία, ἀσθενέω, ἀληθής, ἀνομία, ἀνυπόκριτος, ἄπιστος, ἀδόκιμος, ἀλήθεια.

C 1. 7. ἀβαρής, ἀγρυπνία, ἄμετρος, ἀνεκδιήγητος, ἀπαρασκεύαστος, ἄρρητος,—ἀμεταμέλητος.

C 2. 9. ἀφροσύνη,—ἀκαταστασία, ἀπορέω, ἀχειροποίητος,—ἀδικέω, ἀκαθαρτός, ἀσέλγεια, ἀσθενής, ἄφρων.

(4) Gal. 12 } B 2. 5. ἀγνοέω, ἀθετέω, ἀσθένεια, ἀνόητος, ἀλήθεια.
a. p. p. 1·5 } C 1. 1. ἀληθεύω.
C 2. 6. ἀκυρόω,—ἀπορέω,—ἀδικέω, ἀκαθαρσία, ἀσέλγεια, ἀσθενής.

(5) Eph. 17 } B 1. 1. ἀφθαρσία.
a. p. p. 1·9 } B 2. 3. ἄκαρπος, ἀσωτία, ἀλήθεια.
C 1. 4. ἄθεος, ἄσοφος,—ἀληθεύω, ἀνεξιχνίαστος.
C 2. 9. ἄγνοια, ἀγρυπνέω,—ἀκριβῶς,—ἀκαθαρσία, ἀκαθαρτός, ἄμωμος, ἀπείθεια, ἀσέλγεια, ἄφρων.

(6) Phil. 11 } B 2. 3. ἀσθενέω, ἀληθής, ἀλήθεια.
a. p. p. 1·8 } C 1. 2. ἀκαιρέομαι, ἄλυπος.
C 2. 6. ἀσφαλής,—ἀκέραιος, ἀπρόσκοπος, ἀφόβως,—ἄμεμπτος, ἄμωμος.

APPENDIX I

(7) Col. 10
a. p. p. 1·7
- B 1. 1. ἀνέγκλητος.
- B 2. 2. ἀόρατος, ἀλήθεια.
- C 1. 2. ἀθυμέω, ἀφειδία.
- C 2. 5. ἀχειροποίητος,—ἀδικέω, ἀκαθαρσία, ἄμωμος, ἀπείθεια.

(8) 1 Thess. 12
a. p. p. 2·2
- B 2. 2. ἀγνοέω, ἀθετέω.
- C 1. 3. ἀμέμπτως, ἄτακτος,—ἀδιαλείπτως.
- C 2. 7. ἀληθινός, ἀληθῶς, ἀσφάλεια,—ἀκριβῶς,—ἀκαθαρσία, ἄμεμπτος, ἀσθενής.

(9) 2 Thess. 7
a. p. p. 2·3
- B 2. 4. ἄνομος, ἀδικία, ἀνομία, ἀλήθεια.
- C 1. 2. ἀτακτέω, ἀτάκτως.
- C 2. 1. ἄτοπος.

(10) Philem. 2
a. p. p. 1·6
- C 1. 1. ἄχρηστος.
- C 2. 1. ἀδικέω.

(11) 1 Tim. 26
a. p. p. 4·1
- A 1. 7. ἀδηλότης, ἀνεπίλημπτος, ἀπέραντος, ἀπρόσιτος,—ἀνόσιος, ἀστοχέω,—ἄμαχος.
- A 2. 5. ἀμελέω, ἄσπιλος, ἀφιλάργυρος,—ἀνυπότακτος, ἀργός.
- B 1. 2. ἀθανασία, ἀνέγκλητος.
- B 2. 12. ἀγνοέω, ἀθετέω, ἄνομος, ἀόρατος, ἀπιστία, ἀσεβής, ἀσθένεια, ἄφθαρτος,—ἀνυπόκριτος, ἀνόητος, ἄπιστος, ἀλήθεια.

(12) 2 Tim. 24
a. p. p. 5·1
- A 1. 10. ἀκαίρως, ἀκρατής, ἀνεξίκακος, ἀνεπαίσχυντος, ἀνήμερος, ἀπαίδευτος, ἄσπονδος, ἀφιλάγαθος, ἀνόσιος, ἀστοχέω.
- A 2. 2. ἄνοια, ἀχάριστος.
- B 1. 4. ἀδιάλειπτος, ἄστοργος, ἀτιμία, ἀφθαρσία.
- B 2. 8. ἀδικία, ἀπιστέω, ἀσθενέω, ἀνυπόκριτος,—ἀδόκιμος, ἀπειθής, ἀσέβεια, ἀλήθεια.

(13) Titus. 18
a. p. p. 6·75
- A 1. 4. ἀκατάγνωστος, ἀφθορία, ἀψευδής, ἄμαχος.
- A 2. 3. ἀνωφελής,—ἀνυπότακτος, ἀργός.
- B 1. 1. ἀνέγκλητος.
- B 2. 10. ἄκαρπος, ἀληθής, ἀνομία, ἀσωτία,—ἀνόητος, ἄπιστος,—ἀδόκιμος, ἀπειθής, ἀσέβεια, ἀλήθεια.

Total   Paul 105, a. p. p. 1.   Pastorals 54, a. p. p. 4.

KEY TO DIAGRAMS

Diagr.	p.	PAUL, 140 ff.	PASTS. 137 f.		Rom.	1 Cor.	2 Cor.	Gal.	Eph.	Phil.	Col.	1 Thess.	2 Thess.	Philem.	Pastorals	1 Tim.	2 Tim.	Titus.
				Number of pages in W. H.	26	24	16½	8¼	8¾	6	6	5½	3	1¼	13¾	6⅔	4⅔	2⅔
				Total vocabulary, excluding proper names	993	934	762	503	523	429	409	353	243	129	848	529	413	293
I A I B	21	C 1	A 1 i–vii i–iii	Not elsewhere A including in the N.T. B excluding { words shared by the Pastorals with one another }	103	98	92	32	40	37	33	20	10	5	175	96 75	60 48	43 30
				ditto ... average per page	4	4.1	5.6	3.9	4.6	6.2	5.5	3.6	3.3	4	12.8 11.8	15.2 11.8	12.9 10.3	16.1 11.25
II A	23	BC	A	Not elsewhere in the ten Paulines	261 10	266 11.1	197 12	85 10.3	93 10.6	76 12.7	58 9.7	41 7.5	26 8.7	10 8	306 22.4	173 27.3	114 24.4	81 30.4
				a. p. p.														
II B	23	C	A i–iii	Not elsewhere in the thirteen epistles	228 8.8	237 9.9	177 10.7	80 9.7	84 9.6	67 11.2	55 9.2	33 6	21 7	8 6.4	253 18.5	127 20.1	81 17.4	45 16.9
				a. p. p.														
III	25	BC (r.)	A (r.)	Not elsewhere in the ten Paulines A eliminating { genuine notes } including repetitions B including	336	415	264	100	106	81	60	47	31	10	437	223	107 124	88 90
				a. p. p.	12.9	17.3	16	12.1	12.1	13.5	10	8.5	10.3	8	32	35.4	33.5 26.4	37.2 33.7
IV	34	See pp. 32, 37		Number of words, including repetitions, which occur in at least five Paulines, but not in the Pastorals	360 13.8	448 18.7	306 18.5	146 17.7	127 14.5	122 20.3	109 18.2	96 17.5	55 18.3	22 17.6				
				a. p. p.														

			Description	Rom.	1 Cor.	2 Cor.	Gal.	Eph.	Phil.	Col.	1 Thess.	2 Thess.	Philem.	Pastorals	1 Tim.	2 Tim.	Titus.
V	35	p. 37	Number of particles, prepositions, &c., including repetitions—not in the Pastorals a. p. p.	187 / 7·2	288 / 12	163 / 9·9	89 / 10·8	38 / 4·3	54 / 9	31 / 5·2	51 / 9·3	15 / 5	16 / 12·8		26 / 4·1	24 / 5·1	18 / 6·75
VI	44	G pp. 155 ff.	Compounds with α-privative a. p. p.	48 / 1·8	47 / 2	27 / 1·6	12 / 1·5	17 / 1·9	11 / 1·8	10 / 1·7	12 / 2·2	7 / 2·3	2 / 1·6	54 / 4			
VII	62		Shakespearean Hapax Legomena														
VIII	63		Pauline N.T. Hapax Legomena, acc. Workman														
IX A	69	C1 +*x A1 +*x	Not elsewhere in the N.T., but in the Apostolic Fathers or Apologists a. p. p.	50 / 1·9	54 / 2·3	37 / 2·2	15 / 1·8	14 / 1·6	19 / 3·2	13 / 2·2	10 / 1·8	5 / 1·7	3 / 2·4	93 / 6·8	50 / 7·9	35 / 7·5	23 / 8·6
IX B	69	C1 +* A1 +*	Not elsewhere in the N.T., but in the Apostolic Fathers a. p. p.	26 / 1	34 / 1·4	20 / 1·2	11 / 1·3	10 / 1·1	14 / 2·3	8 / 1·3	6 / 1·1	5 / 1·7	3 / 2·4	61 / 4·5	28 / 4·4	26 / 5·6	19 / 7·1
X A	71	BC +*x A +*x	Not elsewhere in the ten Paulines, but in the Apostolic Fathers or Apologists a. p. p.	195 / 7·5	197 / 8·2	131 / 7·9	59 / 7·2	62 / 7·1	52 / 8·7	34 / 5·7	28 / 5·1	19 / 6·3	8 / 6·4	211 / 15·4	118 / 18·6	84 / 18	57 / 21·4
X B	71	BC +* A +*	Not elsewhere in the ten Paulines, but in the Apostolic Fathers a. p. p.	147 / 5·6	156 / 6·5	95 / 5·8	47 / 5·7	52 / 5·9	42 / 7	26 / 4·3	22 / 4	17 / 5·7	7 / 5·6	161 / 11·8	86 / 13·6	65 / 13·9	50 / 18·7
XI C	72	BC *x A *x	Not elsewhere in the ten Paulines, but in the Apologists a. p. p.	165 / 6·3	158 / 6·6	104 / 6·3	52 / 6·3	46 / 5·3	36 / 6	25 / 4·2	24 / 4·4	15 / 5	6 / 4·8	156 / 11·4	92 / 14·5	62 / 13·3	44 / 16·5
XI D	72	BC * A *	Not elsewhere in the ten Paulines, but both in the Apostolic Fathers and in the Apologists a. p. p.	117 / 4·5	117 / 4·9	68 / 4·1	40 / 4·8	36 / 4·1	26 / 4·3	17 / 2·8	18 / 3·3	13 / 4·3	5 / 4	106 / 7·8	60 / 9·5	43 / 9·2	37 / 13·9

CLASSIFICATION OF PAUL'S VOCABULARY

ACCORDING TO THE NUMBER OF EPISTLES IN WHICH EACH WORD OCCURS.

NUMBER OF EPISTLES	1	2	3	4	5	6	7	8	9	10	Total
B. *In Paul and in the Pastorals.*											
B 1. Not elsewhere in the N.T.	30	10	6	1	3						50
B 2. In other N.T. books also:											
α. nouns, verbs, adjectives, &c.	86	71	69	39	44	26	24	19	19	18	415
β. particles, prepositions, pronouns, &c.	7	5	2	5	2	4	6	6	11	29	77
Total	123	86	77	45	49	30	30	25	30	47	542
C. *In Paul, but not in the Pastorals.*											
C 1. Not elsewhere in the N.T.:											
α. nouns, &c.	462	83	21	7							573
β. particles, &c.	7	1		1							9
C 2. In other N.T. books:—											
α. nouns, verbs, adjectives, &c.	494	205	120	61	41	19	10	6	4		960
β. particles, prepositions, &c.	27	21	12	12	6	4	6	4	1		93
Total	990	310	153	81	47	23	16	10	5		1635
Total in Paul	1113	396	230	126	96	53	46	35	35	47	2177

APPENDIX I

THE RESIDUE

82 Words found in the Pastorals, but not elsewhere in the N. T., nor in Goodspeed's *Indices* (*Patristicus et Apologeticus*).

ἀδηλότης i. Plut. *J. Caes.* 7; Polyb., Dion. Hal., Philo (ἄδηλος 1 Clem. xviii. 6; Ath. 5. 2; Ptolemaeus ii. 33).

αἱρετικός iii. Aelian, *N. A.* vi. 59; Schol. in Lucian 216. 19; (προαιρετικός Cleomedes i. 6. 29).

αἰσχροκερδής v. Plut. (Passow's *Wörterbuch*), Hdt., Xen., Plat.; *Test. XII Patr.* Jud. xvi. 1

ἀκαίρως ii. Epict. *Diss.* ii. 7. 1, iii. 22. 50 &c.; M. Aur. *Com.* iv. 19; Galen, *De Temp.* 97. 29.

ἀκατάγνωστος iii. 2 Macc. iv. 47 (ἀκατάληπτος 1 Clem., Ath., -σκεύαστος Jus.).

ἄμαχος v. Aelian, *N.A.* ix. 41. 49 and *passim*; Lucian, *Praec.* 1, *Vit. Auct.* 22.

ἀνδραποδιστής i. Lucian, *Deor. D.* iv. 1. 209, *Mar. D.* vi. 3. 304; Polyb. xii. 9. 2; Dio Chrys. Or. lxix (ed. Dindorf, vol. ii, p. 238, l. 3).

ἀνεπαίσχυντος ii. Joseph. *Ant.* xviii. 7. 1.

ἀντιδιατίθεμαι ii. Longinus, *de Sublim.* 17. 1 (ἀντιτίθεμαι Jus. *Ap.* 30. 1, διατίθεμαι Jus. *D.* 22. 7, ἀντιδιατάξομαι Epict. iii. 24. 24).

ἀντίθεσις i. Galen, *De Temp.* (ed. Helmreich, p. 4, l. 10); Lucian i. *Mort. Dial.* x. 374; Plato, Aristotle.

ἀντίλυτρον i. Polyaenus, *Excerpt.* 52. 7, *Orph. Lith.* 587; Uncert. transl. of Ps. xlviii (xlix). 9.

ἀπόβλητος i. Dio Chrys. i, p. 169; Galen i, p. 10; Lucian, *De Merc. Cond.* c. 27, *Toxar.* 37, *Philops.* 29.

ἀποθησαυρίζω i. Aelian, *N.A.* iii. 10; Lucian, *Alex.* 23; Epict. *Diss.* iii. 22. 50; Joseph. *B. I.* vii. 5. 2 &c.

ἄρτιος ii. Epict. i. 28. 3; M. Aurel. *Com.* i. 16.

ἄσπονδος ii. Galen, *D. U. P.* ii. 195. 15; Polyaenus, *Strat.* viii. 35, 65; Philo, *De Sacrif.* 4.

αὐθεντέω i. [*P. Tebt.* ii. 276. 28, late second or third century A.D.] (αὐθέντης Hermes, *Sim.* ix. 5. 6, αὐθεντικός 2 Clem. xiv. 3).

αὐτοκατάκριτος iii. Philo ii. 652 (αὐτεπαίνετος 1 Clem., κατάκριτος Ign.).

ἀφθορία iii. (ἄφθορος Justin, Diod.—ἀδιάφθορος Galen, *D. U. P.* i. 494. 14; Plut. *Mor.* v, p. 115 (820 A).

ἀφιλάγαθος ii. (φιλάγαθος Plut. *Mor.* 140 C.—ἀφιλόκαλος Plut., ἀπειράγαθος Diod. &c.)

APPENDIX I

βαθμός i. Hadrian. Imp. (*Sententiae*—cf. Estienne, *Thes. Gr. Ling.* xii. 2. 490 f.), Lucian, Appian &c.; Joseph. *B. I.* iv. 3. 10. (171).

γάγγραινα ii. Galen, *De Tumor* 8, *Com.* 4 εἰς τὸ π. Ἄρθρων, vol. xii, p. 437; Plut. *Discr. cm. et adul.* 36, 2. 65 D.

γενεαλογία v. Joseph. *c. Ap.* 1. 3, *Ant. Iud.* xi. 3. 10; Polyb. ix. 2. 1 γενεαλ. κ. μύθους. LXX, Philo i. 525 (γενεαλογέω Aristeides, Lucian, *Phal.* ii. 9).

γραώδης i. Cleomedes, *De MCCC.* ii. 1. 89 (162. 14); Galen v. 120 B; Strabo i. 16.

γυμνασία. i. Epict. i. 7. 12, 8. 7 &c.; Arrian, *Tact.* xxxii. 2, xxxiii. 3; Galen, *D. U. P. passim.*

γυναικάριον ii. M. Aurel. *Com.* v. 11; Epict. *Diss.* ii. 18. 18, 22. 23 &c.

διαπαρατριβή i. (παρατριβή Ath. 18. 3, διατριβή Dio Chry. iv. 81. 23, Jus., Lucian, Hipp. 5 &c.; M. Aur. i. 4 &c.—ἀποδιατρίβειν Schol. in Lucian 98. 23.)

διδακτικός iv. Philo, *Praem. et poen.* 4, *De Congr. Erud.* 7.

ἑδραίωμα i. (ἑδραῖος Ign., ἑδράζω 1 Clem., Ign., Jus., Ath.—ἑδραιότης Dio Chrys.)

ἔκδηλος ii. Dio Chrys. iv. 79. 17, vii. 141. 13 (272 R); 2 Macc. iii. 19, vi. 5.

ἐκζήτησις i. (ἐκζητέω 1 Clem. &c.—ζήτησις Justin, Melito.)

ἔλεγμος ii. LXX. Sir. xxi. 6; 2 Kings xix. 3 &c.

ἐπανόρθωσις ii. Epict. *Diss.* iii. 21. 15 &c., *Ench.* xxxiii. 10; Ptolemaeus, *Synt. Math.* xiii. fin.; Galen, *De Temp.* 26. 12; Philo, *De Inebr.* 22 &c.

ἐπαρκέω i. Dio Chrys. vii, p. 122. l. 29 (243 R), 124. l. 13 (244 R); Epict. iii. 26. 8 &c.; Hom., Xen.

ἐπιδιορθόω iii. (διορθόομαι 1 Clem.)

ἐπιστομίζω iii. Lucian, *Dionys.* 7; Plut., Plato.

εὐμετάδοτος i. M. Aur. i. 14, iii. 14, vi. 48.

θεόπνευστος ii. Plut. *De Plac. Phil.* v. 2. 3 (904 f.), *Orac. Sib.* 5. 406.

ἱεροπρεπής iii. Lucian, *De Sacr.* 13; Joseph.; 4 Macc. ix. 25, xi. 20; Plato, Philo.

καλοδιδάσκαλος iii. (κακοδιδασκαλέω 2 Clem. x. 5, -ία Ign. *Eph.* vi. 2 &c.)

καταστολή i. Epict. *Diss.* ii. 10. 15, 21. 11; Plut. *Pericl.* 5; Joseph. *B. I.* ii. 8. 4.

καταστρηνιάω i. Ign. *ad Antioch.* c. 11.

APPENDIX I

καυστηριάζομαι i. Schol. in Lucian 137. 11; Strabo v. 1. 9 (p. 215) [*B. G.* v. 952. 4, ii/A. D.]

κενοφωνία iv. Dioscorides, *De Mat. Med.* praef. 2 (κενοδοξία 1 Clem., Ign., Herm.—ὁμοφωνίαι 1 Clem.).

κνήθω ii. Moeris, *Lex. Att.* p. 215; Aristotle, *H.A.* ix. 1 (609 A) (κνῆσθαι Galen, *D. U. P.* i. 11. 15 &c.).

κοινωνικός i. Epict. *Diss.* iii. 13. 5 and *passim*; Lucian, *Tim.* 56; M. Aurel. *Com.* iii. 4. 2 &c.; Galen i. 12. 28; Polyb. ii. 44. 1; Plat., Aristot.

λογομαχέω ii. (λογοποιέω Ath. *Suppl.* 2. 1, 31. 1, 32. 1; Lucian, *Cont.* 12. 506.)

λογομαχία i. (λογοποιία Ath. *Suppl.* 3. 1.)

μάμμη ii. Epict. ii. 16. 28, 43 &c.; Plut., Appian, Joseph.; 4 Macc. xvi. 9; Philo.

ματαιολόγος iii. (ματαιολογία Plut. *Mor.* 6 f.; Polycarp, *Php.* ii. 1.— ματαιοπονία 1 Clem., Galen, *D. U. P.* i. 56. 25.)

μεμβράνα ii. Cf. Horace, *Serm.* ii. 3. 1 f. 'Sic raro scribis, ut toto non quater anno | membranam poscas', and Gai. *Inst.* ii. 77 'quod in chartulis sive membranis meis aliquis scripserit, meum est'.

μητραλῴης i. Lucian, *Deor. Conc.* 12; Aesch., Plat.

νεόφυτος i. (νεόγαμοι Arrian, *Hist.* i. 24. 2; Lucian, *Mort. D.* xix. 1. 410. νεόνυμφος Lucian, *Asin.* 34. 603 and numerous compds. of νεο- in Lucian.)

νηφάλιος v. Appian, *De Reb. Macc.* ix. 9; Joseph. *Ant.* iii. 12. 2; Plut. *Mor.* 132 E.

νομικός (adj.) iii. As subs. cf. Matt. xxii. 35, Luke x. 25, vii. 30.

νομίμως iv. Galen, *ad Hipp. Aphor.* 18; Athen. 1, p. 20 E; Dio Chrys. *De Ex. Or.* xiii, p. 246, l. 18 (427 R); Plut. *Galb.* 15; Thuc., Xen., Plat.

ξενοδοχέω i. Moeris, *Lex. Att.* p. 248; (ξενοδόχος Plut. *V. Alex.* 51; ξενοκτονέω Ta.).

οἰκοδεσποτέω i. Lucian, *De Astrol.* 20; Plut. *De Plac. Phil.* v. 18, p. 1672 [908 B] (οἰκοδεσπότης Epict. *Diss.* ii. 20. 20, iii. 22. 4).

οἰκουρ(γ)ός iii. Plut. *Mor.* 953 B (οἰκουργέω 1 Clem., i. 3, οἰκουρέω Galen, *De Temp.* ii. 606, *De Vic. Att.* 61. 20; Aelian, *N. A.* i. 22.

ὀρθοτομέω ii. LXX. Prov. xi. 5 (καινοτομέω Ta. 35. 2; Lucian, *Phal.* ii. 9, ὀρθογνώμονες Justin).

πάροινος v. Lucian, *Tim.* 55; Plut. *De Loq.* 504 B, *Symp.* 8 (716 F) (παροινία, Dio Chrys. xxxii. 421. 22).

πατραλῴης i. M. Aur. *Com.* vi. 34.

περιπείρω i. Plut. *Galb.* 27; Lucian, Joseph., Philo.

περιφρονέω iii. Plut. *Pericl.* 31, *Mor.* 762 E; 4 Macc. vi. 9, vii. 16.

πλέγμα i. Joseph. *Ant.* ii. 9. 4 (πλεγμάτιον M. Aur. ii. 2).
πορισμός i. Joseph. *B. I.* ii. 21. 3; Plut. *Mor.* 524 D, *Cat. Mai.* 25; Polyb. iii. 122. 2.
πρόκριμα i. (προκρίνω Jus. *D.* v. 5; Melito; Euseb. *H. E.* iv. 26. 13.)
σκέπασμα i. Joseph. *B. I.* ii. 8. 5; Aristot. (σκέπαρνον M. Aur. x. 38, σκεπαστήριος Galen, *D. U. P.* i. 22. 4 &c.)
στόμαχος i. Dioscorides, *De M. M.* i. 17. 2 &c.; Galen, *D. U. P.* iv. 15 &c.; M. Aur. x. 31. 35; *Test. XII Patr.* Neph. ii. 8.
στρατολογέω ii. Plut., Joseph. (see Thayer, *s. v.*); Diod. Sic.; Dion. Hal.
συνκακοπαθέω ii. (συμπαθέω Jus. *D.* xxxviii. 2, κακοπαθέω 2 Clem. xix. 3.)
σωφρονισμός ii. Appian, *Pun.* viii. 65; Joseph. *Ant.* xvii. 9. 2, *B. I.* i. 3; Plut. *Mor.* 712 C.
τεκνογονία i. Aristot. *H. A.* vii. 1. 8 (τεκνογονέω Diogn. v. 6).
τεκνοτροφέω i. Epict. i. 23. 3; Aristot. (τεκνοκτονέω Ath. 20. 2, 35. 2).
ὑδροποτέω i. Dioscorides, *De M. M.* v. 7. 1; Lucian, *Bis Acc.* 16; Macrob. 5; Aelian, *Var. Hist.* ii. 38; Xenophon.
ὑποτύπωσις iv. Galen (see Stephanus, *Thes.* s. v. 'etiam inter Galeni scripta, sed Latine tantum exstat ἐμπειρικῆς ἀγωγῆς ὑποτύπωσις).
ὑψηλοφρονέω i. (ὑψηλοφροσύνη, -φρων Herm., ταπεινοφροσύνη, -έω 1 Clem., Herm.)
φαιλόνης ii. = *paenula*. Epict. iv. 8. 24; M. Aur. i. 16 (cf. Varr. ap. Non. 537, 12; Juv. v. 79; Lampr. *Alex. Sev.* 27). C. H. Dodd has drawn attention to two extremely interesting notes given in Grenfell and Hunt's *Oxyrrhynchus Papyri*, vol. xii. 1916, (1) 1583. Second cent. A. D. . . . Γενοῦ παρὰ Ἰσίδωρον χάριν τοῦ φαινόλου καὶ τοῦ ἐπικαρσίου καὶ ἀπένεγκον παρὰ Καλύκην . . . (2) 1489. Third cent. A. D. τὸ κιθώνιν (=χιτώνιον) ἐπιλέλησμαι παρὰ Τεκοῦσαν εἰς τὸν πυλῶνα· πέμψον μοι . . . (Expositor, viii. 88. April 1918.
φιλάγαθος iii. Plut. *Mor.* 140 c, *Praec. Coni.* 17; LXX. Sap. vii. 22; Philo, Aristot.
φίλανδρος iii. Polyaenus, *Strat.* viii. 32. 34; Plut. *Praec. coni.* 28; Lucian, *Halc.* 8, *de Mer.* 73.
φλύαρος i. Plut. *Symp.* 7 (701 A), *V. Cicer.* 2, *V. Anton.* 29, *Mor.* 39 A &c.; 4 Macc. v. 10 (φλυαρέω Ta. xxxiii. 1, -ία Ta. xxvi. 2 &c., ἀφλύαρος M. Aur. v. 5).
φρεναπάτης iii. (φρεναπατάω Gal. vi. 3.—φρενήρης M. Aur. viii. 51.)
ψευδώνυμος i. Aelian, *N. A.* ix. 18; Plut. *Mor.* 479 E; Philo, Aeschyl.

APPENDIX I

Phrases in the Pastorals and in early second-century non-Christian Writers.

(1) Οἱ γυμνασταὶ καὶ οἱ γε νομίμως ἀθλοῦντες Galen, *ad Hippocr. Aphor.* 18; cf. 2 Tim. ii. 5.

(2) Ἐὰν καλὸς στρατιώτης γένῃ, τρίτῳ βαθμῷ (promotion) δυνήσῃ εἰς πραιτώριον μεταβῆναι, Hadriani Sententiae (Estienne, *Thes. Graec. Ling.* vol. xii. 2. 490 f.); cf. 2 Tim. ii. 3 ὡς καλὸς στρατιώτης, 1 Tim. iii. 13 οἱ καλῶς διακονήσαντες βαθμὸν ἑαυτοῖς καλὸν περιποιοῦνται.

(3) γυναῖκας μὴ ὁμιλεῖν οἴνῳ ἀλλὰ ὑδροποτεῖν Aelian, *Var. Hist.* ii. 38; cf. 1 Tim. v. 23 μηκέτι ὑδροπότει, ἀλλὰ οἴνῳ ὀλίγῳ χρῶ διὰ τὸν στόμαχον κ. τ. . . . ἀσθενείας. Dioscorides, *De M. M.* v. 7. 1 ὁ δὲ καλούμενος μελίτης οἶνος δίδοται μὲν . . . τοῖς ἀσθενῆ τὸν στόμαχον ἔχουσι . . . καὶ . . . τοῖς ἀσθενῆ τ. κεφαλὴν ἔχουσι· χρήσιμος δὲ καὶ γυναιξὶν ὑδροποτούσαις.

(4) εἰ μὲν . . . ὡς μῦθόν τις γραὸς ἀναγινώσκοι τὸν λόγον Galen, *D. U. P.* iii. 15; cf. 1 Tim. iv. 7. μυθαρίῳ γραώδει πιστεύσας Cleomedes, *MCCC.* ii. 1 (162. 14): cf. Philo Byblius (Fragm. Hist. Graec. viii, p. 564); M. Aurel. 8. 25.

(5) ἀπόθου τῶν ῥημάτων τὴν τοσαύτην ἀπεραντολογίαν καὶ ἀντιθέσεις καὶ παρισώσεις . . . καὶ βαρβαρισμοὺς κ. τ. ἄλλα βάρη τ. λόγων Lucian, *Mort. D.* x. 373 f.; 1 Tim. i. 6, vi. 20.

(6) εἰ Πλάτωνος . . . κ. Ἀριστοτέλους ἐκλαθόμενος καθῆσαι, τ. ὅμοιον πεπονθὼς τοῖς τὰ ὦτα πτερῷ κνωμένοις . . . Lucian, *Rhet.* praec 11. 12, 2 Tim. iv. 3.

(7) ὑγιὴς λόγος M. Aurel. viii. 30; Titus ii. 8. ὀρθῷ καὶ ὑγιεῖ καὶ ἀνεπιλήπτῳ βίῳ χρώμενος Lucian, *Demon.* 3; ἐν ὑγιαινούσῃ τῇ ψυχῇ Lucian, *Longaev.* 209; cf. Titus i. 13, 1 Tim. iii. 2 &c.

(8) πλανῶνται κατὰ τὸν βίον ὅσαι ψυχαὶ . . . δεδουλωμέναι δὲ ἡδοναῖς, φιλήδονοι, καὶ φιλοσώματοι, βίον αἰσχρὸν . . . οὐχ ἑλόμεναι ζῶσιν, ἀλλὰ ἐνεχθεῖσαι πρὸς αὐτόν Dio Chrys. iv, p. 85 (178 R); cf. Titus iii. 3 πλανώμενοι, δουλεύοντες . . . ἡδοναῖς. 2 Tim. iii. 5 f. φιλήδονοι . . . ἀγόμενα ἐπιθυμίαις . . .

(9) ἐκ προγόνων Phlegon Trallianus 31; cf. οἱ πρόγονοί σου . . . ὁ μὲν πάππος σου Ἀριανὸς . . . ὁ δὲ πατήρ σου . . . σὺ δὲ . . . πεπείσμεθα πάντα πράσσειν Melito (Eus. *H. E.* iv. 26); cf. 2 Tim. i. 5.

(10) Ἄνθρωπον μὲν εἶναι σοφὸν κ. δίκαιον κ. τῶν οἰκείων παίδων προμηθέστατον, κ. τῶν γειναμένων ποιεῖσθαι τὴν προσήκουσαν φροντίδα, Aelian *N. A. proem.*; cf. 1 Tim. iii. 4 f., v. 8.

APPENDIX II

A.

STEREOTYPED PHRASES IN THE PASTORALS

παράγγελλε ταῦτα κ. δίδασκε, I. iv. 11; ταῦτα δίδασκε κ. παρακάλει, I. vi. 2.
καὶ ταῦτα παράγγελλε, I. v. 7; ταῦτα ὑπομίμνησκε, II. ii. 14.
ταῦτα λάλει, καὶ παρακάλει καὶ ἔλεγχε, Titus ii. 15; ταῦτα φεῦγε I. vi. 11.
Cf. ταῦτα ὑποτιθέμενος &c., I. iv. 6; ταῦτα μελέτα, I. iv. 15; ταῦτα παράθου, II. ii. 2.
μύθους (κτλ.) παραιτοῦ, I. iv. 7, v. 11, II. ii. 23, Titus iii. 10.
κενοφωνίας (μάχας) περιίστασο, II. ii. 16, Titus iii. 9.
δι' ἣν αἰτίαν, II. i. 6, 12; Titus i. 13.
εἰ παντὶ ἔργῳ ἀγαθῷ ἐπηκολούθησε, I. v. 10.
εἰς πᾶν ἔργον ἀγαθὸν ἡτοιμασμένον, II. ii. 21.
πρὸς πᾶν ἔργον ἀγαθὸν ἐξηρτισμένος, II. iii. 17.
πρὸς πᾶν ἔργον ἀγαθὸν ἀδόκιμοι, Titus i. 16; (ἑτοίμους), Titus iii. 1.
ἐν τῷ νῦν αἰῶνι, I. vi. 17; II. iv. 10; Titus ii. 12. Paul writes ἐν τ. αἰῶνι τούτῳ, Rom. xii. 2; 1 Cor. i. 20, ii. 6, 8, iii. 18; 2 Cor. iv. 4; Eph. i. 21.
τῆς (τῇ) ἐν Χριστῷ Ἰησοῦ, I. i. 14, iii. 13; II. i. 1. 9, 13, ii. 1. 10, iii. 15.
ἔργα καλά, I. iii. 1, v. 10, 25, vi. 18; Titus ii. 7, 14, iii. 8, 14.
(κατὰ) εἰς ἐπίγνωσιν ἀληθείας, I. ii. 4; II. ii. 25, iii. 7; Titus i. 1.
ἐμπίπτειν εἰς παγίδα, I. iii. 7, vi. 9; cf. II. ii. 26.
ζῆν εὐσεβῶς, II. iii. 12; Titus ii. 12; cf. I. ii. 2.
περὶ τὴν πίστιν ἐναυάγησαν, I. i. 19, (ἠστόχησαν) vi. 21; (ἀδόκιμοι) II. iii. 8.
περὶ τὴν ἀλήθειαν ἠστόχησαν, II. ii. 18.
(Paul uses περί with accusative only once, Phil. ii. 23 τὰ περὶ ἐμέ.)
τὸν καλὸν ἀγῶνα ἀγωνίζειν, II. iv. 7; I. vi. 12.
ἄνθρωπος θεοῦ, I. vi. 11; II. iii. 17.
διαπαρατριβαὶ διεφθαρμένων ἀνθρώπων τ. νοῦν, I. vi. 5.
ἄνθρωποι κατεφθαρμένοι τ. νοῦν, II. iii. 8.
μεμίανται αὐτῶν ... ὁ νοῦς, Titus i. 15.
μιᾶς γυναικὸς ἀνήρ, I. iii. 2, 12; Titus i. 6; ἑνὸς ἀνδρὸς γυνή, I. v. 9.

ἐν καθαρᾷ συνειδήσει, I. iii. 9 ; II. i. 3.
ἐκ καθαρᾶς καρδίας (κ. συνειδήσεως ἀγαθῆς), I. i. 5 ; II. ii. 22.
ἔχων ἀγαθὴν συνείδησιν, I. i. 19 ; cf. I. iv. 2 ; Titus i. 15.
πιστὸς ὁ λόγος, I. i. 15, iii. 1, iv. 9 ; II. ii. 11.
τοῦ κατὰ τὴν διδαχὴν πιστοῦ λόγου, Titus i. 9.
τῆς καλῆς διδασκαλίας ᾗ παρηκολούθηκας, I. iv. 6.
παρηκολούθησάς μου τῇ διδασκαλίᾳ, II. iii. 10.
ἡ ὑγιαίνουσα διδασκαλία, I. i. 10 ; II. iv. 3 ; Titus i. 9, ii. 1.
ὑγιαίνοντες λόγοι, I. vi. 3 ; II. i. 13 ; Titus ii. 8.
ὑγιαίνειν τῇ πίστει, Titus i. 13, ii. 2.

B.

PAULINE PHRASES IN THE PASTORALS

The reference before a phrase applies to the Pastorals, that after a phrase applies to the Pauline epistle in question.

i. *Romans*.

1 Tim. i. 1 κατ᾽ ἐπιταγὴν Θεοῦ, xvi. 26.
  i. 5 τὸ δὲ τέλος . . ., vi. 22 ; cf. πλήρωμα νόμου ἡ ἀγάπη, xiii. 10.
  i. 8 οἴδαμεν δὲ ὅτι καλὸς ὁ νόμος . . . : cf. οἴδαμεν δὲ ὅτι ὅσα ὁ νόμος λέγει τοῖς ἐν τ. νόμῳ λέγει, iii. 19 ; σύνφημι τῷ νόμῳ ὅτι καλός, vii. 16.
  i. 10 καὶ εἴ τι ἕτερον ; cf. καὶ εἴ τις ἑτέρα ἐντολή, xiii. 9.
  i. 14 ὑπερεπλεόνασε δὲ ἡ χάρις τοῦ Κυρίου ἡμῶν : cf. οὗ δὲ ἐπλεόνασεν ἡ ἁμαρτία ὑπερεπερίσσευσεν ἡ χάρις, v. 20 ; ἡ χάρις τ. Κυρίου ἡμῶν Ἰησοῦ, xvi. 20.
  i. 15 Χ. Ι. ἦλθεν εἰς τ. κόσμον ἁμαρτωλοὺς σῶσαι : cf. ἔτι ἁμαρτωλῶν ὄντων Χ. ὑπὲρ ἡμῶν ἀπέθανε . . . ἡ ἁμαρτία εἰς τ. κόσμον εἰσῆλθε, v. 8, 12.
  i. 16 πιστεύειν ἐπ᾽ αὐτῷ, ix. 33, x. 11 ; cit. Isa. xxviii. 16 ; εἰς ζωὴν αἰώνιον, v. 21.
  i. 17 τῷ δὲ . . . μόνῳ Θεῷ . . . δόξα εἰς τ. αἰῶνας· ἀμήν, xvi. 25, 27.
  ii. 1 πρῶτον . . . ποιεῖσθαι εὐχαριστίας : cf. πρῶτον μὲν εὐχαριστῶ, i. 8.
  ii. 7 ἀλήθειαν λέγω, οὐ ψεύδομαι, ix. 1 ; ἐγὼ . . . ἀπόστολος . . . ἐθνῶν, xi. 13.
  iii. 7, vi. 9 εἰς παγίδα, xi. 9 ; cit. Ps. lxix. 23.
  iv. 13 τῇ παρακλήσει, τῇ διδασκαλίᾳ : cf. xii. 8.
  v. 18 λέγει γὰρ ἡ γραφή, ix. 17, x. 11.
  vi. 4 φθόνος, ἔρις . . . διεφθαρμένων ἀνθρώπων τ. νοῦν κ. ἀπεστερημένων τ. ἀληθείας : cf. ἀνθρώπων τῶν τ. ἀλήθειαν ἐν ἀδικίᾳ κατεχόντων . . . εἰς ἀδόκιμον νοῦν . . . μεστοὺς φθόνου . . . ἔριδος, i. 18, 28 f.
  vi. 11 δίωκε δικαιοσύνην : cf. ix. 30 (τὰ μὴ διώκοντα δικαιοσύνην), xii. 13.

2 Tim. i. 1, 13, ii. 1, 10, iii. 15 τῆς (τῇ) ἐν Χριστῷ Ἰησοῦ, iii. 24, viii. 39.

i. 3 f. Χάριν ἔχω τ. Θεῷ ᾧ λατρεύω ... ὡς ἀδιάλειπτον ἔχω τ. περὶ σοῦ μνείαν ἐν ταῖς δεήσεσί μου, ἐπιποθῶν σε ἰδεῖν ἵνα : cf. χάρις τ. Θεῷ, vi. 17 ; εὐχαριστῶ τ. Θεῷ ... ᾧ λατρεύω, ὡς ἀδιαλείπτως μνείαν ὑμῶν ποιοῦμαι ... ἐπὶ τῶν προσευχῶν μου, δεόμενος ... ἐπιποθῶ γὰρ ἰδεῖν ὑμᾶς, ἵνα ..., i. 8–11.

i. 5 τῆς ἐν σοὶ ... πίστεως ..., i. 12 ; οἶδα γὰρ ᾧ πεπίστευκα : cf. ἡ πίστις ὑμῶν, i. 8 ; ... διὰ τῆς ἐν ἀλλήλοις πίστεως ὑμῶν τε καὶ ἐμοῦ, i. 12.

i. 5 πεπείσμαι δὲ ὅτι καί, xv. 14.

i. 6 χάρισμα, i. 11.

i. 6 τὸ χάρισμα τοῦ Θεοῦ, vi. 23.

i. 7 οὐ γὰρ ἔδωκεν ἡμῖν ὁ Θεὸς πνεῦμα δειλίας, ἀλλὰ δυνάμεως καί : cf. οὐ γὰρ ἐλάβετε πνεῦμα δουλείας πάλιν εἰς φόβον, ἀλλά ..., viii. 15 ; ἐν δυνάμει πνεύματος ἁγίου, xv. 13 ; ἔδωκεν αὐτοῖς ὁ Θεὸς πνεῦμα κατανύξεως, xi. 8 ; cit. Isa. xxix. 10.

i. 8 μὴ ἐπαισχυνθῇς τὸ μαρτύριον, ... i. 12 οὐκ ἐπαισχύνομαι cf. i. 16.

i. 9 τοῦ καλέσαντος ... οὐ κατὰ τ. ἔργα ἡμῶν : cf. οὐκ ἐξ ἔργων ἀλλ' ἐκ τ. καλοῦντος, ix. 11 ; contrast ἀποδώσει ἑκάστῳ κατὰ τὰ ἔργα αὐτοῦ, ii. 6.

i. 9 ἀλλὰ κατὰ ἰδίαν πρόθεσιν καὶ χάριν, τὴν δοθεῖσαν ἡμῖν ἐν Χ. Ι. πρὸ χρόνων αἰωνίων, φανερωθεῖσαν δὲ νῦν διά ... : cf. τοῖς κατὰ πρόθεσιν κλητοῖς, viii. 28 ; κατὰ τὴν χάριν τὴν δοθεῖσαν ἡμῖν, xii. 6 ; ἐν Χ. Ι. vi. 11 &c. ; χρόνοις αἰωνίοις σεσιγημένου, φανερωθέντος δὲ νῦν διά ..., xvi. 25.

i. 10 ζωὴν καὶ ἀφθαρσίαν : cf. ii. 7.

i. 12 οἶδα καὶ πέπεισμαι ὅτι δυνατός ἐστιν, xiv. 14, xi. 23.

i. 13 ἀγάπῃ τῇ ἐν Χριστῷ Ἰησοῦ, viii. 39.

i. 14 διὰ Πνεύματος Ἁγίου τοῦ ἐνοικοῦντος ἐν ἡμῖν, v. 5, viii. 11.

ii. 1 ἐν τ. χάριτι τῇ ἐν Χ. Ι. : cf. v. 15, iii. 24.

ii. 8 Ἰ. Χ. ἐγηγερμένον ἐκ νεκρῶν : cf. iv. 24, vi. 4, 9. ἐκ σπέρματος Δαβίδ, i. 3 ; κατὰ τὸ εὐαγγέλιόν μου, ii. 16, xvi. 25.

ii. 11 εἰ γὰρ συναπεθάνομεν, κ. συνζήσομεν, vi. 8.

ii. 12 εἰ ὑπομένομεν, καὶ συν- ... : cf. εἴπερ συμπάσχομεν ἵνα κ. συνδοξασθῶμεν, viii. 17 : cf. 1 Cor. iv. 8.

ii. 13 εἰ ἀπιστοῦμεν κτλ. : cf. iii. 3.

ii. 15 σεαυτὸν δόκιμον παραστῆσαι τ. Θεῷ : cf. vi. 13, xiv. 18.

ii. 20 σκεύη ἃ μὲν εἰς τιμὴν ἃ δὲ εἰς ἀτιμίαν, ix. 21.

ii. 22 δίωκε δικαιοσύνην ... εἰρήνην : cf. ix. 30, xiv. 19.

ii. 25 μήποτε δῴη αὐτοῖς ὁ Θεὸς μετάνοιαν : cf. ii. 4.

iii. 1 τοῦτο γίνωσκε, ὅτι, vi. 6.
iii. 2 ἀλαζόνες, ὑπερήφανοι, γονεῦσιν ἀπειθεῖς, ἄστοργοι, i. 30 f.
Titus i. 2 ἣν ἐπηγγείλατο πρὸ χρόνων αἰωνίων, ἐφανέρωσεν δὲ . . . κατ᾽ ἐπιταγὴν τοῦ . . . Θεοῦ: cf. ὃ προεπηγγείλατο, i. 2 ; χρόνοις αἰωνίοις . . . φανερωθέντος δὲ . . . κατ᾽ ἐπιταγὴν τ. Θεοῦ, xvi. 26.
i. 2 ὁ ἀψευδὴς Θεός : cf. iii. 3.
i. 15 πάντα καθαρὰ τοῖς καθαροῖς : cf. πάντα μὲν καθαρά, xiv. 20 : cf. xiv. 14.
ii. 5 ἵνα μὴ ὁ λόγος τ. Θεοῦ βλασφημῆται : cf. ii. 24 ; cit. Isa. lii. 5 (ὄνομα τ. Θεοῦ). Cf. 1 Tim. vi. 1 ἵνα μὴ τὸ ὄνομα τ. Θεοῦ . . . βλασφημῆται.
iii. 1 ἐξουσίαις ὑποτάσσεσθαι, xiii. 1.
iii. 4 ἡ χρηστότης Θεοῦ, xi. 22.
iii. 7 δικαιωθέντες τῇ ἐκείνου χάριτι, iii. 24 : cf. v. 1.

ii. 1 *Corinthians*.

1 Tim. i. 2 Τιμοθέῳ τέκνῳ, iv. 17.
i. 3 ἐν Ἐφέσῳ, xvi. 8.
i. 12 εἰς διακονίαν, xvi. 15.
i. 12 πιστόν με ἡγήσατο . . . ἠλεήθην : cf. ἠλεημένος ὑπὸ Κυρίου πιστὸς εἶναι, vii. 25.
i. 20 οὓς παρέδωκα τῷ Σατανᾷ ἵνα . . . : cf. κέκρικα παραδοῦναι τ. τοιοῦτον τ. Σατανᾷ ἵνα, v. 5.
ii. 3 τοῦτο καλόν, vii. 26.
ii. 7 ἐτέθην ἐγὼ ἀπόστολος κ. διδάσκαλος : cf. οὓς μὲν ἔθετο ὁ Θεὸς ἀποστόλους . . . τρίτον διδασκάλους, xii. 28.
ii. 8 προσεύχεσθαι τ. ἄνδρας : cf. xi. 4.
ii. 9 ὃ πρέπει γυναιξίν : cf. πρέπον ἐστὶ γυναῖκα ἀκατακάλυπτον τ. Θεῷ προσεύχεσθαι, xi. 13.
ii. 11 f. γυνὴ μανθανέτω ἐν πάσῃ ὑποταγῇ, διδάσκειν δὲ γυναικὶ οὐκ ἐπιτρέπω . . . ἀλλ᾽ εἶναι ἐν ἡσυχίᾳ : cf. αἱ γυναῖκες ἐν τ. ἐκκλησίαις σιγάτωσαν, οὐ γὰρ ἐπιτρέπεται αὐταῖς λαλεῖν, ἀλλ᾽ ὑποτασσέσθωσαν . . ., xiv. 34 f.
ii. 13 Ἀδὰμ γὰρ πρῶτος κτλ. : cf. xi. 8, xv. 22, 45.
ii. 15 σωθήσεται δὲ διά, iii. 15 : cf. vii. 16. ἐὰν μείνωσιν, vii. 8, 20, 40.
iii. 6 ἵνα μὴ εἰς κρίμα, xi. 34.
v. 18 Βοῦν ἀλοῶντα οὐ φιμώσεις, ix. 9 : cit. Deut. xxv. 4.
v. 19 ἐκτὸς εἰ μή, xiv. 5, xv. 2.
vi. 11 ταῦτα φεῦγε : cf. vi. 18, x. 14. δίωκε ἀγάπην, xiv. 1.
vi. 14 τηρῆσαί σε τ. ἐντολήν : cf. τήρησις ἐντολῶν, vii. 19.
2 Tim. i. 2 Τιμοθέῳ ἀγαπητῷ τέκνῳ . . . ἀναμιμνήσκω σε : cf. Τιμόθεον, ὅς ἐστί μου τέκνον ἀγαπητόν . . . ὃς ὑμᾶς ἀναμνήσει, iv. 17.

APPENDIX II

i. 10 καταργήσαντος τὸν θάνατον : cf. καταργεῖται ὁ θάνατος, xv. 26.

ii. 4 f. ἐὰν δὲ καί, vii. 28 (ἀρέσῃ, vii. 33).

ii. 5 οὐ στεφανοῦται ἐὰν μὴ κτλ. : cf. ix. 25.

ii. 6 τὸν κοπιῶντα γεωργὸν κτλ. : cf. ix. 7, 10–14, iv. 12.

ii. 12 καὶ συνβασιλεύσομεν, iv. 8.

ii. 19 f. ὁ στέρεος θεμέλιος ἔστηκεν ἔχων ... (σκεύη) χρυσᾶ κ. ἀργυρᾶ κ. ξύλινα : cf. ἔστηκεν ... ἑδραῖος μὴ ἔχων ..., vii. 37; ἐπὶ τ. θεμέλιον χρυσίον, ἀργύριον, ξύλα, iii. 12.

ii. 22 μετὰ τ. ἐπικαλουμένων τ. κύριον : cf. σὺν πᾶσι τ. ἐπικαλουμένοις τ. ὄνομα τ. Κυρίου, i. 2.

Titus i. 3 τ. λόγον αὐτοῦ ἐν κηρύγματι : cf. ὁ λόγος μου κ. τ. κήρυγμά μου, ii. 4.

i. 5 ὡς ἐγώ σοι διεταξάμην : cf. vii. 17, xi. 34.

i. 7 ὡς Θεοῦ οἰκονόμον : cf. ὡς οἰκονόμους μυστηρίων Θεοῦ, iv. 1.

i. 15 μεμίανται αὐτῶν ἡ συνείδησις, viii. 7 (μολύνεται).

iii. 3–7 ἦμεν πλανώμενοι ... κληρονόμοι ... διὰ λουτροῦ ... δικαιωθέντας ... πνεύματος : cf. vi. 9 f.

iii. 2 Corinthians.

1 Tim. i. 3 εἰς Μακεδονίαν, i. 16, ii. 13, vii. 5.

i. 11 τὸ εὐαγγέλιον τῆς δόξης τοῦ (Θεοῦ), iv. 4 (Χριστοῦ ... Θεοῦ).

i. 12 θέμενος εἰς διακονίαν : cf. θέμενος ἐν ἡμῖν τ. λόγον ... δόντος ... τ. διακονίαν, v. 18 f.

i. 18 ἵνα στρατεύῃ ... τ. καλὴν στρατείαν : cf. στρατευόμεθα ... τ. ὅπλα τ. στρατείας, x. 3 f.

ii. 3 καλὸν ἐνώπιον τ. Θεοῦ : cf. καλὰ .. ἐνώπιον Κυρίου, viii. 21.

ii. 13 f. Εὕα ... ἡ γυνὴ ἐξαπατηθεῖσα : cf. ὁ ὄφις ἐξηπάτησεν Εὕαν, xi. 3 ; cit. Gen. iii. 13 (ἠπάτησεν).

iii. 15 ἐν οἴκῳ Θεοῦ ἀναστρέφεσθαι : cf. ἐν χάριτι Θεοῦ ἀνεστράφημεν ἐν τ. κόσμῳ, i. 12.

iii. 16 ἐφανερώθη ἐν σαρκί, iv. 10 f.

iv. 10 ἠλπίκαμεν ἐπὶ Θεῷ ζῶντι : cf. ἐπὶ τ. Θεῷ εἰς ὃν ἠλπίκαμεν, i. 9 f.

iv. 12 ἐν λόγῳ ... ἐν ἀγάπῃ ... ἐν ἁγνείᾳ : cf. ἐν ἁγνότητι ... ἐν ἀγάπῃ ... ἐν λόγῳ, vi. 6 f.

iv. 13 τῇ ἀναγνώσει, iii. 14.

v. 14 μηδεμίαν ἀφορμὴν διδόναι τῷ ἀντικειμένῳ λοιδορίας χάριν : cf. ἀφορμὴν διδόντες, v. 12 ; μηδεμίαν διδόντες προσκοπήν, ἵνα μὴ μωμηθῇ, vi. 3.

v. 19 ἐπὶ ϲτόματοϲ δύο μαρτύρων κ. τριῶν, xiii. 1 : cit. Deut. xix. 15.

2 Tim. i. 15 οἶδας τοῦτο ὅτι ἀπεστράφησάν με πάντες οἱ ἐν τῇ Ἀσίᾳ : cf. οὐ θέλομεν ὑμᾶς ἀγνοεῖν περὶ τ. θλίψεως ἡμῶν τῆς γενομένης ἐν τ. Ἀσίᾳ, i. 8.

ii. 10 δόξης αἰωνίου : cf. αἰώνιον βάρος δόξης, iv. 17. πάντα ὑπομένω διὰ τ.

APPENDIX II 171

ἐκλεκτούς, ἵνα κ. αὐτοὶ σωτηρίας τύχωσιν : cf. (πάντα ὑπομένει, 1 Cor. xiii. 7) ἐν ὑπομονῇ πολλῇ, vi. 4 ; εἴτε θλιβόμεθα, ὑπὲρ τῆς ὑμῶν σωτηρίας, i. 6.

ii. 11 εἰ συναπεθάνομεν κ. συζήσομεν : cf. εἰς τὸ συναποθανεῖν κ. συζῆν, vii. 3.

ii. 20 σκεύη ὀστράκινα, iv. 7.

Titus i. 3 f. κατ᾿ ἐπιταγὴν ... Τίτῳ γνησίῳ : cf. Τίτον ... κατ᾿ ἐπιταγὴν ... τὸ τ. ὑμετέρας ἀγάπης γνήσιον, viii. 6, 8.

iv. Galatians.

1 Tim. i. 2 ἐν πίστει, ii. 20.

i. 7 θέλοντες εἶναι νομοδιδάσκαλοι : cf. ὑπὸ νόμον θέλοντες εἶναι, iv. 21.

i. 13 τὸ πρότερον ὄντα διώκτην : cf. iv. 13, i. 13.

ii. 5 εἷς Θεός, εἷς καὶ μεσίτης ... : cf. ὁ δὲ μεσίτης ἑνὸς οὐκ ἔστιν, ὁ δὲ Θεὸς εἷς ἐστιν, iii. 19 f.

ii. 6, Tit. ii. 14 Ι. Χ. ὁ δοὺς ἑαυτὸν ὑπὲρ πάντων : cf. Ι. Χ. τοῦ δόντος ἑαυτὸν ὑπέρ, i. 4, ii. 20.

iii. 16 ἐκηρύχθη ἐν ἔθνεσιν : cf. ὃ κηρύσσω ἐν ἔθνεσιν, ii. 2.

v. 3 μάλιστα οἰκείων : cf. μάλιστα πρὸς τ. οἰκείους (τ. πίστεως), vi. 10.

vi. 3 εἴ τις ἑτεροδιδασκαλεῖ : cf. μετατίθεσθε εἰς ἕτερον εὐαγγέλιον ὃ οὐκ ἔστιν ἄλλο, i. 6 f. ; εἴ τις ὑμᾶς εὐαγγελίζεται παρ᾿ ὃ ἐλάβετε, i. 9.

2 Tim. i. 1 κατ᾿ ἐπαγγελίαν, iii. 29.

Titus iii. 3-7 ἦμεν ... ποτὲ καὶ ἡμεῖς ἀνόητοι ... δουλεύοντες ... ὅτε δὲ ... κληρονόμοι : cf. καὶ ἡμεῖς, ὅτε ἦμεν νήπιοι, ... ἦμεν δεδουλωμένοι· ὅτε δὲ ... κληρονόμος, iv. 3-7.

v. Ephesians.

1 Tim. i. 14 μετὰ πίστεως καὶ ἀγάπης : cf. ἀγάπη μετὰ πίστεως, vi. 23.

i. 15 ἁμαρτωλοὺς ὧν πρῶτός εἰμι ἐγώ : cf. ἐμοὶ τ. ἐλαχιστοτέρῳ κτλ., iii. 8.

iii. 16 ἵνα ἐν ἐμοὶ ἐνδείξηται Χ. Ι. τ. ἅπασαν μακροθυμίαν : cf. ἵνα ἐνδείξηται ... ἐφ᾿ ἡμᾶς ἐν Χ. Ι., ii. 7 ; μετὰ μακροθυμίας, iv. 2 ; Exod. ix. 16.

ii. 1 δεήσεις ὑπὲρ πάντων : cf. δεήσει περὶ πάντων τ. ἁγίων, vi. 18.

ii. 8 προσεύχεσθαι ἐν παντὶ (τόπῳ), vi. 18 (καιρῷ).

iii. 4 τέκνα ἔχοντα ἐν ὑποταγῇ : cf. τέκνα ὑπακούετε τ. γονεῦσιν, vi. 1.

iii. 8 μὴ οἴνῳ πολλῷ προσέχοντας : cf. μὴ μεθύσκεσθε οἴνῳ, v. 18.

iii. 16 μέγα ἐστὶ τὸ τ. εὐσεβείας μυστήριον (cf. ἐκκλησία, vs. 15) : cf. τὸ μυστήριον τοῦτο μέγα ἐστί, λέγω εἰς ... τ. ἐκκλησίαν, v. 32.

vi. 1 f. δοῦλοι ... δουλευέτωσαν : cf. vi. 7.

vi. 13 Θεοῦ τ. ζ. τὰ πάντα : cf. i. 10.

2 Tim. i. 8 ἐμὲ τὸν δέσμιον αὐτοῦ : cf. ἐγὼ ὁ δέσμιος ἐν Κυρίῳ, iii. 1, iv. 1.

i. 10 φωτίσαντος ... διὰ τ. εὐαγγελίου: cf. εὐαγγελίσασθαι καὶ φωτίσαι, iii. 9.
ii. 1 ἐνδυναμοῦ ἐν τ. χάριτι τ. ἐν Χ. Ι.: cf. ἐνδυναμοῦσθε ἐν Κυρίῳ, vi. 10.
ii. 15 τὸν λόγον τῆς ἀληθείας, i. 13.
iv. 3 κατὰ τὰς ἐπιθυμίας τ. ἰδίας: cf. κατὰ τὰς ἐπιθυμίας τ. ἀπάτης, iv. 22.
Titus i. 5 τούτου χάριν, iii. 1, 14.
ii. 5 ὑποτασσομένας τοῖς ἰδίοις ἀνδράσιν, v. 21 f.
ii. 9 δούλους ἰδίοις δεσπόταις ὑποτάσσεσθαι: cf. οἱ δοῦλοι ὑπακούετε τοῖς κατὰ σάρκα κυρίοις, vi. 5.
iii. 3–5 ἦμεν ... ποτε καὶ ἡμεῖς ... ἐπιθυμίαις ... χρηστότης ... οὐκ ἐξ ἔργων ... ἔσωσεν ἡμᾶς διὰ λουτροῦ ... διὰ Ι. Χ. ... πλουσίως ... τῇ ἐκείνου χάριτι: cf. καὶ ἡμεῖς ... ποτε ἐν τ. ἐπιθυμίαις ... ἤμεθα ... πλούσιος ὢν ... τὸ ... πλοῦτος τῆς χάριτος αὐτοῦ ἐν χρηστότητι ἐφ' ἡμᾶς ἐν Χ. Ι. τῇ γὰρ χάριτί ἐστε σεσωσμένοι ... οὐκ ἐξ ἔργων, ii. 3–7; καθαρίσας τῷ λουτρῷ, v. 26.

vi. *Philippians.*

1 Tim. i. 2 Τιμοθέῳ γνησίῳ τέκνῳ: cf. Τιμόθεον ... ὅτι ὡς πατρὶ τέκνον ..., ii. 19, 22 (γνήσιε, iv. 3).
ii. 8 χωρὶς ὀργῆς καὶ διαλογισμοῦ: cf. χωρὶς γογγυσμῶν καὶ διαλογισμῶν, ii. 14.
iv. 3 μέτα εὐχαριστίας, iv. 6.
iv. 12 τύπος γίνου: cf. iii 17.
iv. 15 ἵνα σου ἡ προκοπὴ φανερὰ ᾖ πᾶσιν: cf. i. 12 f., 25.
v. 4 μηδεμίαν ... τῷ ἀντικειμένῳ: cf. i. 28.
vi. 4 φθόνος, ἔρις, i. 15.
2 Tim. i. 3 ἐν τ. δεήσεσί μου: cf. ἐν πάσῃ δεήσει μου, i. 4.
i. 4 ἵνα χαρᾶς πληρωθῶ: cf. πληρώσατέ μου τὴν χαράν, ii. 2.
i. 10 τ. σωτῆρος ἡμῶν Ι. Χ.: cf. σωτῆρα ... Ι. Χ., iii. 20.
i. 13 ὧν παρ' ἐμοῦ ἤκουσας: cf. ἃ ἠκούσατε ἐν ἐμοί, iv. 9.
ii. 3 ὡς καλὸς στρατιώτης Χ. Ι.: cf. τ. συνστρατιώτην μου, ii. 25.
ii. 9 μέχρι δεσμῶν ... ὁ λόγος τ. Θεοῦ οὐ δέδεται: cf. ii. 30, i. 12–17 f.
i. 16–18: cf. ii. 25–30, p. 129 f.
iv. 6–22: cf. p. 112 f.
Titus i. 10 μάλιστα οἱ ἐκ τῆς, iv. 22.
iii. 15 ἀσπάζονταί σε οἱ μετ' ἐμοῦ πάντες, iv. 21 f. (σύν), p. 116.

vii. *Colossians.*

1 Tim. i. 1 Χ. Ι. τῆς ἐλπίδος: cf. i. 27.
i. 4 οἰκονομίαν Θεοῦ, i. 25.
i. 17 ἀοράτῳ Θεῷ, i. 15.

APPENDIX II 173

iii. 7 δεῖ δὲ καὶ μαρτυρίαν καλὴν ἔχειν ἀπὸ τῶν ἔξωθεν : cf. iv. 5.
iii. 15 ἵνα εἰδῇς πῶς δεῖ . . ., iv. 6.
iii. 16 τὸ μυστήριον . . . ὃς ἐφανερώθη : cf. τὸ μυστήριον ἐφανερώθη, i. 26.
iv. 3, 6 τοῖς πιστοῖς κ. ἐπεγνωκόσι τ. ἀλήθειαν . . ἀδελφοῖς : cf. τοῖς πιστοῖς ἀδελφοῖς . . . . ἐπέγνωτε τ. χάριν τ. Θεοῦ ἐν ἀληθείᾳ, i. 2, 6.
iv. 6 καλὸς διάκονος Χ. Ι. : cf. πιστὸς διάκονος τ. Χρ., i. 7.
iv. 10 εἰς τοῦτο κοπιῶμεν κ. ἀγωνιζόμεθα : cf. εἰς ὃ κοπιῶ ἀγωνιζόμενος, i. 29.
vi. 12 εἰς ἣν ἐκλήθης, iii. 15.
vi. 21 ἡ χάρις μεθ᾽ ὑμῶν, iv. 18.
2 Tim. iv. 6–22 : cf. pp. 111 ff., 122 ff.
Titus i. 10 οἱ ἐκ περιτομῆς, iv. 11.

viii. 1 Thessalonians.

1 Tim. i. 14 πίστεως καὶ ἀγάπης, v. 8.
v. 1 παρακάλει ὡς πατέρα : cf. ὡς πατὴρ τέκνα παρακαλοῦντες, ii. 11.
v. 5 νυκτὸς κ. ἡμέρας, iii. 10.
v. 21 καὶ οἱ λοιποί, iv. 13.
2 Tim. i. 3 f. χάριν ἔχω τῷ Θεῷ . . . ὡς . . . ἔχω τὴν περὶ σοῦ μνείαν, ἐν τ. δεήσεσί μου νυκτὸς κ. ἡμέρας ἐπιποθῶν σε ἰδεῖν . . . ἵνα χαρᾶς πληρωθῶ . . . τῆς ἐν σοὶ . . . πίστεως : cf. εὐχαριστοῦμεν τῷ Θεῷ, i. 2, 13 ; ὅτι ἔχετε μνείαν ἡμῶν . . . ἐπιποθοῦντες ἡμᾶς ἰδεῖν καθάπερ κ. ἡμεῖς ὑμᾶς . . . ἐπὶ πάσῃ τ. χαρᾷ ᾗ χαίρομεν δι᾽ ὑμᾶς . . . νυκτὸς κ. ἡμέρας . . . δεόμενοι εἰς τὸ ἰδεῖν κτλ. . . . τῆς πίστεως ὑμῶν, iii. 6, 10.
iv. 18 εἰς τὴν βασιλείαν αὐτοῦ, ii. 12.
Titus ii. 3 πίστει . . . ἀγάπῃ . . . ὑπομονῇ : cf. i. 3.

ix. 2 Thessalonians.

1 Tim. ii. 12 ἐν ἡσυχίᾳ : cf. iii. 12.
ii. 15 σωθήσεται . . . ἐν πίστει καὶ ἁγιασμῷ : cf. εἰς σωτηρίαν ἐν ἁγιασμῷ . . . καὶ πίστει, ii. 13.
vi. 14 μέχρι τ. ἐπιφανείας τ. Κυρίου Ι. Χ. . . . : cf. τ. ἐπιφανείᾳ τ. παρουσίας αὐτοῦ (Κυρίου), ii. 8.
Titus ii. 8 ἵνα ὁ ἐξ ἐναντίας ἐντραπῇ : cf. εἰ δέ τις οὐχ ὑπακούει τ. λόγῳ ἡμῶν . . . τοῦτον σημειοῦσθε . . . ἵνα ἐντραπῇ, iii. 14.

x. Philemon.

1 Tim. i. 9 εἰδὼς ὅτι, 21.
iii. 13 πολλὴν παρρησίαν ἐν Χριστῷ, 8.
v. 13 ἅμα δὲ καί, 22.
vi. 2 οἱ (δοῦλοι) πιστοὺς ἔχοντες δεσπότας . . . ὅτι ἀδελφοί εἰσιν, ἀλλὰ μᾶλλον δουλευέτωσαν, ὅτι πιστοί εἰσι καὶ ἀγαπητοί : cf. τ. πίστιν ἣν

ἔχεις, 5; οὐκέτι ὡς δοῦλον ἀλλὰ ὑπὲρ δοῦλον, ἀδελφὸν ἀγαπητόν ... πόσῳ δὲ μᾶλλον ..., 16.

2 Tim. iv. 11 μοι εὔχρηστος εἰς διακονίαν, 11.

xi. *More than one Pauline Epistle.*

1 Tim. i. 1 Παῦλος ἀπόστολος Χ. Ι., 2 Cor. i. 1; Eph. i. 1; Col. i. 1. κατ' ἐπιταγήν, Rom. xvi. 26; 1 Cor. vii. 6; 2 Cor. viii. 8.

i. 2 χάρις ... εἰρήνη ἀπὸ Θεοῦ πατρὸς καὶ Χ. Ι. τ. Κυρίου ἡμῶν: cf. χάρις ὑμῖν καὶ εἰρήνη ἀπὸ Θεοῦ πατρὸς ἡμῶν κ. Κυρίου Ι. Χ., Rom. i. 7; 1 Cor. i. 3; 2 Cor. i. 2; Gal. i. 3; Eph. i. 2; Phil. i. 2; Philem. 3.

i. 8 οἴδαμεν ὅτι, Rom. ii. 2, iii. 19, viii. 28; 1 Cor. viii. 1, 4; 2 Cor. v. 1.

i. 11 τὸ εὐαγγέλιον ... ὃ ἐπιστεύθην ἐγώ: cf. πεπίστευμαι τὸ εὐαγγέλιον, Gal. ii. 7; δεδοκιμάσμεθα ... πιστευθῆναι τὸ εὐαγγέλιον, 1 Thess. ii. 4.

i. 12 Χ. Ι. τῷ Κυρίῳ ἡμῶν, Rom. vi. 23, viii. 39; 1 Cor. xv. 31; Eph. iii. 11: cf. Phil. iii. 8 (μου).

i. 17 δόξα εἰς τοὺς αἰῶνας τῶν αἰώνων. ἀμήν, Rom. xvi. 27; Gal. i. 5; Phil. iv. 20: cf. Eph. iii. 21.

ii. 1 Παρακαλῶ οὖν, Rom. xii. 1; 1 Cor. iv. 16; Eph. iv. 1.

ii. 3, v. 4, 21, vi. 13. ἐνώπιον τοῦ Θεοῦ, Rom. xiv. 22; 1 Cor. i. 29; 2 Cor. iv. 2, vii. 12; Gal. i. 20.

ii. 5 εἷς Θεός, Rom. iii. 30; 1 Cor. viii. 6; Gal. iii. 20; Eph. iv. 6. εἷς ... ἄνθρωπος Χ. Ι.: cf. Rom. v. 15; 1 Cor. viii. 6; 2 Cor. v. 15; Eph. iv. 5; Gal. iii. 16, 20.

ii. 7 οὐ ψεύδομαι, Rom. ix. 1; 2 Cor. xi. 31; Gal. i. 20. ἐν ἀληθείᾳ, 2 Cor. vii. 14; Eph. v. 9, vi. 14; Col. i. 6.

ii. 8 ἐν παντὶ τόπῳ, 1 Cor. i. 2; 2 Cor. ii. 14; 1 Thess. i. 8.

ii. 15 ἐν ἁγιασμῷ, 1 Thess. iv. 4, 7; 2 Thess. ii. 13.

iii. 13 πολλὴν παρρησίαν, 2 Cor. iii. 12, vii. 4; Philem. 8.

iii. 15 Θεοῦ ζῶντος, Rom. ix. 26: cit. Hos. ii. 1; 2 Cor. iii. 3, vi. 16; 1 Thess. i. 9.

iv. 5 λόγος Θεοῦ, Rom. ix. 6; 1 Cor. xiv. 36; 2 Cor. ii. 17, iv. 2; Phil. i. 14; Col. i. 25; 1 Thess. ii. 13.

iv. 6 διάκονος Χριστοῦ, 2 Cor. xi. 23; Col. i. 7.

v. 10 (2 Tim. ii. 21, iii. 17; Titus i. 16, iii. 1) πᾶν ἔργον ἀγαθόν, 2 Cor. ix. 8; Col. i. 10; 2 Thess. ii. 17; ἔργον ἀγαθόν, Rom. ii. 7, xiii. 3; Eph. ii. 10; Phil. i. 6.

v. 13 οὐ μόνον δὲ ... ἀλλὰ καί, Rom. v. 3; 2 Cor. viii. 19; Eph. i. 21; Phil. i. 29; 1 Thess. i. 5.

APPENDIX II

2 Tim. i. 1 Παῦλος ἀπόστολος Χ. Ι. διὰ θελήματος Θεοῦ, 1 Cor. i. 1; 2 Cor. i. 1; Eph. i. 1; Col. i. 1. διὰ θελήματος Θεοῦ, Rom. xv. 32; 2 Cor. viii. 5.

i. 3 (1 Tim. v. 5) νυκτὸς καὶ ἡμέρας, 1 Thess. ii. 9, iii. 10; 2 Thess. iii. 8. ἐπιποθῶν σε (ὑμᾶς) ἰδεῖν, Rom. i. 11; Phil. ii. 26; 1 Thess. iii. 6.

i. 8 δύναμις Θεοῦ, Rom. i. 16; 1 Cor. i. 18, 24, ii. 5; 2 Cor. vi. 7, xiii. 3 f. (Eph. i. 19 iii. 7 αὐτοῦ).

i. 9 κατὰ χάριν τὴν δοθεῖσαν ἡμῖν, Rom. xii. 6; 1 Cor. iii. 10 (μοι): cf. Rom. xii. 3; 1 Cor. i. 4; 2 Cor. viii. 1; Gal. ii. 9; Eph. iii. 2, 7; Col. i. 25. κατὰ πρόθεσιν, Rom. viii. 28; Eph. i. 11, iii. 11. καλέσαντος κλήσει (ἁγίᾳ): cf. τ. κλήσει ᾗ ἐκλήθη, 1 Cor. vii. 20; τ. κλήσεως ἧς ἐκλήθητε, Eph. iv. 1.

i. 10 (Titus i. 3)... φανερωθεῖσαν δὲ νῦν: cf....φανερωθέντος δὲ νῦν, Rom. xvi. 26; νῦν δὲ ἐφανερώθη, Col. i. 26. διὰ τοῦ εὐαγγελίου, 1 Cor. iv. 15; Eph. iii. 6; 2 Thess. ii. 14.

iii. 15 εἰς σωτηρίαν (Isa. xlix. 6), Rom. i. 16, x. 1, 10; 2 Cor. vii. 10; Phil. i. 19; 2 Thess. ii. 13 (Acts xiii. 47; 1 Pet. i. 5, ii. 2).

Titus i. 1 Παῦλος δοῦλος, Rom. i. 1; Phil. i. 1: cf. 1 Cor. vii. 22; Gal. i. 10; Col. iv. 12. ἐκλεκτῶν Θεοῦ, Rom. viii. 33; Col. iii. 12.

i. 2 ἐπ' ἐλπίδι, Rom. iv. 18, v. 2, viii. 20; 1 Cor. ix. 10.

i. 10 οἱ ἐκ περιτομῆς, Col. iv. 11; Gal. ii. 12.

ii. 11 ἡ χάρις τοῦ Θεοῦ, Rom. v. 15; 1 Cor. i. 4, xv. 10; 2 Cor. i. 12; Gal. ii. 21; Eph. iii. 2; Col. i. 6; 2 Thess. i. 12.

iii. 5 οὐκ ἐξ ἔργων, Rom. iii. 20, xi. 6; Gal. ii. 16; Eph. ii. 9.

C.

1 PETER AND THE PASTORALS

1 Tim. i. 1 Παῦλος ἀπόστολος Χ. Ι. κατ' ἐπιταγὴν Θεοῦ σωτῆρος: cf. Πέτρος ἀπόστολος Ι. Χ. κατὰ πρόγνωσιν Θεοῦ πατρός, i. 1 f.

i. 5 τὸ δὲ τέλος... ἀγάπη ἐκ καθαρᾶς καρδίας κ. συνειδήσεως ἀγαθῆς κ. πίστεως ἀνυποκρίτου: cf. τὸ δὲ τέλος... φιλάδελφοι, iii. 8; εἰς φιλαδελφίαν ἀνυπόκριτον ἐκ καθαρᾶς καρδίας ἀλλήλους ἀγαπήσατε, i. 22, and i. 9.

i. 19 ἔχων... ἀγαθὴν συνείδησιν, iii. 16, 21.

ii. 1–3 παρακαλῶ... ποιεῖσθαι δεήσεις... ὑπὲρ βασιλέων κ. πάντων τῶν ἐν ὑπεροχῇ ὄντων... τοῦτο καλὸν κ. ἀπόδεκτον ἐνώπιον τ. Θεοῦ: cf. παρακαλῶ, ii. 11; ὑποτάγητε πάσῃ ἀνθρωπίνῃ κτίσει,... εἴτε βασιλεῖ, ὡς ὑπερέχοντι, εἴτε ἡγεμόσιν, ii. 13; ὅτι οὕτως ἐστὶ τὸ θέλημα τ. Θεοῦ, ii. 15.

ii. 7 τὸ μαρτύριον ... εἰς ὃ ἐτέθην ἐγώ : cf. τῷ λόγῳ ... εἰς ὃ καὶ ἐτέθησαν, ii. 8 (2 Tim. i. 11).

ii. 9 ὡσαύτως γυναῖκας ἐν καταστολῇ κοσμίῳ ... κοσμεῖν ἑαυτάς, μὴ ἐν πλέγμασι κ. χρυσίῳ ... ἢ ἱματισμῷ πολυτελεῖ, ἀλλ' (ὃ πρέπει γυναιξὶν ἐπαγγελλομέναις θεοσέβειαν) ... : cf. ὁμοίως γυναῖκες ... ὧν ἔστω οὐχ ὁ ἔξωθεν ἐμπλοκῆς τριχῶν κ. περιθέσεως χρυσίων ἢ ἐνδύσεως ἱματίων κόσμος, ἀλλ' ... ὅ ἐστιν ἐνώπιον τ. Θεοῦ πολυτελές, iii. 3.

ii. 15 ἐν ἁγιασμῷ, i. 2.

iii. 2 φιλόξενον, iv. 9.

iii. 7 δεῖ δὲ κ. μαρτυρίαν καλὴν ἔχειν ἀπὸ τῶν ἔξωθεν, ἵνα μὴ εἰς ὀνειδισμόν ..., iii. 15 πῶς δεῖ ... ἀναστρέφεσθαι : cf. τὴν ἀναστροφὴν ὑμῶν ἐν τ. ἔθνεσιν ἔχοντες καλήν, ἵνα ἐν ᾧ καταλαλοῦσιν ὑμῶν, ii. 12.

iii. 8 διακόνους ... μὴ αἰσχροκερδεῖς : cf. πρεσβυτέρους ... μηδὲ αἰσχροκερδῶς, v. 1 f.

iii. 15 ἐν οἴκῳ Θεοῦ, iv. 17.

iii. 16 ἐφανερώθη ἐν σαρκί,   cf. θανατωθεὶς μὲν σαρκί, iii. 18 f.
ἐδικαιώθη ἐν πνεύματι,   ζωοποιηθεὶς δὲ πνεύματι,
ὤφθη ἀγγέλοις,   ὑποταγέντων αὐτῷ ἀγγέλων,
ἐκηρύχθη ἐν ἔθνεσιν,   τοῖς ἐν φυλακῇ πνεύμασι ... ἐκήρυξεν ...
ἐπιστεύθη ἐν κόσμῳ,   εἰς ὃν πιστεύοντες, ii. 6 f.
ἀνελήφθη ἐν δόξῃ.   ὅς ἐστιν ἐν δεξιᾷ τοῦ Θεοῦ κτλ., iii. 22.

iv. 12 μηδείς σου ... καταφρονείτω, ἀλλὰ τύπος γίνου τ. πιστῶν ... ἐν ἀναστροφῇ ... ἐν ἁγνείᾳ : cf. μηδ' ὡς κατακυριεύοντες ... ἀλλὰ τύποι γινόμενοι τ. ποιμνίου, v. 3 ; ἅγιοι ἐν πάσῃ ἀναστροφῇ γενήθητε, i. 15.

iv. 14 μὴ ἀμέλει τοῦ ἐν σοὶ χαρίσματος : cf. ἕκαστος καθὼς ἔλαβε χάρισμα, iv. 10.

v. 1 πρεσβυτέρῳ ... παρακάλει ὡς πατέρα, νεωτέρους ὡς ἀδελφούς : cf. πρεσβυτέρους ... παρακαλῶ, v. 1 ; νεώτεροι, ὑποτάγητε πρεσβυτέροις, v. 5.

v. 5 ἡ δὲ ὄντως χήρα ... ἤλπικεν ἐπὶ Θεόν : cf. αἱ ἅγιαι γυναῖκες αἱ ἐλπίζουσαι εἰς Θεόν, iii. 5.

v. 14 μηδεμίαν ἀφορμὴν διδόναι τῷ ἀντικειμένῳ λοιδορίας χάριν : cf. μὴ ἀποδίδοντες ... λοιδορίαν ἀντὶ λοιδορίας, iii. 9.

vi. 1 δοῦλοι, τοὺς ἰδίους δεσπότας πάσης τιμῆς ἀξίους ἡγείσθωσαν : cf. οἱ οἰκέται ὑποτασσόμενοι ... τοῖς δεσπόταις, ii. 18.

vi. 12 εἰς ἣν ἐκλήθης : cf. εἰς τοῦτο ἐκλήθητε, iii. 19.

vi. 17 f. μὴ ὑψηλοφρονεῖν, ... ἀγαθοεργεῖν : cf. τὴν ταπεινοφροσύνην, v. 5 ; ἀγαθοποιοῦντες, ii. 20.

2 Tim. i. 1 f. Π. ἀπόστολος Χ. Ι. ... Θεοῦ πατρός ... Χ. Ι. ... χάρις, ἔλεος, εἰρήνη, ... Χ. Ι. τ. Κυρίου ἡμῶν, i. 1–3.

i. 5 ἀνυπόκριτος, i. 22, i. 6 χάρισμα, iv. 10.

APPENDIX II

i. 12 δι' ἣν αἰτίαν κ. ταῦτα πάσχω· ἀλλ' οὐκ ἐπαισχύνομαι, οἶδα γὰρ ᾧ πεπίστευκα, κ. πέπεισμαι ὅτι δυνατός ἐστι τ. παραθήκην μου φυλάξαι: cf. μὴ γάρ τις ὑμῶν πασχέτω ὡς... κακοποιὸς ... εἰ δὲ ὡς Χριστιανός, μὴ αἰσχυνέσθω, iv. 15; ὁ πιϲτεγων ἐπ' ἀγτῷ ογ μὴ καταιϲχγνθῇ, ii. 6; ὥστε κ. οἱ πάσχοντες κατὰ τὸ θέλημα τ. Θεοῦ πιστῷ κτίστῃ παρατιθέσθωσαν τὰς ψυχάς, iv. 19.

ii. 3 ὡς καλὸς στρατιώτης: cf. ὡς καλοὶ οἰκονόμοι, iv. 10.

ii. 8 I. X. ἐγηγερμένον ἐκ νεκρῶν: cf. i. 3, 21.

ii. 9 ἐν ᾧ κακοπαθῶ... ὡς κακοῦργος... πάντα ὑπομένω κτλ.: cf. ἐν ᾧ καταλαλοῦσιν ὑμῶν ὡς κακοποιῶν, ... εἰ ἀγαθοποιοῦντες κ. πάσχοντες ὑπομενεῖτε, ii. 12, 20.

ii. 22 ἐκ καρδίας, i. 22.

iii. 15 εἰς σωτηρίαν διὰ πίστεως, i. 5.

iv. 1 τοῦ μέλλοντος κρίνειν ζῶντας καὶ νεκρούς: cf. τῷ ἑτοίμως κρίνοντι ζῶντας καὶ νεκρούς, iv. 5.

Titus i. 1 Π. ἀπόστολος I. X. κατὰ πίστιν ἐκλεκτῶν Θεοῦ: cf. Π. ἀπόστολος I. X. ... ἐκλεκτοῖς ... κατὰ πρόγνωσιν Θεοῦ, i. 1.

iii. 5 κατὰ τὸ αὑτοῦ ἔλεος: cf. κατὰ τὸ πολὺ αὐτοῦ ἔλεος, i. 3.

ii. 3 πρεσβύτιδας ὡσαύτως ... τὰς νέας ... ὑποτασσομένας τοῖς ἰδίοις ἀνδράσιν: cf. ὁμοίως γυναῖκες ὑποτασσόμεναι τοῖς ἰδίοις ἀνδράσιν, iii. 1.

D.

1 CLEMENT AND THE PASTORALS

1 Tim. i. 16 τῶν μελλόντων πιστεύειν, xlii. 4.

i. 17 τῷ δὲ βασιλεῖ τῶν αἰώνων ... δόξα εἰς τοὺς αἰῶνας τῶν αἰώνων. ἀμήν: cf. βασιλεῦ τῶν αἰώνων, lxi. 2 ...; ᾧ ἔστω ἡ δόξα εἰς τοὺς αἰῶνας τῶν αἰώνων. ἀμήν, xxxii. 4.

ii. 3 καλὸν καὶ ἀπόδεκτον ἐνώπιον τοῦ Θεοῦ: cf. καλὸν καὶ πρόσδεκτον ἐνώπιον τοῦ ποιήσαντος ἡμᾶς, vii. 3.

ii. 6 (vi. 15, Titus i. 3) καιροῖς ἰδίοις, xx. 4, 10.

ii. 7 ἐν πίστει καὶ ἀληθείᾳ, lx. 4.

ii. 8 βούλομαι οὖν προσεύχεσθαι τοὺς ἄνδρας ... ἐπαίροντας ὁσίους χεῖρας: cf. προσέλθωμεν οὖν αὐτῷ ἐν ὁσιότητι ψυχῆς, ἁγνὰς καὶ ἀμιάντους χεῖρας αἴροντες, xxix. 1.

ii. 9 f. κοσμεῖν ἑαυτάς ... δι' ἔργων ἀγαθῶν: cf. ἐν ἔργοις ἀγαθοῖς ... ἐκοσμήθησαν, xxxiii. 7.

v. 17 οἱ καλῶς προεστῶτες πρεσβύτεροι διπλῆς τιμῆς ἀξιούσθωσαν: cf. τιμὴν τὴν καθήκουσαν ἀπονέμοντες τοῖς παρ' ὑμῖν πρεσβυτέροις, i. 3; ἐνίους μετηγάγετε καλῶς πολιτευμένους, xliv. 6.

v. 21 μηδὲν ποιῶν κατὰ πρόσκλισιν: cf. μὴ κατὰ προσκλίσεις, xxi. 7, l. 2.

v. 24 f. τινῶν . . . αἱ ἁμαρτίαι πρόδηλοί εἰσι, προάγουσαι εἰς κρίσιν : cf. ὧν τὸ κρῖμα πρόδηλον ἐγενήθη, li. 3.

vi. 1 ὑπὸ ζυγόν, xvi. 17.

vi. 7 f. ἔχοντες διατροφὰς κ. σκεπάσματα, τούτοις ἀρκεσθησόμεθα : cf. τοῖς ἐφοδίοις τοῦ Θεοῦ ἀρκούμενοι, ii. 2.

2 Tim. i. 3 Θεῷ ᾧ λατρεύω . . . ἐν καθαρᾷ συνειδήσει : cf. τῶν ἐν καθαρᾷ συνειδήσει λατρευόντων τῷ . . . ὀνόματι αὐτοῦ, xlv. 7.

ii. 2 ἃ ἤκουσας παρ' ἐμοῦ . . . ταῦτα παράθου πιστοῖς ἀνθρώποις, οἵτινες ἱκανοὶ ἔσονται καὶ ἑτέρους διδάξαι : cf. xliv. οἱ ἀπόστολοι . . . κατέστησαν τοὺς προειρημένους, κ. μεταξὺ ἐπιμονὴν δέδωκασιν ὅπως, ἐὰν κοιμηθῶσιν, διαδέξωνται ἕτεροι δεδοκιμασμένοι ἄνδρες τὴν λειτουργίαν αὐτῶν, xliv. 2 ; ἐπέμψαμεν . . . ἄνδρας πιστοὺς . . . οἵτινες κ. μάρτυρες ἔσονται, lxiii. 3.

ii. 12 ἀρνήσασθαι γὰρ ἑαυτὸν οὐ δύναται, (Titus i. 2 ὁ ἀψευδὴς Θεός) : cf. οὐδὲν γὰρ ἀδύνατον παρὰ τῷ Θεῷ, εἰ μὴ τὸ ψεύσασθαι, xxvii. 2.

ii. 22 τὰς νεωτερικὰς ἐπιθυμίας φεῦγε : cf. φεύγοντες . . . μέθας τε κ. νεωτερισμοὺς κ. βδελυκτὰς ἐπιθυμίας, xxx. 1.

ii. 31 εἰς πᾶν ἔργον ἀγαθὸν ἡτοιμασμένον : cf. εἰς πᾶν ἔργον ἀγαθὸν ἕτοιμοι, ii. 7.

iii. 15 ff. ἱερὰ γράμματα : cf. ἱερὰς γραφάς, liii. 1, xlv. 2 f.

Titus i. 5 ἵνα καταστήσῃς κατὰ πόλιν πρεσβυτέρους κτλ. : cf. κατὰ . . . πόλεις κηρύσσοντες καθίστανον τ. ἀπαρχὰς αὐτῶν, . . . εἰς ἐπισκόπους καὶ διακόνους . . ., xlii. 4.

ii. 5 ἵνα σωφρονίζωσι τὰς νέας φιλάνδρους εἶναι, . . . σώφρονας, ἁγνάς, οἰκουργούς, ὑποτασσομένας τοῖς ἰδίοις ἀνδράσιν : cf. γυναιξίν . . . ἐν ἀμώμῳ κ. σεμνῇ κ. ἁγνῇ συνειδήσει, . . . στεργούσας καθηκόντως τοὺς ἄνδρας ἑαυτῶν· ἔν τε τῷ κανόνι τῆς ὑποταγῆς ὑπαρχούσας τὰ κατὰ τὸν οἶκον σεμνῶς οἰκουργεῖν ἐδιδάσκετε, πάνυ σωφρονούσας, i. 3.

ii. 10 πίστις ἀγαθή, xxvi. 1.

ii. 14 λαὸν περιούϲιον, lxiv. 1.

iii. 1 πρὸς πᾶν ἔργον ἀγαθὸν ἑτοίμους εἶναι, ii. 7 ; ἀρχαῖς ἐξουσίαις ὑποτάσσεσθαι : cf. ὑποτασσόμενοι τοῖς ἡγουμένοις ὑμῶν, i. 3.

iii. 8 καλὰ καὶ ὠφέλιμα, lxi. 2.

APPENDIX III

BIBLIOGRAPHY

1. *Special editions and Introductions to the Pastorals.*

F. Schleiermacher, *1 Tim.* Berl. 1807; H. L. Planck, *1 Tim.* Gött. 1808; J. F. Beckhaus, *Hapax Leg. in 1 Tim.* Ling. 1810; J. A. L. Wegscheider, *1 Tim.* Gött. 1810; C. T. Kuinoel, Titus (in *Com. Theol.* ed. Velthusen), 1812; J. F. C. Löffler, '1 Tim.' (*Kleine Schriften*), Weimar, 1817; H. G. Van den Es, Lugd. Bat. 1819; H. F. Elsner (*Paulus u. Jesaias*, p. 17 ff.), Vratisl. 1819; A. L. C. Heydenreich, Hadamar, 1826-8; A. Curtius, *1 Tim.* Ber. 1828; A. Koraes, *Tit.* Paris, 1828-31; J. Broechner, Hafn, 1829; G. Boehl, Ber. 1829; J. F. v. Flatt (ed. C. F. Kling), Tüb. 1831; E. Demôle, *2 Tim.* Geneva, 1831; F. C. Baur, Stuttgart, 1835; M. J. Mack, Tüb. 1836; G. E. Leo, Lips. 1837-50, Zittau, 1884; M. Baumgarten, Ber. 1837; E. T. Mayerhoff, *Col. mit vorn. Berücksichtigung der drei Past.* Ber. 1838; C. S. Matthies, Greifswald, 1840; L. R. Rolle, Arg. 1841; R. Møller, Copenhagen, 1842; F. Hitzig (*Joh. Markus u. seine Schriften*, p. 154 ff.), Zürich, 1843; A. Barnes, N. York, 1845; Blau, *Tit.* 1846; C. Scharling, Jena, 1846; S. F. Good, Montauban, 1848; J. E. Huther (Meyer's *Comm.*), Gött. 1850, E. Tr., Edin. 1881; J. B. Sumner, Lon. 1851; A. Saintes, Par. 1852; T. Rudow, Gött. 1852; P. Doumergue, *1 Tim.* Strassb. 1856; A. Dubois, *1 Tim.* Strassb. 1856; W. Mangold, *Irrlehrer der PB.* Marburg, 1856; C. J. Ellicott, Lon. 1856, [b]1883; H. E. Vinke, Utrecht, 1859; J. Diedrich, Lips. 1860; W. Graham, *Tit.* Lon. 1860; C. W. Otto, Lips. 1860; F. Märcker, Meiningen, 1861; F. G. Ginella, Vratisl. 1865; E. Belin, Strassb. 1865; A. C. Larsen, Copenh. 1869; J. T. Plitt, Ber. 1872; P. Bordier, *Les Épîtres Pastorales*, 1872; E. Herzog, *Abfassungszeit der PB.* 1872; P. Fairbairn, Edin. 1874; R. Rothe, Wittenb. 1876; E. Reuss, Par. 1878; J. T. Beck, *1 and 2 Tim.* Gütersl. 1879; P. Cassel, *Tit.* Ber. 1880; H. J. Holtzmann, Lips. 1880; H. Koelling, *1 Tim.* Ber. 1882-7; L. Lemme, *Das echte Ermahnungsschreiben des Ap. Paulus an Tim.* Bresl. 1882; J. Cuendet, *La Doctrine des Ép. Past.* Lausanne, 1883; E. Kühl, *Die Gemeindeordnung in den PB.* Ber. 1885; J. Müller, *Verf. der chr. Kirche in den ersten beiden Jhdten. u. . . . Kritik der PB.* Lips. 1885; A. Rowland, Lon. 1887; K. Knoke, Gött. 1887-9; A. Plummer, Lon. 1888; E. Bertrand, Par. 1888; F. H. Hesse, Halle, 1889; M. F. Sadler, Lon. 1890; A. Bourquin, Geneva, 1890; A. E. Humphreys, Camb. 1895; F. Dehninger, *Die Grundbegriffe der*

PB., Gütersl. 1896; H. P. Liddon, *1 Tim.* 1897; E. Riggenbach and O. Zöckler, ²1897; A. Röricht, Gütersl. 1897; J. H. Bernard, Camb. 1899; F. W. Stellhorn, Gütersl. 1899; W. E. Bowen, Lon. 1900; R. F. Horton, Edin. 1901; R. M. Pope, Lon. 1901; J. P. Lilley, Edin. 1901; W. Kelly, *Tit. and Philem.* Lon. 1901; P. Ewald, *Probabilia betr. den Text des 1 Tim.* Erlangen, 1901; E. Krukenberg, Gütersl. 1901; J. v. Andel, Leiden, 1904; A. Schlatter, Stuttg. 1904; T. C. Laughlin, *The P.E. in the Light of One Roman Imprisonment*, California, 1905; J. D. James, Lon. 1906; J. E. Belser, Freiburg, 1907; E. Xantop, *1 Tim.* Neumünster, 1909; F. Maier, *Hauptprobleme der PB.*, Münster, 1910; H. W. Fulford, Camb. 1911; R. St. J. Parry, Camb. 1920.

2. *N. T. Introductions and Commentaries*

J. E. C. Schmidt, Giessen, 1804; J. Macknight, *Apost. Epistles*, Lon. 1809; J. G. Eichhorn, Lips. 1812; T. H. Horne, Lon. 1818; L. Bertholdt, Erlangen, 1819; J. L. Hug, Stuttg. 1808; A. B. Feilmoser, Tüb. 1810–30; W. M. L. de Wette, Ber. 1826; H. C. F. Guerike, Halle, 1828; H. A. Schott, Jena, 1830; M. Schneckenburger, Stuttg. 1832; K. A. Credner, Halle, 1836; C. G. Neudecker, Lips. 1840; J. B. Glaire, Par. 1841; E. Reuss, Halle, 1842, E. Tr., Edin. 1884; H. E. F. Guericke, *N.-T. Isagogik*, Lips. 1842; K. A. Credner, Giessen, 1843; W. M. L. de Wette, Lips. 1844; H. Alford, Lon. 1849–84; J. T. A. Wiesinger (in Olshausen's *Comm.*), 1850, E. Tr., Edin. 1851; A. Maier, Freiburg, 1852; F. Reithmayr, 1852; J. J. van Oosterzee (Lange's *Bibelwerk*, N. T. xi), Bielefeld, 1860, E. Tr., Edin. 1869; F. Bleek, Ber. 1862; J. Langen, Freiburg, 1868; J. H. Friedlieb, Breslau, 1868; H. Ewald, *Sieben Sendschr. des N. Bundes*, pp. 216 ff., Gött. 1870; O. Pfleiderer, *Protestantenbibel*, Lips. 1872; J. C. C. v. Hofmann, Nördlingen, 1874; A. Hilgenfeld, Lips. 1875; M. v. Aberle, Freib. 1877; H. Wace (ed. Cook), Lon. 1881; E. H. Plumptre, *1 and 2 Tim.*, and J. O. Dykes, *Tit.* (Schaff's *Popular Comm.*), Edin. 1882; S. Davidson, Lon. ²1882; B. Weiss (Meyer's *Comm.*) ⁵1885,⁶ ed. J. Weiss, Gött. 1894; W. Mangold (Bleek's *Einl.*), Ber. 1886; B. Weiss, 1886, E. Tr., Lon. 1896; G. Salmon, Lon. ²1886; A. C. Hervey (*Pulpit Comm.*), Lon. 1887; R. Kübel (Strack and Zöckler's *Kurzgef. Komm.*), Nördlingen, 1888; M. A. N. Rovers, Hertogenbosch, ²1888; R. Corneley, Par. 1889; C. Trochon and H. Lesêtre, Par. 1890; H. v. Soden, 1891; H. J. Holtzmann, Freib., 1885–92; J. B. Lightfoot (*Biblical Essays*, xi f., pp. 399–437), Lon. 1893; F. Godet, Par. 1893; A. Jülicher, Freib. 1894; F. S. Trenkle, Freib. 1897; Th. Zahn, Lips. 1897–1906; A. Rüegg (*Aus Schrift u. Gesch.*, pp. 59–108), Basel, 1898; A. Schäfer, Münster, 1890;

APPENDIX III

G. Desjardins, Par. 1900; J. M. S. Baljon, *Gesch. van de Boeken des N. Verbonds*, pp. 150–74, Groningen, 1901; J. Moffatt, *Historical N. T.* Edin. 1901; J. E. Belser, Freib. 1901; O. Cone (*International Handbooks to the N. T.* iii), 1901; B. W. Bacon, N. York, 1902; W. Lock (*Hastings' D. B.* iv, 'Timothy and Titus, Epp.'), Edin. 1902; J. Moffatt, *Enc. Bibl.* iv, 'Timothy and Titus, Epp.'), 1903; E. Jacquier, Par. 1903, E. Tr., 1907; E. Hühn, Tüb. 1904; H. v. Soden, Ber. 1905, E. Tr., Lon. and N. York, 1906; G. Wohlenberg (Zahn's *N.-T. Komm.* xiii), Lips. 1906; F. Koehler (J. Weiss, *Schriften des N. T.* ii), Gött. 1907; F. Barth, Gütersl. 1908; A. S. Peake, Lon. 1909; J. A. Beet, Lon. 1909; C. R. Gregory, Lips. 1909; G. C. Martin, Lon. 1909; N. J. D. White (*Expositor's G. T.* iv), Lon. 1910; J. Moffatt, Edin. 1911; W. F. Adeney, Lon. 1911; M. Dibelius (H. Liezmann's *Handb. zum N.T.*) Tüb. 1913.

3. *Paul and Pauline Epistles*

J. T. Hemsen, Gött. 1830; K. Schrader, Lips. 1832–6; A. F. Dähne, *Entwickelung des paulin. Lehrbegriffes*, p. 14 f., Halle, 1835; H. Böttger, Gött. 1837–8; F. C. Baur, Stuttg. 1845; T. Lewin, Lon. 1851; A. Monod, Par. 1851; W. J. Conybeare and J. S. Howson, Lon. 1852; B. Bauer, Ber. 1852; A. Bisping, *Exeg. Handbuch z. d. Br. d. Ap. Paulus*, iii, Münster 1858; M. Vidal, Par. 1863; A. Hausrath, Heidelb. 1865; E. Renan, Par. 1869; M. Krenkel, Lips. 1869; A. Sabatier, 1870, E. Tr. (*Appendix on the P. E.*, by G. G. Findlay), Lon. [5]1903; F. Märcker, Gütersl. 1871; O. Pfleiderer, 1873, E. Tr., ii, pp. 194 ff., Lon. 1877; P. J. Gloag, Edin. 1874; S. Sharpe, *Hist. of the Heb. Nation and its Literature*, pp. 447 ff., Lon. [3]1876; F. W. Bugge, Christiania, 1879–81; G. A. Berchter, Mülheim, 1885; G. Heinrici, Giessen, 1886; J. R. Boise, *The Epistles of Paul written after he became a prisoner*, N. York, 1887; P. Rambaud, Par. 1888; M. Krenkel, Braunschw. 1890; S. Arosio, Milan 1892; L. Bonnet, Lausanne, 1892; C. Clemen, *Chronol. der paulin. Briefe*, Halle 1893; id. *Einheitlichkeit der paulin. Briefe*, Gött. 1894; G. H. Gilbert, N. York, 1899; W. Lock, *Paul the Master-Builder*, Lon. 1899–1905; J. van Steenkiste, Bruges, 1899; H. Lisco, *Vincula Sanctorum—Gefangenschaftsbriefe des Ap. Paulus*, Ber. 1900; A. S. Way, Lon. 1901; R. D. Shaw, Edin. 1903–4; Th. Zahn (Herzog's *Realencycl.*), Lips. 1904; C. Clemen, Giessen, 1904; M. Goguel, Par. 1904; H. Weinel, Tüb. 1904; B. W. Bacon, *Story of S. Paul*, 1905; R. J. Knowling, *Testimony of S. Paul*, pp. 121 ff., Lon. 1905; Th. Nägeli, *Wortschatz des Ap. Paulus*, Gött. 1905; R. Scott, Edin. 1906; H. S. Nash (*New Schaff-Herzog Encycl.*, viii), N. York, 1910; A. Schweitzer, *Gesch. der paulin. Forschung*, Tüb. 1911; A. Deissmann, Tüb. 1911.

4. *Second Imprisonment and Death of Paul*

R. Wolf, Lips. 1819; D. Schenkel (*St. u. Krit.* xiv. i, pp. 53–87), 1841; A. O. Kunze, Gött. 1848; A. Bisping, Monast. Guestphal., 1852; H. Opitz, *Schicksale u. Schriften des Ap. Paulus während seiner Gefang. zu Rom*, Zür. 1858; G. Astro, Tr. ad Rhen., 1859; L. Ruffet, Paris, 1860; F. Spitta (*Gesch. u. Litteratur des Urchristenthums*, i. 1. 1–108), Gött. 1893; R. Steinmetz, Lips. 1897; C. Fouard, Par. 1897; C. Erbes (*Texte u. Untersuchungen* ... *N. F.* iv. 1. pp. 1–66), Lips. 1899; J. Frey, Jurjew (Dorpat), 1900; J. Strachan (*Westminster N. T.*, pp. 23 ff.), Lon. 1910; F. Frey (*Bibl. Zeit- u. Streitfragen*, vi. 3), Ber. 1911.

JOURNALS, ETC.

G. Reuterdahl, 'Tit.' (*Theologisk Quartalschrift*, iii. 1, pp. 1–77), Lund, 1831; H. Böttger, 'Ueber einige die Einl. in die Pastoralbriefe betreffende Punkte' (*Z.f.g. L. T. u. K.* III. iv, 1842–3); Fr. Delitzsch, 'Zur krit. Frage über die Past. (*Z.f. g. L. T. u. K.* xii, pp. 722 ff., Lips. 1851; Aberle, 'Ueber die Abfassungszeit des 1 Tim.' (*Theol. Quartalschrift*, pp. 120 ff.), Tübingen, 1863; Wettler, ' Ueber die Hauptgrundsätze der Pastoral theologie, Tim. u. Tit.' (*St. u. Krit.*, pp. 329 ff.), 1864; D. Schenkel, *Bibel-Lexicon*, iv. 393–402, Lips. 1872; Stirm, 'Die pastoraltheol. Winke der Pastoral briefe' (*J. f. d. Th.* xviii. 1. pp. 34–86), Gotha, 1872; C. Weizsäcker, ' Die Kirchenverfassung des apost. Zeitalters' (*J.f. d. Th.*, pp. 660 ff.), Gotha, 1873; O. Holtzmann, *Z.f. w. Th.*, pp. 121–8, 1875; id. *Prot. Kirchenzeitung*, pp. 260 ff., 1875; F. Spitta, ' Ueber die persönlichen Notizen im 2 Tim.' (*Th. Stud. u. Krit.*, pp. 582 ff.), Gotha, 1878; H. R. Reynolds, 'The Pastoral Epistles' (*Expositor*, i. i–iv, viii, x), 1875–9; A. Hilgenfeld, 'Die Irrlehrer der Hirtenbriefe des Paulus' (*Z. f. w. Th.*, pp. 448 ff.), Lips. 1880; O. Holtzmann, ' 2 Tim. u. d. neueste ... Rettungsversuch' (*Z. f. w. Th.*, pp. 45–72), Lips. 1883; A. Hilgenfeld, ' Die Gemeindeordnung der Hirtenbriefe'(*Z.f. w. Th.*, xxix, pp. 456 ff.), Lips. 1886; R. Seyerlen, 'Entstehung des Episcopals ...' (*Z.f. prakt. Th.* ix, pp. 212, 224 ff., 329 ff.), 1887; W. H. Simcox, 'The Pauline Antilegomena' (*Expositor*, III. viii, pp. 180 ff.), London, 1888; H. Bois, 'Zur Exegese der PB.' (*J.f. prot. Th.*, pp. 145 ff.), Lips. 1888; Baljon, '... de conjectural critiek der I. en tweede Brief aan Tim.' (*Th. Stud.*), 1888–9; W. P. Workman, ' The Hapax Legomena of St. Paul' (*Exp. Times*, vii, pp. 418 f.), 1896; E. Y. Hincks, 'Authorship of the Pastoral Epp.' (*J. of Bibl. Lit.* xvi, pp. 94–117), Boston, 1897; A. Hilgenfeld, ' Die Hirtenbriefe des Paulus neu untersucht' (*Z. f. w. Th.*, pp. 1–86), Lips. 1897; B. Weiss,'Present state of the inquiry concerning the genuineness of the Pauline Epp.' (*American J. Theol.*, pp. 392 ff.), Chicago,

1897; J. Turmel, 'Histoire de l'interpr. de 1 Tim. ii. 4' (*Rev. d'Hist. et de Lit. Rel.*), 1900; A. Klöpper, 'Christologie der PB.' (*Z. f. w. Th.*, pp. 339 ff.), 1902; E. J. Wolf, 'Peculiarities of the Pastoral Epp.' (*Bible Student*, pp. 326 ff.), 1903; J. Albani, 'Bildersprache der PB.' (*Z.f. w. Th.*, pp 40-58), Lips. 1903; K. v. Burger, '1 Tim.' (*J. f. d. ev. luth. Landeskirche Bayerns*), 1903; H. J. Holtzmann, 'James Wohlenberg on the Past. Epp.' (*Th. L.-Z.* 31, pp. 702 ff.), Lips. 1906; J. Fischer, 'Die Bestimmung der PB.' (*Weidenauer St.* i, pp. 176-226), 1906; W. Zenker, 'Tit.'(*Pastoralbl.*), 1906; J. D. James, 'Authorship of the Pastoral Epp.' (*Church Quarterly Review*), 1906-7; W. M. Ramsay, 'Hist. Com. on 1 Tim.' (*Expositor*), 1908-11; W. Lütgert, 'Die Irrlehrer der PB.' (*Beiträge zur F. chr. Theol.* ed. Schlatter, xiii. 3), Gütersl. 1909; W. M. Ramsay, 'Dr. Moffatt on the Lit. of the N. T.' (*Expositor*, viii. 7, pp. 77 f.), 1911; H. B. Swete, 'The Faithful Sayings' (*J. of Theol. St.* xviii. pp. 1-6), 1916; F. Torm, 'Die Sprache in den PB.' (*Z.f. d. N.-T. W.* xviii. iv, pp. 215-43), 1918.

CHURCH HISTORY, ETC.

J. A. W. Neander, *Ch. History*, Hamburg, 1832 f.; W. O. Dietlein, *Das Urchristenthum*, pp. 153-271, Halle, 1845; C. C. J. Bunsen, *Ignatius ... u. seine Zeit*, pp. 173 ff., Hamburg, 1847; K. Wieseler, *Chronol. des apost. Zeitalters*, Göttingen, 1848; J. A. B. Lutterbeck, *Die N.T.lichen Lehrbegriffe*, ii, pp. 31 ff., Mainz, 1852; W. J. Thiersch, *Die Kirche im apost. Zeitalter* ... Frankfurt u. Erlangen, 1852; J. P. Lange, *Die Gesch. der Kirche*, 1. i. pp. 134 ff., ii. pp. 374 ff., Braunschweig, 1853-4; F. C. Baur, *Das Christenthum u. die christl. Kirche der 3 ersten Jhdte*, p. 251 ff., Tüb. 1853; C. H. Weisse, *Philosophische Dogmatik*, i. p. 146 f., Lips. 1855; J. J. I. v. Döllinger, *Christenthum u. Kirche in der Zeit der Grundlegung*, Regensb. 1860; J. C. M. Laurent, *N.T.liche Studien*, p. 104 f., Gotha, 1866; H. J. Holtzmann, *Judenthum u. Christenthum im Zeitalter der apokr. u. N.T.lichen Literatur*, p. 551 f., Lips. 1867; R. F. Grau, *Entwickelungsgesch. des N.T.lichen Schriftthums*, ii, p. 185 f., 208 f., Gütersl. 1871; E. Renan, *L'Antéchrist*, pp. 100 ff., 186 f., Paris, 1873; R. Seyerlen, *Entstehung u. erste Schicksale der Christengemeinde in Rom*, pp. 26-48, Tübingen, 1874; K. Hackenschmidt, *Die Anfänge des catholischen Lehrbegriffs*, pp. 32 ff., Strassb. 1874; A. Ritschl, *Die christl. Lehre v. d. Rechtfertigung*, etc., ii, p. 221, Bonn, 1874; W. Beyschlag, *Die christl. Gemeindeverfassung im Zeitalter des N.T.s*, pp. 485 f., Harlem, 1874; A. Immer, *Theol. des N.T.s*, pp. 382-99, Bern, 1877; H. Usener, *Acta Timothei*, 1877; D. Schenkel, *Das Christusbild der Apostel*, etc., pp. 92 f., 161 ff., Lips. 1878-9; J. E. Renan, *L'Église Chrétienne*, vi, pp. 85 ff., Paris, 1879; E. Hatch, *Organization of the early Christian Churches*, pp. 44 f.,

50 f., 83, 113, 136, London, 1880; E. Havet, *Le Christianisme et ses Origines*, iv, pp. 376–82, Paris, 1884; O. Pfleiderer, *Urchristenthum*, 1887, E. Tr. iii, pp. 373–99, London, 1910; J. Heron, *The Church of the Sub-Apostolic Age*, p. 226, London, 1888; E. Loening, *Die Gemeindeverf. des Urchristenthums*, p. 69 f., Halle, 1888–9; W. M. Ramsay, *The Church in the Roman Empire before* A. D. *170*, pp. 246 ff., 365, 380, 416 (ed. 7)., London, 1893, [8]1904; W. Sanday, *Inspiration*, pp. 19, 25, 340, 363 ff., London, 1893; J. Réville, *Les Origines de l'Épiscopat*, i, pp. 262–356, Paris, 1894; F. Blass, *Acta Apostolorum*, pp. 21 ff., Göttingen, 1895; H. Lesetre, *La Sainte Église au siècle des Apôtres*, pp. 383 ff., 393 ff., 409 ff., Paris, 1896; A. Harnack, *Chronol. der altchristlichen Litteratur*, i, pp. 480 ff., Lips. 1897; A. C. McGiffert, *Apostolic Age*, pp. 399–414, Edinb. 1897; F. J. A. Hort, *The Christian Ecclesia*, xi, pp. 171–217, London, 1898; M. Friedländer, *Der vorchristliche jüdische Gnosticismus*, pp. 97 ff., Göttingen, 1898; J. V. Bartlet, *Apostolic Age*, pp. 178–84, 192 ff., 198–202, 511–15, Edinb. 1899, [2]1907; E. P. Gould, *Biblical Theol. of the N. T.* v. ii, pp. 142 ff., London and N. York, 1900; J. W. Falconer, *From Apostle to Priest*, iv, pp. 109–42, Edinb. 1900; G. T. Purves, *Apostolic Age*, pp. 169-76, London, 1900; H. St. J. Thackeray, *Relation of S. Paul to Contemp. Jewish Thought*, pp. 55, 194, 215, 240, London, 1900; E. v. Dobschütz, *Die urchristlichen Gemeinden*, pp. 9, 177 ff., 207 ff., Lips. 1902; E. C. Moore, *The N. T. in the Christian Church*, pp. 47 ff., N. York, 1904; R. Knopf, *Nachapostolische Zeitalter*, pp. 196 ff., 300 ff., Tübingen, 1905; C. R. Gregory, *Canon and Text of the N. T.*, pp. 210 f., Edinb. 1907; P. Feine, *Theol. des N.T.s*, pp. 538–49, Lips. 1910.

APPENDIX IV

TEXT OF 1 & 2 TIMOTHY AND TITUS

1. Words which do not occur in the ten Paulines are printed in red

2. 'Hapax Legomena' are marked with an asterisk

3. Words which occur, in Paul, only as part of quotations from the LXX are marked †

4. Pauline phrases are underlined

5. The genuine notes are written in uncials.

ΠΡΟΣ ΤΙΜΟΘΕΟΝ Α

ΠΑΥΛΟΣ ἀπόστολος Χριστοῦ Ἰησοῦ κατ' ἐπιταγὴν　2 Cor i.1, Eph i.1, Col i.1
Θεοῦ σωτῆρος ἡμῶν καὶ Χριστοῦ Ἰησοῦ τῆς ἐλπίδος ἡμῶν　Ro xvi.26.　Col i.27
Τιμοθέῳ γνησίῳ τέκνῳ ἐν πίστει· χάρις, ἔλεος, εἰρήνη　1 Cor iv.17, Pp ii.19,22, Ga ii.20
ἀπὸ Θεοῦ πατρὸς καὶ Χριστοῦ Ἰησοῦ τοῦ Κυρίου ἡμῶν.　Ro i.7 etc., i.4, vi.23 etc.
　Καθὼς παρεκάλεσά σε　　ἐν Ἐφέσῳ πορευό-　Ac xviii.18, xx.1, 1 Cor xvi.8
μενος εἰς Μακεδονίαν, ἵνα παραγγείλῃς τισὶ μὴ　2 Cor i.16 etc.
　　μηδὲ　　καὶ
　αἵτινες　　παρέχουσι μᾶλλον ἢ οἰκονο-　　Col i.25
μίαν Θεοῦ τὴν ἐν πίστει,— τὸ δὲ τέλος τῆς παραγγελίας　Ga ii.20,　Ro vi.22
ἐστὶν ἀγάπη ἐκ καθαρᾶς καρδίας καὶ συνειδήσεως ἀγαθῆς　Ro v.5, vi.17
καὶ πίστεως ἀνυποκρίτου· ὧν τινες
　εἰς　　, θέλοντες εἶναι　　Ga iv.21
μὴ νοοῦντες μήτε ἃ λέγουσι μήτε περὶ τίνων
　　οἴδαμεν δὲ ὅτι καλὸς ὁ νόμος ἐάν τις αὐτῷ　Ro iii.19, vii.14,16
　χρῆται εἰδὼς τοῦτο, ὅτι δικαίῳ νόμος οὐ κεῖται, Eph v.5, Phm 21
ἀνόμοις δὲ καὶ　　ἀσεβέσι καὶ ἁμαρτωλοῖς,
　　καὶ　　　καὶ
　πόρνοις, ἀρσενοκοίταις,　　ψεύσταις,
　, καὶ εἴ τι ἕτερον τῇ　διδασκαλίᾳ ἀντί- Ro xiii.9
κειται, κατὰ τὸ εὐαγγέλιον τῆς δόξης τοῦ μακαρίου Θεοῦ Ro ii.16, xvi.25, i.1. 2 Cor iv.4
ὃ ἐπιστεύθην ἐγώ.　Χάριν ἔχω τῷ [a]ἐνδυναμώ- Ga ii.7　Pp iv.13
σαντί με Χριστῷ Ἰησοῦ τῷ Κυρίῳ ἡμῶν, ὅτι πιστόν με　Ro vi.23, Eph iii.11. 1 Cor vii.25
ἡγήσατο, θέμενος εἰς διακονίαν, τὸ πρότερον ὄντα　2 Cor v.19, 1 Cor xvi.15, Ga iv.13
　καὶ　　καὶ ὑβριστήν· ἀλλ' ἠλεήθην ὅτι ἀγνοῶν Ga i.13, 1 Cor xv.9, 2 Cor iv.1
ἐποίησα ἐν ἀπιστίᾳ,　δὲ ἡ χάρις τοῦ Κυ-　Ro 20f, xvi.20, 2 Cor iv.15
ρίου ἡμῶν μετὰ πίστεως καὶ ἀγάπης τῆς ἐν Χριστῷ Ἰησοῦ. Eph vi.23, 1 Th v.8, Ro viii.39
πιστὸς ὁ λόγος καὶ πάσης　ἄξιος, ὅτι Χριστὸς 2 Cor i.18,　1 Cor xv.3
Ἰησοῦς ἦλθεν εἰς τὸν κόσμον ἁμαρτωλοὺς σῶσαι· ὧν　Ro v.8f, 12
πρῶτός εἰμι ἐγώ· ἀλλὰ διὰ τοῦτο ἠλεήθην, ἵνα ἐν ἐμοὶ　1 Cor xv.9, Ro iv.16, Eph ii.4,7
πρώτῳ ἐνδείξηται Ἰησοῦς Χριστὸς τὴν ἅπασαν μακροθυ- Ro ix.22
μίαν πρὸς　τῶν μελλόντων πιστεύειν ἐπ' αὐτῷ Ro ix.33
εἰς ζωὴν αἰώνιον. τῷ δὲ βασιλεῖ τῶν αἰώνων, ἀφθάρτῳ, Ro v.21, i.23, 20, xvi.25, 27

[a] ἐνδυναμοῦντι

ΠΡΟΣ ΤΙΜΟΘΕΟΝ Α

Ro ii.7. Ga i.5, Pp iv.20	ἀοράτῳ, μόνῳ Θεῷ, τιμὴ καὶ δόξα εἰς τοὺς αἰῶνας τῶν αἰώνων. ἀμήν. Ταύτην τὴν παραγγελίαν παρα-
1 Cor iv.17	τίθεμαί σοι, ΤΕΚΝΟΝ Τιμόθεε, κατὰ τὰς ἐπὶ
2 Cor x.3f	σὲ προφητείας, ἵνα στρατεύῃ ἐν αὐταῖς τὴν καλὴν
Ro xiv.22, 1 Cor xiii.2	στρατείαν ἔχων πίστιν καὶ ἀγαθὴν συνείδησιν, ἥν τινες ἀπω-
† Ro xi.1f cit. Ps xciv.14	σάμενοι περὶ τὴν πίστιν ἐναυάγησαν· ὧν ἐστὶν Ὑμέναιος
1 Cor v.5	καὶ Ἀλέξανδρος, οὓς παρέδωκα τῷ Σατανᾷ, ἵνα παιδευθῶσι μὴ βλασφημεῖν.
Ro xii.1, 1 Cor iv.16, Eph iv.1, Pp i.4	Παρακαλῶ οὖν πρῶτον πάντων ποιεῖσθαι δεήσεις,
Ro i.8, Eph v.20	προσευχάς, εὐχαριστίας, ὑπὲρ πάντων ἀνθρώπων, ὑπὲρ βασιλέων καὶ πάντων τῶν ἐν ὑπεροχῇ ὄντων, ἵνα
	καὶ ἐν πάσῃ
1 Cor vii.26, 2 Cor vii.12, viii.21	καὶ τοῦτο καλὸν καὶ ἐνώπιον τοῦ σωτῆρος ἡμῶν Θεοῦ, ὃς πάντας ἀνθρώπους θέλει σωθῆ-
Ro iii.30, v.15, 1 Cor viii.6	ναι καὶ εἰς ἐπίγνωσιν ἀληθείας ἐλθεῖν. εἷς γὰρ Θεός, εἷς καὶ
Ga iii.19f	μεσίτης Θεοῦ καὶ ἀνθρώπων ἄνθρωπος Χριστὸς Ἰησοῦς,
Ga i.4, ii.20	ὁ δοὺς ἑαυτὸν ὑπὲρ πάντων, τὸ μαρτύριον
Ga vi.9	καιροῖς ἰδίοις, εἰς ὃ ἐτέθην ἐγὼ καὶ ἀπόστολος
Ro ix.1, xi.13 Ga ii.20	(ἀλήθειαν λέγω, οὐ ψεύδομαι), διδάσκαλος ἐθνῶν ἐν
2 Cor vii.14, Col i.6	πίστει καὶ ἀληθείᾳ. Βούλομαι οὖν προσεύχεσθαι τοὺς
1 Cor xi.4, i.2, 2 Cor ii.14, 1 Th i.8	ἄνδρας ἐν παντὶ τόπῳ, ἐπαίροντας χεῖρας χωρὶς
Pp ii.14	ὀργῆς καὶ ᵃδιαλογισμοῦ· ὡσαύτως γυναῖκας ἐν
	μετὰ καὶ
	ἑαυτάς, μὴ ἐν καὶ ἢ ἢ
1 Cor xi.13	ἀλλ' ὃ πρέπει γυναιξὶν ἐπαγγελ-
Eph ii.10	λομέναις, δι' ἔργων ἀγαθῶν. γυνὴ ἐν ἡσυ-
1 Cor xiv.34f	χίᾳ μανθανέτω ἐν πάσῃ ὑποταγῇ. διδάσκειν δὲ γυναικὶ οὐκ ἐπιτρέπω, οὐδὲ ἀνδρός, ἀλλ' εἶναι ἐν ἡσυ-
Ro v.14, 1 Cor xi.8	χίᾳ. Ἀδὰμ γὰρ πρῶτος ἐπλάσθη, εἶτα Εὔα· καὶ Ἀδὰμ
2 Cor xi.3	οὐκ ἠπατήθη, ἡ δὲ γυνὴ ἐξαπατηθεῖσα ἐν παραβάσει γέγο-
1 Cor iii.15, vii.8	νε· σωθήσεται δὲ διὰ τῆς ἐὰν μείνωσιν ἐν
2 Th ii.13	πίστει καὶ ἀγάπῃ καὶ ἁγιασμῷ μετὰ πιστὸς
	ὁ λόγος. Εἴ τις καλοῦ ἔρ-
	γου ἐπιθυμεῖ. δεῖ οὖν τὸν ἐπίσκοπον εἶναι,
	μιᾶς γυναικὸς ἄνδρα,
	μὴ μὴ ἀλλ' ἐπιεικῆ
	τοῦ ἰδίου οἴκου καλῶς προϊστάμενα
	τέκνα ἔχοντα ἐν ὑποταγῇ μετὰ πάσης (εἰ δέ

ᵃ διαλογισμῶν W.H.

ΠΡΟΣ ΤΙΜΟΘΕΟΝ Α   III 5-IV 8

τις τοῦ ἰδίου οἴκου προστῆναι οὐκ οἶδε, πῶς ἐκκλησίας   1 Cor xi.22 etc.
6 Θεοῦ   ) μὴ   ἵνα μὴ   εἰς   1 Cor xi.34
7 κρῖμα   τοῦ διαβόλου. δεῖ δὲ καὶ   καλὴν
   ἔχειν ἀπὸ τῶν ἔξωθεν, ἵνα μὴ εἰς †ὀνειδισμὸν   καὶ †Ro xv.3 cit Ps lxix.10
8 †παγίδα τοῦ διαβόλου.   διακόνους ὡσαύτως σεμνούς, μὴ †Ro xi.9 cit Ps lxix.23
       μὴ οἴνῳ πολλῷ   μὴ
9 ἔχοντας τὸ μυστήριον τῆς πίστεως ἐν καθαρᾷ συνειδήσει.
10 καὶ οὗτοι δὲ δοκιμαζέσθωσαν πρῶτον, εἶτα διακονείτωσαν 1 Cor xvi.3, 2 Cor viii.22
11 ἀνέγκλητοι ὄντες. γυναῖκας ὡσαύτως σεμνάς, μὴ
12   πιστὰς ἐν πᾶσι.   διάκονοι ἔστωσαν
   μιᾶς γυναικὸς ἄνδρες, τέκνων καλῶς προϊστάμενοι καὶ τῶν
13 ἰδίων οἴκων. οἱ γὰρ καλῶς διακονήσαντες   ἑαυτοῖς
   καλὸν   καὶ πολλὴν παρρησίαν ἐν πίστει τῇ Phm 8, Ga ii.20, Col i.4
14 ἐν Χριστῷ Ἰησοῦ.   Ταῦτά σοι γράφω ἐλπί- 2 Cor xiii.10 etc.
15 ζων ἐλθεῖν πρός σε ἐν τάχει· ἐὰν δὲ   ἵνα εἰδῇς Ro xv.22,24, xvi.20
   πῶς δεῖ ἐν οἴκῳ Θεοῦ ἀναστρέφεσθαι, ἥτις ἐστὶν ἐκκλησία Col iv.6. 1 Cor xv.9 etc.
16 Θεοῦ ζῶντος, στῦλος καὶ   τῆς ἀληθείας. καὶ Ro ix.26 etc.
            μέγα ἐστὶ τὸ τῆς   μυστήριον· Eph v.32
   ὃς   ἐφανερώθη ἐν σαρκί,   Col i.26, 2 Cor iv.11
      ἐδικαιώθη ἐν πνεύματι,
         ὤφθη ἀγγέλοις,
      ἐκηρύχθη ἐν ἔθνεσιν,   Ga ii.2
         ἐπιστεύθη ἐν κόσμῳ,
         ἀνελήφθη ἐν δόξῃ.
1   Τὸ δὲ Πνεῦμα   λέγει, ὅτι ἐν   καιροῖς
   ἀποστήσονταί τινες τῆς πίστεως,   πνεύμασι
2 πλάνοις καὶ διδασκαλίαις δαιμονίων, ἐν ὑποκρίσει
3   τὴν ἰδίαν συνείδησιν, κωλυ-
   όντων γαμεῖν, ἀπέχεσθαι βρωμάτων, ἃ ὁ Θεὸς ἔκτισεν εἰς
       μετὰ εὐχαριστίας τοῖς πιστοῖς καὶ ἐπεγνωκόσι Pp iv.6
4 τὴν ἀλήθειαν. ὅτι πᾶν   Θεοῦ καλόν, καὶ οὐδὲν
5   μετὰ εὐχαριστίας λαμβανόμενον· ἁγιάζεται γὰρ cf. 1 Cor xi.23
6 διὰ λόγου Θεοῦ καὶ   Ταῦτα ὑποτιθέμε- Ro ix.6 etc. 1 Pet.i.23
   νος τοῖς ἀδελφοῖς καλὸς ἔσῃ διάκονος Χριστοῦ Ἰησοῦ, Col i.7
       τοῖς λόγοις τῆς πίστεως καὶ τῆς καλῆς διδα-
7 σκαλίας ᾗ   τοὺς δὲ   καὶ
              δὲ σεαυτὸν πρὸς
8 ἡ γὰρ   πρὸς ὀλίγον ἐστὶν

ΠΡΟΣ ΤΙΜΟΘΕΟΝ Α

ἡ δὲ πρὸς πάντα ἐστιν, ἐπαγγελίαν
ἔχουσα ζωῆς τῆς νῦν καὶ τῆς μελλούσης. πιστὸς ὁ λόγος 9
Col i.29 καὶ πάσης ἄξιος. εἰς τοῦτο γὰρ κοπιῶμεν 10
2 Cor i.10. 1 Th i.9 etc. καὶ ἀγωνιζόμεθα, ὅτι ἠλπίκαμεν ἐπὶ Θεῷ ζῶντι, ὅς
Ro i.16, iii.22 etc. Ga vi.10 ἐστι σωτὴρ πάντων ἀνθρώπων, μάλιστα πιστῶν.
παράγγελλε ταῦτα καὶ δίδασκε. μηδείς σου τῆς
1 Th i.7 καταφρονείτω, ἀλλὰ τύπος γίνου τῶν πιστῶν ἐν 12
2 Cor vi.6f., Ga ii.20 λόγῳ, ἐν ἀναστροφῇ, ἐν ἀγάπῃ, ἐν πίστει, ἐν ἕως 13
Jo xxi.22f. 2 Cor iii.14. Ro xii.8 ἔρχομαι, τῇ ἀναγνώσει, τῇ παρακλήσει, τῇ διδασκαλίᾳ. μὴ τοῦ ἐν σοὶ χαρίσματος, ὃ ἐδόθη σοι 14
διὰ προφητείας μετὰ τῶν χειρῶν τοῦ
ταῦτα ἐν τούτοις ἴσθι, ἵνα σου ἡ προ- 15
Pp i.12f κοπὴ φανερὰ ᾖ πᾶσιν. ἔπεχε σεαυτῷ καὶ τῇ διδασκαλίᾳ 16
Ro xii.20 ἐπίμενε αὐτοῖς· τοῦτο γὰρ ποιῶν καὶ σεαυτὸν σώσεις καὶ
τοὺς ἀκούοντάς σου.

μὴ ἀλλὰ παρακάλει ὡς πα- V
τέρα, ὡς ἀδελφούς, ὡς μητέρας, 2
ὡς ἀδελφὰς ἐν πάσῃ χήρας τίμα τὰς 3
ὄντως χήρας. εἰ δέ τις χήρα τέκνα ἢ ἔχει, μανθα- 4
νέτωσαν πρῶτον τὸν ἴδιον οἶκον καὶ ἀπο-
Ro xiv.22 διδόναι τοῖς τοῦτο γάρ ἐστιν ἐνώπιον
2 Cor i.9f τοῦ Θεοῦ. ἡ δὲ ὄντως χήρα καὶ ἤλπικεν ἐπὶ 5
Eph vi.18 Θεόν, καὶ ταῖς δεήσεσι καὶ ταῖς προσευχαῖς
1 Th iii.10 νυκτὸς καὶ ἡμέρας. ἡ δὲ ζῶσα τέθνηκε. 6
καὶ ταῦτα παράγγελλε, ἵνα ὦσιν. εἰ δέ τις 7
τῶν ἰδίων καὶ μάλιστα οἰκείων οὐ προνοεῖ, τὴν πίστιν 8
καὶ ἔστιν ἀπίστου χήρα 9
μὴ ἐτῶν γεγονυῖα, ἑνὸς ἀνδρὸς γυνή,
ἐν ἔργοις καλοῖς μαρτυρουμένη, εἰ εἰ 10
εἰ ἁγίων πόδας εἰ θλιβομένοις
Col i.10 εἰ παντὶ ἔργῳ ἀγαθῷ 11
δὲ χήρας ὅταν γὰρ τοῦ
Χριστοῦ, γαμεῖν θέλουσιν, ἔχουσαι κρῖμα ὅτι τὴν πρώτην 12
Phm 22 πίστιν ἠθέτησαν. ἅμα δὲ καὶ μανθάνουσιν, 13
2 Cor vii.7 etc. τὰς οἰκίας, οὐ μόνον δὲ ἀλλὰ καὶ
καὶ λαλοῦσαι τὰ μὴ δέοντα. βούλομαι οὖν 14
2 Cor vi.3, v.12, xi.12 γαμεῖν, μηδεμίαν
ἀφορμὴν διδόναι τῷ ἀντικειμένῳ χάριν· ἤδη γὰρ 15

ΠΡΟΣ ΤΙΜΟΘΕΟΝ Α

16 τινες ὀπίσω τοῦ Σατανᾶ. εἴ τις πιστὴ ἔχει
χήρας, αὐταῖς, καὶ μὴ βαρείσθω ἡ ἐκκλησία·
17 ἵνα ταῖς ὄντως χήραις Οἱ καλῶς
προεστῶτες τιμῆς ἀξιούσθωσαν, μά-
18 λιστα οἱ κοπιῶντες ἐν λόγῳ καὶ διδασκαλίᾳ. λέγει γὰρ ἡ Ro ix.17 etc.
γραφή, Βοῦν ἀλοῶντα οὐ φιμώσεις· καὶ, Ἄξιος ὁ ἐργάτης 1Cor ix.9 cit. Deut. xxv.4
19 τοῦ μισθοῦ αὐτοῦ. κατὰ Lk x.7
μὴ ἐκτὸς εἰ μὴ ἐπὶ Δύο ἢ τριῶν μαρτύρων· 1Cor xiv.5,xv.2. 2Cor xiii.1
20 τοὺς ἁμαρτάνοντας ἐνώπιον πάντων ἔλεγχε, ἵνα καὶ οἱ 1Th iv.13 cit.Deut.xix.15
21 λοιποὶ φόβον ἔχωσι. διαμαρτύρομαι ἐνώπιον τοῦ Θεοῦ 2Cor vii.12
καὶ Χριστοῦ Ἰησοῦ καὶ τῶν ἐκλεκτῶν ἀγγέλων, ἵνα ταῦτα
φυλάξῃς χωρὶς μηδὲν ποιῶν κατὰ
22 χεῖρας ταχέως μηδενὶ μηδὲ κοινώνει
23 ἁμαρτίαις ἀλλοτρίαις· σεαυτὸν ἁγνὸν τήρει. μηκέτι
ἀλλ' οἴνῳ ὀλίγῳ χρῶ διὰ τὸν καὶ τὰς
24 σου ἀσθενείας. τινῶν ἀνθρώπων αἱ ἁμαρτίαι
εἰσί, εἰς κρίσιν, τισὶ δὲ καὶ
25 ὡσαύτως καὶ τὰ ἔργα τὰ καλὰ καὶ
τὰ ἔχοντα κρυβῆναι οὐ δύναται.
I 1 Ὅσοι εἰσὶν ὑπὸ ζυγὸν δοῦλοι τοὺς ἰδίους πάσης τι-
μῆς ἀξίους ἡγείσθωσαν, ἵνα μὴ τὸ ὄνομα τοῦ Θεοῦ καὶ ἡ δι- Ro ii.24 cit. Isa.lii.5
2 δασκαλία βλασφημῆται. οἱ δὲ πιστοὺς ἔχοντες
μὴ καταφρονείτωσαν, ὅτι ἀδελφοί εἰσιν· ἀλλὰ μᾶλλον Phm 16
δουλευέτωσαν, ὅτι πιστοί εἰσι καὶ ἀγαπητοὶ οἱ τῆς

3 Ταῦτα δίδασκε καὶ παρακάλει. εἴ τις
καὶ μὴ λόγοις, τοῖς τοῦ Κυρίου Ro v.1 etc.
ἡμῶν Ἰησοῦ Χριστοῦ, καὶ τῇ κατ' διδασκαλίᾳ,
4 μηδὲν ἀλλὰ περὶ
καὶ ἐξ ὧν γίνεται φθόνος, ἔρις, βλασφημίαι, Ro i.18.28f
5 πονηραί, διεφθαρμένων ἀνθρώπων
τὸν νοῦν καὶ ἀπεστερημένων τῆς ἀληθείας, νομιζόντων
6 εἶναι τὴν ἔστι δὲ μέγας ἡ
7 μετὰ αὐταρκείας· οὐδὲν γὰρ εἰς τὸν Ro v.12
8 κόσμον, ὅτι οὐδὲ τι δυνάμεθα· ἔχοντες δὲ
10 καὶ τούτοις ἀρκεσθησόμεθα. οἱ δὲ
βουλόμενοι πλουτεῖν εἰς πειρασμὸν καὶ †πα-
γίδα καὶ ἐπιθυμίας πολλὰς ἀνοήτους καὶ αἵτινες

ΠΡΟΣ ΤΙΜΟΘΕΟΝ Α

1 Cor v.5

     τοὺς ἀνθρώπους εἰς ὄλεθρον καὶ ἀπώλειαν. ῥίζα 10
γὰρ πάντων τῶν κακῶν ἐστιν ἡ   ἧς τινες
      ἀπὸ τῆς πίστεως, καὶ ἑαυτοὺς

Ro xi.17 etc. ix.20 etc.
1 Cor vi.18, x.14. Ro ix.30
1 Cor xiv.1, ix.25
Ro ii.7, Pp i.30
Col iii.15
2 Cor vii.12 etc.
Eph i.11,23

    ὀδύναις πολλαῖς.   Σὺ δέ, ὦ ἄν- 11
θρωπε Θεοῦ, ταῦτα φεῦγε· δίωκε δὲ δικαιοσύνην,
πίστιν, ἀγάπην, ὑπομονήν,   ἀγωνίζου 12
τὸν καλὸν ἀγῶνα τῆς πίστεως,   τῆς αἰωνίου ζωῆς,
εἰς ἣν ἐκλήθης, καὶ ὡμολόγησας τὴν καλὴν ὁμολογίαν ἐνώπιον πολλῶν μαρτύρων. παραγγέλλω σοι ἐνώπιον τοῦ 13
Θεοῦ τοῦ   τὰ πάντα καὶ Χριστοῦ Ἰησοῦ τοῦ
μαρτυρήσαντος ἐπὶ Ποντίου Πιλάτου τὴν καλὴν ὁμολογίαν,

1 Cor vii.19
Ro v.1 etc.
Ga vi.9

τηρῆσαί σε τὴν ἐντολὴν   μέχρι 14
τῆς ἐπιφανείας τοῦ Κυρίου ἡμῶν Ἰησοῦ Χριστοῦ· ἣν και- 15
ροῖς ἰδίοις δείξει ὁ μακάριος καὶ μόνος   ὁ βασι-
λεὺς τῶν βασιλευόντων καὶ κύριος τῶν κυριευόντων, ὁ 16
μόνος ἔχων ἀθανασίαν, φῶς οἰκῶν   ὃν εἶδεν οὐ-
δεὶς ἀνθρώπων οὐδὲ ἰδεῖν δύναται, ᾧ τιμὴ καὶ κράτος
αἰώνιον. ἀμήν.

  Τοῖς πλουσίοις ἐν τῷ νῦν αἰῶνι παράγγελλε μὴ 17
   μηδὲ ἠλπικέναι ἐπὶ πλούτου   ἀλλ᾽
ἐπὶ Θεῷ τῷ παρέχοντι ἡμῖν πάντα πλουσίως εἰς
    πλουτεῖν ἐν ἔργοις καλοῖς, 18
  εἶναι,   ἑαυτοῖς 19

Lk xiii.9
θεμέλιον καλὸν εἰς τὸ μέλλον, ἵνα   τῆς ὄντως ζωῆς.
  Ὦ Τιμόθεε, τὴν   φύλαξον, 20
τὰς   καὶ   τῆς
  γνώσεως, ἥν τινες ἐπαγγελλόμενοι περὶ τὴν πίσ- 21
τιν

Col iv.18   Ἡ χάρις μεθ᾽ ὑμῶν.

ΠΡΟΣ ΤΙΜΟΘΕΟΝ Β

ΠΑΥΛΟΣ ΑΠΟΣΤΟΛΟΣ ΧΡΙΣΤΟΥ ΙΗΣΟΥ διὰ θελήμα-   2 Cor i.1, Eph i.1
τος Θεοῦ κατ' ἐπαγγελίαν ζωῆς τῆς ἐν Χριστῷ Ἰησοῦ ΤΙΜΟ-   Ga iii.29, Ro viii.2, 39
ΘΕΩΙ ΑΓΑΠΗΤΩΙ τέκνῳ· ΧΑΡΙΣ, ΕΛΕΟΣ, ΕΙΡΗΝΗ ΑΠΟ ΘΕΟΥ   1 Cor iv.17, i.2f. etc
ΠΑΤΡΟΣ ΚΑΙ ᵃΚΥΡΙΟΥ ΙΗΣΟΥ ΧΡΙΣΤΟΥ.

Χάριν ἔχω τῷ Θεῷ, ᾧ λατρεύω ἀπὸ   ἐν κα-   Ro i.8ff., vi.17, 1 Clem xv.7
θαρᾷ συνειδήσει, ὡς ἀδιάλειπτον ἔχω τὴν περὶ σοῦ μνείαν   1 Th iii.6, 10
ἐν ταῖς δεήσεσί μου, νυκτὸς καὶ ἡμέρας ἐπιποθῶν σε ἰδεῖν,
μεμνημένος σου τῶν δακρύων, ἵνα χαρᾶς πληρωθῶ·   Pp ii.2
λαβὼν τῆς ἐν σοὶ ἀνυποκρίτου πίστεως, ἥτις ἐνῴκησε
πρῶτον ἐν τῇ   σου Λωΐδι καὶ τῇ μητρί σου Εὐνείκῃ,
πέπεισμαι δὲ ὅτι καὶ ἐν σοί. δι' ἣν   ἀναμιμνήσκω   Ro xv.14
σε   τὸ χάρισμα τοῦ Θεοῦ, ὅ ἐστιν ἐν σοὶ διὰ   1 Clem xxvii.3, Ro vi.23
τῆς   τῶν χειρῶν μου. οὐ γὰρ ἔδωκεν ἡμῖν ὁ Θεὸς   Ac viii.18, Ro viii.15, xi.8, xv.13
πνεῦμα   , ἀλλὰ δυνάμεως καὶ ἀγάπης καὶ
 . μὴ οὖν ἐπαισχυνθῇς τὸ μαρτύριον τοῦ Κυρίου   1 Cor i.6f.
ἡμῶν, μηδὲ ἐμὲ τὸν δέσμιον αὐτοῦ· ἀλλὰ   Eph iii.1, Phm.9
τῷ εὐαγγελίῳ κατὰ δύναμιν Θεοῦ τοῦ σώσαντος ἡμᾶς καὶ   Eph iii.20, Ro i.16, 1 Cor i.24
καλέσαντος κλήσει ἁγίᾳ, οὐ κατὰ τὰ ἔργα ἡμῶν, ἀλλὰ κατ'   Ga i.6, 1 Cor vii.20, Ro ix.11
ἰδίαν πρόθεσιν καὶ χάριν τὴν δοθεῖσαν ἡμῖν ἐν Χριστῷ   Eph i.11, Ga ii.9, Ro xii.5f
Ἰησοῦ πρὸ χρόνων αἰωνίων φανερωθεῖσαν δὲ νῦν διὰ τῆς   Ro xvi.25f
ἐπιφανείας τοῦ σωτῆρος ἡμῶν Χριστοῦ Ἰησοῦ, καταργή-   Pp iii.20
σαντος μὲν τὸν θάνατον φωτίσαντος δὲ ζωὴν καὶ ἀφθαρ-   1 Cor xv.26, Ro ii.7
σίαν διὰ τοῦ εὐαγγελίου, εἰς ὃ ἐτέθην ἐγὼ   καὶ ἀπό-   1 Cor iv.15, xii.28, 1 Pe ii.8
στολος καὶ διδάσκαλος. δι' ἣν   καὶ ταῦτα πάσχω·   1 Pe ii.6, 20
ἀλλ' οὐκ ἐπαισχύνομαι, οἶδα γὰρ ᾧ πεπίστευκα, καὶ πέ-   Pp i.20, Ro i.16, xv.14
πεισμαι ὅτι δυνατός ἐστι τὴν   μου φυλάξαι   Ro iv.21, xi.23
εἰς ἐκείνην τὴν ἡμέραν.   ἔχε   2 Th i.10 cit Is ii.11
λόγων, ὧν παρ' ἐμοῦ ἤκουσας, ἐν πίστει καὶ ἀγάπῃ τῇ ἐν   Ro xi.27, 1 Th ii.13, Pp iv.9, Ga ii.20
Χριστῷ Ἰησοῦ. τὴν καλὴν   φύλαξον διὰ   Ro viii.39
Πνεύματος Ἁγίου τοῦ ἐνοικοῦντος ἐν ἡμῖν. Οἶδας   Ro v.5, viii.11
τοῦτο, ὅτι †ἀπεστράφησάν με πάντες οἱ ἐν τῇ Ἀσίᾳ· ὧν   †Ro xi.26. 2 Cor i 8
ἐστι Φύγελος καὶ Ἑρμογένης.

ΔΩΙΗ ΕΛΕΟΣ Ο ΚΥΡΙΟΣ ΤΩΙ ΟΝΗΣΙΦΟΡΟΥ ΟΙΚΩΙ· ΟΤΙ
ΠΟΛΛΑΚΙΣ ΜΕ   , ΚΑΙ ΤΗΝ ΑΛΥΣΙΝ ΜΟΥ ΟΥΚ
ΕΠΗΙΣΧΥΝΘΗ, ΑΛΛΑ ΓΕΝΟΜΕΝΟΣ ΕΝ ΡΩΜΗΙ ΣΠΟΥΔΑΙΩΣ
ΕΖΗΤΗΣΕ ΜΕ ΚΑΙ ΕΥΡΕ (ΔΩΙΗ ΑΥΤΩΙ Ο ΚΥΡΙΟΣ ΕΥΡΕΙΝ
ΕΛΕΟΣ ΠΑΡΑ ΚΥΡΙΟΥ ΕΝ ΕΚΕΙΝΗΙ ΤΗΙ ΗΜΕΡΑΙ)· ΚΑΙ ΟΣΑ ΕΝ   2 Th i.10 cit Is ii.11
ΕΦΕΣΩΙ ΔΙΗΚΟΝΗΣΕ,   ΣΥ ΓΙΝΩΣΚΕΙΣ.

Σὺ οὖν, τέκνον μου, ἐνδυναμοῦ ἐν τῇ χάριτι τῇ ἐν   Eph vi.10, 2 Cor viii.19, 1 Cor i.4

a. so W.H.m.

ΠΡΟΣ ΤΙΜΟΘΕΟΝ Β II 2-22

Pp iv.9, Ro xi.27	Χριστῷ Ἰησοῦ. καὶ ἃ ἤκουσας παρ' ἐμοῦ διὰ πολλῶν μαρτύ-	2
1 Clem xliv.1-6, lxii.3, lxiii.3	ρων, ταῦτα παράθου πιστοῖς ἀνθρώποις, οἵτινες ἱκανοὶ	
	ἔσονται καὶ ἑτέρους διδάξαι. ὡς καλὸς	3
1 Cor ix.7-10,14,23	Χριστοῦ Ἰησοῦ. οὐδεὶς στρατευόμενος	4
	ταῖς τοῦ , ἵνα τῷ ἀ-	
	ρέσῃ. ἐὰν δὲ καὶ τις, οὐ ἐὰν μὴ	5
	τὸν κοπιῶντα δεῖ πρῶτον τῶν	6
	καρπῶν νόει ὃ λέγω· δώσει γάρ σοι	7
	ὁ Κύριος σύνεσιν ἐν πᾶσι. μνημόνευε Ἰησοῦν Χριστὸν	8
Ro iv.24, i.3f	ἐγηγερμένον ἐκ νεκρῶν ἐκ σπέρματος Δαβὶδ κατὰ τὸ	
Ro ii.16, xvi.25	εὐαγγέλιόν μου· ἐν ᾧ μέχρι δεσμῶν	9
Pp i.12-18, Col iv.3	ὡς , ἀλλ' ὁ λόγος τοῦ Θεοῦ οὐ δέδεται.	
2 Cor i.v.1, 1 Cor xiii.7	διὰ τοῦτο πάντα ὑπομένω διὰ τοὺς ἐκλεκτούς, ἵνα καὶ	10
Pp i.28, Ro viii.39	αὐτοὶ σωτηρίας τύχωσι τῆς ἐν Χριστῷ Ἰησοῦ μετὰ	
Ro vi.8, 2 Cor vii.3	δόξης αἰωνίου. πιστὸς ὁ λόγος· εἰ γὰρ συναπεθά-	11
1 Cor viii.8, Ro viii.17	νομεν, καὶ συζήσομεν· εἰ ὑπομένομεν, καὶ συμβασι-	12
Matt. x.33	λεύσομεν· εἰ , κἀκεῖνος ἡμᾶς	
Ro iii.3f	εἰ ἀπιστοῦμεν, ἐκεῖνος πιστὸς μένει·	13
	γὰρ ἑαυτὸν οὐ δύναται. Ταῦτα	14
2 Cor viii.21	διαμαρτυρόμενος ἐνώπιον τοῦ Κυρίου μὴ	
	ἐπ' οὐδὲν ἐπὶ τῶν ἀκουόντων.	
Ro vi.13, xiv.18	σπούδασον σεαυτὸν δόκιμον παραστῆσαι τῷ Θεῷ, ἐργά-	15
Eph i.13	την τὸν λόγον τῆς	
	ἀληθείας. τὰς δὲ	16
Ac iv.17	ἐπὶ πλεῖον γὰρ προκόψουσιν ἀσεβείας, καὶ ὁ λόγος	17
	αὐτῶν ὡς ἕξει· ὧν ἐστιν Ὑμέναιος	
	καὶ Φιλητός, οἵτινες περὶ τὴν ἀλήθειαν λέ-	18
	γοντες τὴν ἀνάστασιν ἤδη γεγονέναι, καὶ	
	τὴν τινῶν πίστιν. ὁ θεμέλιος τοῦ	19
Numb. xvi.5,26f	Θεοῦ ἕστηκεν, ἔχων τὴν σφραγῖδα ταύτην, Ἔγνω	
	Κύριος τοὺς ὄντας αὐτοῦ, καὶ Ἀποστήτω ἀπὸ ἀδικίας	
Ro x.13 cit Is xxvi.13	πᾶς ὁ ὀνομάζων τὸ ὄνομα Κυρίου. ἐν μεγάλῃ δὲ	20
	οἰκίᾳ οὐκ ἔστι μόνον σκεύη καὶ ἀλλὰ	
2 Cor iv.7, Ro ix.21	καὶ καὶ ὀστράκινα, καὶ ἃ μὲν εἰς τιμήν, ἃ δὲ εἰς	
1 Cor v.7	ἀτιμίαν. ἐὰν οὖν τις ἐκκαθάρῃ ἑαυτὸν ἀπὸ τούτων, ἔσται	21
	σκεῦος εἰς τιμήν, ἡγιασμένον, εὔχρηστον τῷ	
2 Cor ix.8	εἰς πᾶν ἔργον ἀγαθὸν ἡτοιμασμένον. τὰς δὲ	22
Ro ix 30, xiv.19	ἐπιθυμίας φεῦγε, δίωκε δὲ δικαιοσύνην,	

ΠΡΟΣ ΤΙΜΟΘΕΟΝ Β II.22–III.16

πίστιν, ἀγάπην, εἰρήνην, μετὰ τῶν ἐπικαλουμένων τὸν Κύ- 1Cor xiv.1, i.2
23 ριον ἐκ καθαρᾶς καρδίας.   τὰς δὲ μωρὰς καὶ
                  εἰδὼς ὅτι γεννῶσι μάχας.
24 δοῦλον δὲ Κυρίου οὐ δεῖ   ἀλλ' ἤπιον εἶναι   1Cor vii.22
25 πρὸς πάντας,   ἐν πραότητι
   παιδεύοντα τοὺς   δῴη
26 αὐτοῖς ὁ Θεὸς μετάνοιαν εἰς ἐπίγνωσιν ἀληθείας, καὶ
       ἐκ τῆς τοῦ διαβόλου †παγίδος   †Ro xi.9 cit Ps lxix.23
   ὑπ' αὐτοῦ εἰς τὸ ἐκείνου θέλημα.
III 1 Τοῦτο δὲ γίνωσκε, ὅτι ἐν ἐσχάταις ἡμέραις ἐνστή- Ro vi.6.   Is. ii.2
2 σονται καιροὶ   ἔσονται γὰρ οἱ ἄνθρωποι
             ἀλαζόνες, ὑπερήφανοι, _ _ _ _ γονεῦ- Ro i.30f
3 σιν ἀπειθεῖς, _ _ _ _ _ _ _ _ _   ἄστοργοι,
4
                   μᾶλλον ἢ
5 ἔχοντες μόρφωσιν   τὴν δὲ δύναμιν αὐτῆς   Ro ii.20
6   καὶ τούτους   ἐκ τούτων γάρ εἰσιν
   οἱ   εἰς τὰς οἰκίας καὶ αἰχμαλωτίζοντες
       †σεσωρευμένα ἁμαρτίαις, ἀγόμενα ἐπιθυμίαις †Ro xii.20 cit.Prov.xxv.22
7   πάντοτε μανθάνοντα καὶ   εἰς ἐπί-
8 γνωσιν ἀληθείας ἐλθεῖν δυνάμενα. ὃν τρόπον δὲ Ἰαννῆς
   καὶ Ἰαμβρῆς ἀντέστησαν Μωϋσεῖ, οὕτως καὶ οὗτοι ἀνθί-
   στανται τῇ ἀληθείᾳ, ἄνθρωποι   τὸν νοῦν, Ro i.28
9 ἀδόκιμοι περὶ τὴν πίστιν. ἀλλ' οὐ προκόψουσιν ἐπὶ πλεῖον·
   ἡ γὰρ   αὐτῶν   ἔσται πᾶσιν, ὡς καὶ ἡ ἐκεί-
   νων ἐγένετο.
10   ΣΥ ΔΕ   ΜΟΥ ΤΗΙ ΔΙΔΑΣΚΑΛΙΑΙ, ΤΗΙ
        ΤΗΙ ΠΡΟΘΕΣΕΙ, ΤΗΙ ΠΙΣΤΕΙ, ΤΗΙ ΜΑΚΡΟΘΥΜΙΑΙ, ΤΗΙ 2Cor vi.4-7
11 ΑΓΑΠΗΙ, ΤΗΙ ΥΠΟΜΟΝΗΙ, ΤΟΙΣ ΔΙΩΓΜΟΙΣ, ΤΟΙΣ ΠΑΘΗΜΑΣΙΝ,–ΟΙΑ
   ΜΟΙ ΕΓΕΝΕΤΟ ΕΝ ΑΝΤΙΟΧΕΙΑΙ, ΕΝ ΙΚΟΝΙΩΙ, ΕΝ ΛΥΣΤΡΟΙΣ, ΟΙΟΥΣ ΔΙΩΓ- Ac xiii.14.44-52.xiv.1f
   ΜΟΥΣ ΥΠΗΝΕΓΚΑ, ΚΑΙ ΕΚ ΠΑΝΤΩΝ ΜΕ ΕΡΡΥΣΑΤΟ Ο ΚΥΡΙΟΣ. 2Cor i.10
12 καὶ πάντες δὲ οἱ θέλοντες   ζῆν ἐν Χριστῷ Ἰησοῦ Ro viii.39 etc
13 διωχθήσονται. πονηροὶ δὲ ἄνθρωποι καὶ   προκόψου- 2Th iii.2
14 σιν ἐπὶ τὸ   πλανῶντες καὶ πλανώμενοι. σὺ δὲ μένε ἐν
15 οἷς ἔμαθες καὶ   εἰδὼς παρὰ τίνων ἔμαθες, καὶ
   ὅτι ἀπὸ   ἱερὰ γράμματα οἶδας τὰ δυνάμενά σε
16   εἰς σωτηρίαν διὰ πίστεως τῆς ἐν Χριστῷ Ἰησοῦ. πᾶσα 1Pe i.5, Ro i.16,iii.22, viii.39
   γραφὴ   καὶ   πρὸς διδασκαλίαν, πρὸς Ro xv.4

ΠΡΟΣ ΤΙΜΟΘΕΟΝ Β III 16–IV 15

Eph iv.24, vi.4 πρὸς   πρὸς παιδείαν τὴν ἐν δικαιοσύ- 17
2 Cor ix.8   νη· ἵνα   ᾖ ὁ τοῦ Θεοῦ ἄνθρωπος, πρὸς πᾶν ἔργον
                 ἀγαθόν.

Ga i.20 etc   ΔΙΑΜΑΡΤΥΡΟΜΑΙ ΕΝΩΠΙΟΝ ΤΟΥ ΘΕΟΥ ΚΑΙ ΧΡΙΣΤΟΥ I 1
                 ΙΗΣΟΥ ΤΟΥ ΜΕΛΛΟΝΤΟΣ ΚΡΙΝΕΙΝ ΖΩΝΤΑΣ ΚΑΙ ΝΕΚΡΟΥΣ,
                 ΚΑΙ ΤΗΝ ΕΠΙΦΑΝΕΙΑΝ ΑΥΤΟΥ ΚΑΙ ΤΗΝ ΒΑΣΙΛΕΙΑΝ ΑΥΤΟΥ,
                 ΚΗΡΥΞΟΝ ΤΟΝ ΛΟΓΟΝ, ΕΠΙΣΤΗΘΙ 2

Col i.11, 2 Cor vi.6   ἔλεξον,   παρακάλεσον, ἐν πάσῃ μακροθυμίᾳ
1 Cor xiv.6   καὶ διδαχῇ.
                 ἔσται γὰρ καιρὸς ὅτε τῆς   διδασκαλίας οὐκ 3
Eph iv.22   ἀνέξονται, ἀλλὰ κατὰ τὰς ἐπιθυμίας τὰς ἰδίας ἑαυτοῖς
                                  διδασκάλους   τὴν ἀκοήν, καὶ 4
† Ro xi.26 cit Is.lix.20 ἀπὸ μὲν τῆς ἀληθείας τὴν ἀκοὴν ἀποστρέψουσιν, ἐπὶ δὲ
                 τοὺς

Pp iv.12   Eph iv.11f   σὺ δὲ νῆφε ἐν πᾶσι,   ΕΡΓΟΝ ΠΟΙΗΣΟΝ 5
Ro xi.13, Col iv.17   ΕΥΑΓΓΕΛΙΣΤΟΥ, ΤΗΝ ΔΙΑΚΟΝΙΑΝ ΣΟΥ ᵃΠΛΗΡΟΦΟΡΗΣΟΝ. ΕΓΩ 6
Pp iii.12, ii.17, i.23 ΓΑΡ ΗΔΗ ΣΠΕΝΔΟΜΑΙ, ΚΑΙ Ο ΚΑΙΡΟΣ ΤΗΣ ΕΜΗΣ
Pp i.30   ΕΦΕΣΤΗΚΕ. ΤΟΝ ΑΓΩΝΑ ΤΟΝ ΚΑΛΟΝ ΗΓΩΝΙΣΜΑΙ, 7
Pp ii.16, Ac xx.24, Eph iv.3f ΤΟΝ   ΤΕΤΕΛΕΚΑ, ΤΗΝ ΠΙΣΤΙΝ ΤΕΤΗΡΗΚΑ· ΛΟΙΠΟΝ 8
Col i.5, 1 Cor ix.24f, Pp iv.1 ΑΠΟΚΕΙΤΑΙ ΜΟΙ Ο ΤΗΣ ΔΙΚΑΙΟΣΥΝΗΣ ΣΤΕΦΑΝΟΣ, ΟΝ ΑΠΟ-
Pp iii.14   ΔΩΣΕΙ ΜΟΙ Ο ΚΥΡΙΟΣ ΕΝ ΕΚΕΙΝΗ ΤΗ ΗΜΕΡΑΙ, Ο ΔΙΚΑΙΟΣ
                        ΟΥ ΜΟΝΟΝ ΔΕ ΕΜΟΙ, ΑΛΛΑ ΚΑΙ ΠΑΣΙ ΤΟΙΣ ΗΓΑΠΗΚΟΣΙ
                        ΤΗΝ ΕΠΙΦΑΝΕΙΑΝ ΑΥΤΟΥ.

Pp ii.19-23   ΣΠΟΥΔΑΣΟΝ ΕΛΘΕΙΝ ΠΡΟΣ ΜΕ ΤΑΧΕΩΣ· ΔΗΜΑΣ ΓΑΡ 9/10
Col iv.10-14, Phm 24   ΜΕ ΕΓΚΑΤΕΛΙΠΕΝ, ΑΓΑΠΗΣΑΣ ΤΟΝ ΝΥΝ ΑΙΩΝΑ, ΚΑΙ ΕΠΟΡ-
                        ΕΥΘΗ ΕΙΣ ΘΕΣΣΑΛΟΝΙΚΗΝ, ΚΡΗΣΚΗΣ ΕΙΣ ΓΑΛΑΤΙΑΝ, ΤΙΤΟΣ
                        ΕΙΣ ΔΑΛΜΑΤΙΑΝ· ΛΟΥΚΑΣ ΕΣΤΙ ᵇΜΟΝΟΣ ΜΕΤ' ΕΜΟΥ. ΜΑΡ- 11
Phm 11f   ΚΟΝ ΑΝΑΛΑΒΩΝ ΑΓΕ ΜΕΤΑ ΣΕΑΥΤΟΥ· ΕΣΤΙ ΓΑΡ ΜΟΙ ΕΥΧΡΗ-
Eph vi.21f, Col iv.7f   ΣΤΟΣ ΕΙΣ ΔΙΑΚΟΝΙΑΝ. ΤΥΧΙΚΟΝ ΔΕ ΑΠΕΣΤΕΙΛΑ ΕΙΣ ΕΦΕΣΟΝ. 12

2 Cor ii.12f   ΤΟΝ   ΟΝ   ΕΝ ΤΡΩΑΔΙ ΠΑΡΑ 13
                        ΚΑΡΠΩΙ ΕΡΧΟΜΕΝΟΣ ΦΕΡΕ, ΚΑΙ ΤΑ ΒΙΒΛΙΑ, ΜΑΛΙΣΤΑ ΤΑΣ
Ac xix.24f, 33f   ΑΛΕΞΑΝΔΡΟΣ Ο   ΠΟΛ- 14
Ro ii 6 cit Ps xxiv.12 ΛΑ ΜΟΙ ΚΑΚΑ ΕΝΕΔΕΙΞΑΤΟ· ΑΠΟΔΩΣΕΙ ΑΥΤΩΙ Ο
                        ΚΥΡΙΟΣ ΚΑΤΑ ΤΑ ΕΡΓΑ ΑΥΤΟΥ· ΟΝ ΚΑΙ ΣΥ ΦΥ- 15
                        ΛΑΣΣΟΥ,ᶜ   ΓΑΡ ΑΝΤΕΣΤΗ ΤΟΙΣ ΗΜΕΤΕΡΟΙΣ
                        ΛΟΓΟΙΣ.

a ΠΛΗΡΩΣΟΝ cf. Col iv.17.   *b* ? ΣΥΝ ΕΜΟΙ ΜΟΝΟΣ 1D etc.
c cf 2 Cor xi.5, xii.11 ὑπερλίαν.

ΠΡΟΣ ΤΙΜΟΘΕΟΝ Β IV 16-22

16 ΕΝ ΤΗΙ ΠΡΩΤΗΙ ΜΟΥ ΑΠΟΛΟΓΙΑΙ ΟΥΔΕΙΣ ΜΟΙ ΠΑΡΕΓΕ- Ac xxii.1, xxiii.1
ΝΕΤΟ, ΑΛΛΑ ΠΑΝΤΕΣ ΜΕ ΕΓΚΑΤΕΛΙΠΟΝ· ΜΗ ΑΥΤΟΙΣ
17 ΛΟΓΙΣΘΕΙΗ. Ο ΔΕ ΚΥΡΙΟΣ ΜΟΙ ΠΑΡΕΣΤΗ, ΚΑΙ ΕΝΕΔΥΝΑ- Ac xxiii.11 (xxvii.23). Pp ñ
ΜΩΣΕ ΜΕ, ΙΝΑ ΔΙ' ΕΜΟΥ ΤΟ ΚΗΡΥΓΜΑ ^{a}ΠΛΗΡΟΦΟΡΗΘΗΙ, Ro x.14, xvi.25f, 2 Cori.1
ΚΑΙ ΑΚΟΥΣΗΙ ΠΑΝΤΑ ΤΑ ΕΘΝΗ· ΚΑΙ ΕΡΡΥΣΘΗΝ ΕΚ ΣΤΟ- Ac xxviii.27f
18 ΜΑΤΟΣ   ΡΥΣΕΤΑΙ ΜΕ Ο ΚΥΡΙΟΣ ΑΠΟ ΠΑΝ- Ps xxii.22
ΤΟΣ ΕΡΓΟΥ ΠΟΝΗΡΟΥ, ΚΑΙ ΣΩΣΕΙ ΕΙΣ ΤΗΝ ΒΑΣΙΛΕΙΑΝ 2 Cor i.10, Ga i.4
18 ΑΥΤΟΥ ΤΗΝ ΕΠΟΥΡΑΝΙΟΝ.   Col iv.11, 1 Th ii.12

ΩΙ Η ΔΟΞΑ ΕΙΣ ΤΟΥΣ ΑΙΩΝΑΣ ΤΩΝ ΑΙΩΝΩΝ. ΑΜΗΝ. Ga i.5, Pp iv.20f
19 ΑΣΠΑΣΑΙ ΠΡΙΣΚΑΝ ΚΑΙ ΑΚΥΛΑΝ, ΚΑΙ ΤΟΝ ΟΝΗΣΙΦΟΡΟΥ ΟΙΚΟΝ. Ro xvi.3

20 ΕΡΑΣΤΟΣ ΕΜΕΙΝΕΝ ΕΝ ΚΟΡΙΝΘΩΙ· ΤΡΟΦΙΜΟΝ ΔΕ Ro xvi.23 Ac xix.22
21   ΕΝ ΜΙΛΗΤΩΙ ΑΣΘΕΝΟΥΝΤΑ. ΣΠΟΥΔΑΣΟΝ ΠΡΟ
ΕΛΘΕΙΝ.   Tit iii.12

ΑΣΠΑΖΕΤΑΙ ΣΕ ΕΥΒΟΥΛΟΣ, ΚΑΙ ΠΟΥΔΗΣ, ΚΑΙ ΛΙΝΟΣ, Pp iv.21f
22 ΚΑΙ ΚΛΑΥΔΙΑ, ΚΑΙ ΟΙ ΑΔΕΛΦΟΙ ΠΑΝΤΕΣ. Ο ΚΥΡΙΟΣ^b
ΜΕΤΑ ΤΟΥ ΠΝΕΥΜΑΤΟΣ ΣΟΥ.

Η ΧΑΡΙΣ ΜΕΘ' ΥΜΩΝ.   Col iv.18

---

^{a} ΠΛΗΡΩΘΗΙ cf Ro. viii.4
^{b} ΙΗΣΟΥΣ. W.H m., v S txt.

ΠΡΟΣ ΤΙΤΟΝ

Ro i.1, 1Cor i.1	**ΠΑΥΛΟΣ** δοῦλος Θεοῦ ἀπόστολος δὲ Ἰησοῦ Χριστοῦ, 1 I
Ro viii.33	κατὰ πίστιν ἐκλεκτῶν Θεοῦ καὶ ἐπίγνωσιν ἀληθείας τῆς
Ro v.2 etc., 21, i.2	κατ' ἐπ' ἐλπίδι ζωῆς αἰωνίου, ἣν ἐπηγγείλατο 2
Ro xvi.26, Col i.25f	ὁ Θεὸς πρὸ χρόνων αἰωνίων, ἐφανέρωσε δὲ 3
Ga vi.9,1Cor ii.4, Ga ii.7	καιροῖς ἰδίοις τὸν λόγον αὐτοῦ ἐν κηρύγματι ὃ ἐπιστεύθην
Ro xvi.26	ἐγὼ κατ' ἐπιταγὴν τοῦ σωτῆρος ἡμῶν Θεοῦ, Τίτῳ γνη- 4
Ro i.7 etc.	σίῳ τέκνῳ κατὰ κοινὴν πίστιν· χάρις καὶ εἰρήνη ἀπὸ Θε-
	οῦ πατρὸς καὶ Χριστοῦ Ἰησοῦ τοῦ σωτῆρος ἡμῶν.
Eph iii.1,14	Τούτου χάριν σε ἐν Κρήτῃ ἵνα τὰ 5
	καὶ καταστήσῃς κατὰ πόλιν
1Cor xvi.1	ὡς ἐγώ σοι διεταξάμην· εἴ τίς ἐστιν ἀνέγκλητος, 6
	μιᾶς γυναικὸς ἀνήρ, τέκνα ἔχων πιστά, μὴ ἐν
	ἀσωτίας ἢ δεῖ γὰρ τὸν ἐπίσκοπον ἀνέγ-7
1Cor iv.1	κλητον εἶναι, ὡς Θεοῦ οἰκονόμον, μὴ μὴ
	, μὴ , μὴ μὴ ἀλ- 8
	λὰ δίκαιον,
	ἀντεχόμενον τοῦ κατὰ τὴν διδαχὴν πιστοῦ 9
	λόγου, ἵνα δυνατὸς ᾖ καὶ παρακαλεῖν ἐν τῇ διδασκαλίᾳ
	τῇ καὶ τοὺς ἀντιλέγοντας ἐλέγχειν. Εἰσὶ γὰρ 10
	πολλοὶ καὶ
Php iv.22, Ga ii.12	μάλιστα οἱ ἐκ περιτομῆς, οὓς δεῖ οἵτινες 11
	ὅλους οἴκους διδάσκοντες ἃ μὴ δεῖ αἰσχροῦ
	κέρδους χάριν. εἶπέ τις ἐξ αὐτῶν ἴδιος αὐτῶν προφήτης, 12
	Κρῆτες ἀεὶ ψεῦσται, κακὰ θηρία, γαστέρες
	ἡ αὕτη ἐστὶν ἀληθής. δι' ἣν ἔλεγχε 13
1Cor xvi.13 etc.	αὐτοὺς ἀποτόμως, ἵνα ἐν τῇ πίστει, μὴ 14
	καὶ ἐντολαῖς ἀνθρώπων
† Ro xi.26 cit. Is. lix.20 Ro xiv.20	†ἀποστρεφομένων τὴν ἀλήθειαν. πάντα καθαρὰ τοῖς 15
	καθαροῖς· τοῖς δὲ καὶ ἀπίστοις οὐδὲν καθαρόν,
1Cor viii.7	ἀλλὰ αὐτῶν καὶ ὁ νοῦς καὶ ἡ συνείδησις. Θεὸν 16
	ὁμολογοῦσιν εἰδέναι, τοῖς δὲ ἔργοις
2Cor ix.8	ὄντες καὶ ἀπειθεῖς καὶ πρὸς πᾶν ἔργον ἀγαθὸν ἀδόκιμοι.
	Σὺ δὲ λάλει ἃ πρέπει τῇ διδασκαλίᾳ· 1 II
	πρεσβύτας εἶναι, σεμνούς, 2
cf. 1Th i.3	τῇ πίστει, τῇ ἀγάπῃ, τῇ ὑπομονῇ 3
	ὡσαύτως ἐν μὴ
	μηδὲ οἴνῳ πολλῷ δεδουλωμένας, ἵνα 4
	τὰς νέας εἶναι,

ΠΡΟΣ ΤΙΤΟΝ II 5-III 9

5 ἁγνάς, ἀγαθάς, ὑποτασσομένας Eph v.21f
τοῖς ἰδίοις ἀνδράσιν, ἵνα μὴ ὁ λόγος τοῦ Θεοῦ βλασφημῆται· Ro ix.6, ii.24
6 τοὺς ὡσαύτως παρακάλει σωφρονεῖν· περὶ πάν-
7 τα σεαυτὸν παρεχόμενος τύπον καλῶν ἔργων, ἐν τῇ διδα-
8 σκαλίᾳ λόγον
ἵνα ὁ ἐξ ἐναντίας ἐντραπῇ μηδὲν ἔχων λέγειν περὶ ἡμῶν φαῦ- 2 Th iii.14
9 λον. δούλους ἰδίοις ὑποτάσσεσθαι, ἐν πᾶσιν εὐ- Col iii.22
10 αρέστους εἶναι, μὴ ἀντιλέγοντας, μὴ
ἀλλὰ πᾶσαν πίστιν ἐνδεικνυμένους ἀγαθήν, ἵνα τὴν διδασκαλίαν τοῦ σωτῆρος ἡμῶν Θεοῦ ἐν
11 πᾶσιν. γὰρ ἡ χάρις τοῦ Θεοῦ Ro v.15ff 1 Cor xv.10 etc.
12 πᾶσιν ἀνθρώποις, παιδεύουσα ἡμᾶς, ἵνα
τὴν ἀσέβειαν καὶ τὰς ἐπιθυμίας
13 καὶ δικαίως καὶ ζήσωμεν ἐν τῷ νῦν αἰῶνι, προσδεχόμενοι τὴν μακαρίαν ἐλπίδα καὶ ἐπιφάνειαν τῆς δόξης cf. 1 Cor i.7.
14 τοῦ μεγάλου Θεοῦ καὶ σωτῆρος ἡμῶν Ἰησοῦ Χριστοῦ, ὃς 2 Cor iv.6
ἔδωκεν ἑαυτὸν ὑπὲρ ἡμῶν, ἵνα ἡμᾶς ἀπὸ Ga i.4
πάσης ἀνομίας καὶ καθαρίσῃ ἑαυτῷ λαὸν ζηλω-
15 τὴν καλῶν ἔργων. Ταῦτα λάλει, καὶ παρακάλει καὶ Ga i.14
ἔλεγχε μετὰ πάσης ἐπιταγῆς. μηδείς σου

III 1 αὐτοὺς ἀρχαῖς ἐξουσίαις ὑποτάσσεσ- Ro xiii.1
θαι, πρὸς πᾶν ἔργον ἀγαθὸν ἑτοίμους εἶναι, 2 Cor ix.8
2 μηδένα βλασφημεῖν, εἶναι, ἐπιεικεῖς, πᾶσαν ἐν- Pp iv.5
3 δεικνυμένους πραότητα πρὸς πάντας ἀνθρώπους. ἦμεν 2 Cor viii.24, x.1
γάρ ποτε καὶ ἡμεῖς ἀνόητοι, ἀπειθεῖς, πλανώμενοι, δου- Ga iv.3, Eph ii.3
λεύοντες ἐπιθυμίαις καὶ , ἐν κακίᾳ καὶ Ro vi.6,12, Col iii.5ff
4 φθόνῳ , μισοῦντες ἀλλήλους. ὅτε δὲ Ga iv.4
ἡ χρηστότης καὶ ἡ τοῦ σωτῆρος Ro ii.4, xi.22
5 ἡμῶν Θεοῦ, οὐκ ἐξ ἔργων τῶν ἐν δικαιοσύνῃ, ἃ ἐποιή- Eph ii.8f
σαμεν ἡμεῖς ἀλλὰ κατὰ τὸ αὐτοῦ ἔλεος ἔσωσεν ἡμᾶς
διὰ λουτροῦ καὶ ἀνακαινώσεως Πνεύ-
6 ματος Ἁγίου, οὗ †ἐξέχεεν ἐφ᾿ ἡμᾶς πλουσίως διὰ Ἰησοῦ † Ro iii.15 cit Is. lix.7
7 Χριστοῦ τοῦ σωτῆρος ἡμῶν, ἵνα δικαιωθέντες τῇ ἐκεί- Ro vii.25 etc. iii.24, v.1,2
νου χάριτι κληρονόμοι γενηθῶμεν κατ᾿ ἐλπίδα ζωῆς αἰω- Ro viii.17, iv.14
8 νίου. πιστὸς ὁ λόγος· καὶ περὶ τούτων βούλομαί
σε ἵνα καλῶν ἔργων προ-
ΐστασθαι οἱ πεπιστευκότες Θεῷ. ταῦτά ἐστι καλὰ καὶ Ro iv.3
9 τοῖς ἀνθρώποις· μωρὰς δὲ καὶ

ΠΡΟΣ ΤΙΤΟΝ

καὶ ἔρεις καὶ μάχας
1 Cor iii.20 cit Ps. xciv.11   εἰσὶ γὰρ   καὶ μάταιοι.   ἄνθρωπον
μετὰ μίαν καὶ δευτέραν νουθεσίαν   εἰδὼς
Phm 21 ὅτι   ὁ τοιοῦτος καὶ ἁμαρτάνει ὢν

1 Cor xvi.3-24   ΟΤΑΝ ΠΕΜΨΩ ΑΡΤΕΜΑΝ ΠΡΟΣ ΣΕ Η ΤΥΧΙΚΟΝ, ΣΠΟΥΔΑΣΟΝ ΕΛΘΕΙΝ ΠΡΟΣ ΜΕ ΕΙΣ ΝΙΚΟΠΟΛΙΝ· ΕΚΕΙ ΓΑΡ ΚΕΚΡΙΚΑ ΠΑΡΑΧΕΙΜΑΣΑΙ. ΖΗΝΑΝ ΤΟΝ ΚΑΙ ΑΠΟΛΛΩ ΣΠΟΥΔΑΙΩΣ ΠΡΟΠΕΜΨΟΝ, ΙΝΑ ΜΗΔΕΝ ΑΥΤΟΙΣ ΜΑΝΘΑΝΕΤΩΣΑΝ ΔΕ ΚΑΙ ΟΙ ΗΜΕΤΕΡΟΙ ΚΑΛΩΝ ΕΡΓΩΝ ΠΡΟΙΣΤΑΣΘΑΙ ΕΙΣ ΤΑΣ ΑΝΑΓΚΑΙΑΣ ΧΡΕΙΑΣ, ΙΝΑ ΜΗ ΩΣΙΝ ΑΚΑΡΠΟΙ. ΑΣΠΑΖΟΝΤΑΙ ΣΕ ΟΙ ΜΕΤ' ΕΜΟΥ ΠΑΝΤΕΣ. ΑΣΠΑΣΑΙ ΤΟΥΣ ΦΙΛΟΥΝΤΑΣ ΗΜΑΣ ΕΝ ΠΙΣΤΕΙ. Η ΧΑΡΙΣ ΜΕΤΑ ΠΑΝΤΩΝ ΥΜΩΝ.

www.ingramcontent.com/pod-product-compliance
Lightning Source LLC
Chambersburg PA
CBHW050147170426
43197CB00011B/1999